MW00559031

In Other Words

In Other Words
40 Years of Writing on Indonesia and the Wider World

selected, translated, and with an introduction by
Jennifer Lindsay

and a foreword by
Terence Ward

Arcade Publishing · New York

Arcade Publishing books may be purchased in bulk at special discounts for sales promotion, corporate gifts, fund-raising, or educational purposes. Special editions can also be created to specifications. For details, contact the Special Sales Department, Arcade Publishing, 307 West 36th Street, 11th Floor, New York, NY 10018 or arcade@skyhorsepublishing.com.

Arcade Publishing® is a registered trademark of Skyhorse Publishing, Inc.®, a Delaware corporation.

Visit our website at www.arcadepub.com.

10 9 8 7 6 5 4 3 2 1

Library of Congress Cataloging-in-Publication Data is available on file.

Cover design by Erin Seaward-Hiatt

Print ISBN: 978-1-62872-731-9
Ebook ISBN: 978-1-62872-732-6

Printed in the United States of America

Contents

Foreword

On a balmy June day in 2012, the writer Michael Ondaatje delivered his *Lectio Magistralis* speech in Florence. From the Palazzo Medici Riccardi, he reflected on our epoch, and spoke of *Mongrel Art*. Ondaatje described his work belonging to Art that reaches across the divide, art that draws inspiration over the waters, art that communes freely with literary co-conspirators, past and present, and draws associations beyond one's culture. He mapped out how this Art moves between forms—from literature into film, from music to writing—with such a fearless sweep that it is not bound by culture, mindsets or tradition. To create such work, a 360 degree inter-connected vision is needed. And inspiration. While leaving the halls painted by Florentine masters, I thought, is this the profile of a "Renaissance man" in our brave new world?

Goenawan Mohamad, activist, journalist, editor, essayist, poet, commentator, theatre director and playwright, has been doing just that for 40 years in his weekly column for *Tempo*, the Indonesian weekly magazine that he founded in 1971. His output of essays is staggering. His vision is uniquely Indonesian, yet breathtakingly universal, setting his work apart from his contemporary South-Asian writers. He too is a purveyor of Mongrel Art.

As much at home in Paris as in Java, Goenawan is the leading political thinker in Indonesia. But his reach is far deeper than mere politics. His writing is stirring and original – a sledgehammer of thought. Just as Orhan Pamuk offers his cosmopolitan view from Istanbul, Goenawan offers the same from his window in Jakarta.

His writing is lucid, illuminating, urgent, timeless. Critics have called him the "Borges of Southeast Asia" and compared his best essays to Italo Calvino (whose *Invisible Cities*, he often cites).

Goenawan is as much at home drawing lessons from Indonesia's complex history as he is reflecting on world cultural figures, events and places (Martin Luther King, 9/11, or the Ka'aba). He enjoys engaging with philosophers (Aristotle, Kant or Confucius), writers (Goethe, Garcia Marquez or Camus), and psychoanalysts (Jung, Freud, or Lacan). He delights in exploring the ancient myths of the Mahabharata, the Arabian Nights, Exodus, or the thoughts of Laozi, Maimonides, and Thomas Aquinas, or even the mystic revelations of al-Hallaj, Meister Eckhart, and Rumi.

Who else would insert in an essay on *Jerusalem*, a quote of the poet William Blake, and then draw parallels with Oedipus, Hamlet, and Arjuna of the *Bhagavad Gita,* before ending with the words of the guitarist John Lennon, 'God is a concept by which we measure pain'?

Who would begin an essay entitled *Tso Wang*, by comparing fundamentalism to digital technology and then suggest 'both are virtual. They don't touch the soil,' before citing the German philosopher Martin Heidegger, a 10th century Javanese mystical poem described as '*sepi, sepah, samun*' (silent, vacant, secret), and ending with the 4th century Chinese philosopher, Zhuangzi, of the Daoist School who said 'the highest stage of knowledge is stillness without movement within what cannot be known absolutely with reason, a state called *tso wang*?

Who else would describe a forest in north Bali with such an arresting poetry: 'At that moment, in that green half-light, the everlasting appeared. Eternity moved. Each second seemed to slip and fuse into the chlorophyll of the trees. Centuries seemed to tremble in the forks of the tree trunks.'?

Or capture this solar eclipse over Borobudur: 'It was as though the Buddha statues in their stupas had suddenly gone mute. These stones had been standing for centuries at Borobudur without movement. But when the eclipse happened and the strange filtered light fell even to the distant hills, the sensation of silence was sudden. Astonishing.'?

Few contemporary writers possess such dexterity and immediacy. Or cut so cleanly with their samurai pen.

The essay is an important literary form in Indonesia, where much significant writing is first published in newspapers and journals (and now blogs and other web-based forms). Goenawan Mohamad has developed the essay as no other Indonesian writer. Far from being merely a journalistic column commenting on recent events, Goenawan's essays speak to the universal, drawing deep insights from the commonplace and far afield, always linking Indonesia to the wider world.

In Part 1, Goenawan fearlessly narrates the contradictions of Indonesian identity, questioning colonial ancestors, Javanese spirits and origins. He plunges deep into Hindu epics and myth. He meditates on the contrasting faces of Islam and grapples with his country's struggle with modernism and its discontents. Always curious, always probing, he peels off the layers of nationalist myths, from the god-king Sukarno to the dreaded year when a nightmare of massacres swept across the country. His essay, *1965*, may be the best explanation why. Reacting to the recent film *The Act of Killing*, he deftly compares Anwar Congo to an infamous Khmer Rouge mass-murderer known as Douch described in *The Gate* by Francois Bizot to widen our vision as witnesses.

In Part 2, he packs his pen and bags. Although he writes mostly in Jakarta, he is also well-worn traveler. His essays drift in from Borobudur, North Bali, Ambon, East Timor and far Papua.

He surfaces in Amsterdam, and walks the streets of Mecca and Shanghai. He witnesses the twin towers fall in Manhattan, and the oil fires burn in Baku. He meditates on architecture in Damascus, Granada and Amalfi, and stands witness in cursed conflict-zones of Srebrenica, Troy, Ayodhya and Baghdad. The journalist in him will not shy away. And from each new city, he offers his fresh take.

In Part 3, he wields his sledge-hammer of thought, leading the reader into shadowed realms, grappling with giants, prophets, and legends – Tolstoy, Shiva, Mohammad, Jesus, Siddharta, Marx, Euclid, Moses, Marlene Dietrich, Khomeini, Akhenaten, Yeats, Spinoza, Agamemnon, Saladin, Jackie Chan, Plato, Hammurabi, Rembrandt, Naipal, Krishna, Noel Coward, Hegel, Kafka, Zhivago, Tagore, Keats, Vonnegut, Kierkegaard, Sophocles, and the red-headed Tintin to name a few.

Foreign readers who hope to understand the complex cultural tapestry that shapes the vast Malay Archipelago and broader Southeast Asia are well served. This collection draws his finest essays from the Indonesian originals of which there are now ten volumes.

His comrade-in-arms, Jennifer Lindsay, has been translating Goenawan's columns since 1992 and she has ingeniously captured Goenawan's broad sweep of themes and extraordinary dexterity in Indonesian prose with her own striking clarity. Jennifer's literary choices are always to the point. They carry weight and gravitas. She too writes with a sharp pen.

In closing, it is important to remind Western readers of a perspective shared by Mircea Eliade. As an exile from Romania, he noted the importance of the work of intellectuals in societies that lived under dictatorships or police states, as Indonesia was for thirty years. To this day, Indonesia remains a country in transition. Precariously. The military stands poised to protect its fiefdoms and powers. For them, Goenawan is only a witness. Alone. And exposed. But, they still have yet to grasp, his voice will outlive them all as Eliade explains in *Labyrinth by Ordeal:*

I do think that the presence of the intellectual in the true sense of the word – great poets, great novelists, great philosophers – I think that their very presence is terribly disturbing for a police state or a dictatorship, whether of the left or the right. The intellectual, as enemy number 1, is entrusted by history with a political mission. In the war of religions, in which we are presently engaged, the enemy is embarrassed solely by 'elites,' which a well-organized police force can easily suppress. In consequence, 'making culture' is today the only efficacious form of politics open to writers. And one must go on 'creating culture'. The traditional positions are reversed: it is no longer the politicians who stand at the concrete center of history but the great minds, the 'intellectual elites'.

In his poem, *The Keeper of the Books*, Jorge Luis Borges describes the aftermath of the Mongol invasion, '…cut throats and sent up pyramids of fire, slaughtering the wicked and the just, …the slave chained to his master's door, using the women and casting them off. And on to the South they rode.' No, he does not condemn the Mongols. He simply sees them as *'innocent as animals of prey, cruel as knives.'* But when he turns to the keeper of the books, we learn the most precarious duty in such sharp times.

> *In the faltering dawn*
> *my father's father saved the books.*
> *Here they are in this tower where I lie*
> *calling back days that belonged to others,*
> *distant days, the days of the past.*

Goenawan has indeed been a keeper of the books, in good

times and bad. As a writer, he narrates his nation's memory, and in 'creating culture' he ensures that the past will be interlinked to Indonesia's future and reach lands beyond the horizon, in times beyond our own.

Terence Ward

Introduction

Goenawan Mohamad was born in 1941 in a coastal town in central Java. He was five years old when President Sukarno read Indonesia's proclamation of independence on 17 August 1945 after three and a half years of Japanese occupation during WWII, and a long history of Dutch colonial rule. He was nine years old when Indonesia's independence was finally recognized internationally in December 1949 after four years of bitter revolutionary struggle against the Dutch. He was still at high school when he began translating poetry (Apollinaire and Emily Dickinson) and nineteen when he moved to Jakarta in 1960 and began contributing his own poetry and essays to various journals. By 1963 he had fallen foul of the government for his public stance against ideologically-directed art. From late 1965-early 1967 he was in Europe, during the bloody aftermath of the 1965 coup d'état in Indonesia which was blamed on the communists, and which led to mass killings, leftist-cleansing, the fall of Sukarno, and the beginning of Soeharto's 'New Order' in 1966. In 1971, he was one of the founders of the Indonesian language weekly journal, *Tempo*, and remained its chief editor until 2000, with a gap from 1994-1999 when the journal was banned because of its uncompromising investigative journalism. Since the fall of the Soeharto regime in 1999, Goenawan's boundless energy has been more directed towards artistic pursuits – establishing a venue and forum for arts and discussion in Jakarta, directing theater, and working on his own performance projects.*⁾

In Indonesia, Goenawan is a towering figure. He is Indonesia's most well known public intellectual, and has a huge following among young people on Twitter and on-line media. He is a multi-faceted man and it is difficult to pin him down to any one description or to find comparison for him. He moves fluidly between generations, and between the worlds of creative writing, performance, academia, journalism and activism. At different times in his life he has given priority to different facets of these worlds.

Goenawan's life spans the history of the Indonesian republic, and his depth of involvement with its history informs his writing and his life. This collection of essays covers nearly five decades of his writing. The earliest is from 1968, the most recent from late 2014.

I have been translating Goenawan's short essays, written as a weekly column called *'Catatan Pinggir'* meaning 'notes on the margins', since 1992, and we have published three collections of them to date: *Sidelines* (1994, 2005); *Conversations with Difference* (2002, 2005) and *Sharp Times* (2011). **)

Some of the most enduring essays in these collections are included here, but almost half the essays in *In Other Words* have not appeared in any of those earlier publications.

---

*) For a fuller discussion about Goenawan and his writing, see my essay 'Goenawan Mohamad: Man on the Margins' in *Australian Book Review* October 2012: 29-41

**) *Sidelines: Writings from Tempo, by Goenawan Mohamad,* translated and with an introduction by Jennifer Lindsay. Melbourne: Hyland House and Monash Asia Institute. Republished 1994 *as Sidelines: Thought Pieces from Tempo* magazine, Jakarta: the Lontar Foundation. This edition republished by Equinox, Jakarta 2005. *Conversations with Difference:* essays from *Tempo* magazine by Goenawan Mohamad translated from the Indonesian by Jennifer Lindsay. Jakarta: PT Tempo Inti Media Tbk, 2002 (reprinted 2005). Republished Singapore University Press, 2005. *Sharp Times. Selections from Sidelines* by Goenawan Mohamad, translated by Jennifer Lindsay. Jakarta: Grafiti, 2011.

The original Indonesian language versions were published as a weekly column in *Tempo* which Goenawan began writing in March 1976, with one exception, 'From Ambon and Scorched Ruins' which also appeared in *Tempo*, but is a longer essay, not from the weekly column. It is included here because it covers an important subject, and also to give readers a comparative glimpse at Goenawan's longer essay writing style. The earliest essay in this book (Sacred Poetry) appeared pre-*Tempo*, in another publication, but is included to show his early essay style and a recurring theme – the power of language. Another (La Patrie) appeared in an unlicensed magazine during the period *Tempo* was banned. Other than that, all the essays in this book are from *Tempo,* and the date of the original publication is noted at the foot of each essay. In Indonesia, all of Goenawan's columns are also collected and published in book form, titled *Catatan Pinggir*, of which to date there are ten volumes. The volume where each essay appears is also noted beside the original *Tempo* publication date. The essays in each section are presented in order from the present to the past, with a few exceptions.

Goenawan has developed the short essay form within the constraints of a column of around 800 words. He explores different voices and language as he approaches a staggeringly wide range of issues from various points of view – sometimes intensely private and poetic, sometimes more public and detached. The short essay is only one form of Goenawan's writing – he also writes longer essays, poetry and plays – but the demand of producing a regular weekly column for over forty years has honed his mastery of this particular form.

The column itself is written for Indonesian readers, of course. Goenawan has described its purpose as to comment, muse, and raise questions rather than draw conclusions. It is not a forum for polemics, but to bring the outside world to Indonesian readers, discussing philosophy, new books he has read, history and current events, and relating these to something local and immediate. Or the other way around. This context has changed over the years. In 1976 when the column began, Goenawan was an important and influential conduit to the outside world. Since the Internet, however, his Indonesian readers have their own instant links to news and ideas, and these days they read his columns as a less authorial voice.

In 2000, an English language edition of *Tempo* was launched (also called *Tempo*), published alongside the Indonesian language edition, which remains Indonesia's most influential weekly. Since then, I have been translating Goenawan's columns every week for the English magazine, so the original and the English translation appear a week apart, and both are available on line. This simultaneous publication has contributed to a shift in Goenawan's focus in his column. Foreign readers are now just as curious to read his perception of world, regional and local events or topics of discussion. Goenawan's awareness of this foreign readership at the time of first writing also feeds into his writing. He tends these days to write more about broader topics than more specifically Indonesian ones. Whatever he writes about, however, he has a unique Indonesian vision and voice that spring from his particular experience and deep commitment to his country. He is able to bring together something very broad with something grounded locally, to make comparisons, and to speak across readerships.

He does this while masterfully exploring the potential of the Indonesian language. In this, he speaks directly to his fellow Indonesians, showing them what their national language can do. He is of the generation that helped forge this language, of which he is rightfully proud. For readers of this book who are unfamiliar with Indonesian, allow me to provide a brief note here. Indonesian is a version of Malay, which for centuries was used as a lingua franca over a wide area covering southern Thailand, the Malay Peninsula, Brunei, Indonesia and Timor Leste. Indonesian nationalists adopted Malay (*bahasa Melayu*) as Indonesia's national language in 1928 and renamed it *bahasa Indonesia* (the language of Indonesia, or Indonesian). This was a bold rejection of the Dutch language, which was spoken by a small, educated elite but was not widespread in the colony. In 1942, the occupying Japanese banned all use of Dutch. When Indonesia declared its independence in 1945, Indonesian was made the national language and has remained the success story of the nation – its true binding force. Indonesian exists alongside other local languages, but has become a first language with the current young generation. Literature and journalism were an important force in developing the language in the first few decades of the republic after independence, and Goenawan was right at the forefront of this mission to forge the nation in language and writing.

The journal he edited, *Tempo,* declared its commitment to promoting jargon-free language, clarity of journalistic style, and to extending vocabulary. Goenawan's own column, however, is far from journalistic. He is often opaque as he pushes the language to express complex ideas, and pushes his prose towards poetry. He stretches the Indonesian language every which way – and continues to do so. This makes translation of his short essays an exciting challenge, for he is at once concerned with meaning – the ability of this wonderfully flexible and fast-growing language to express ideas – and the creative potential of the language itself. He enriches vocabulary, uses alliteration and rhythm extensively, and experiments with structure and tone. And he continues to do this even when many Indonesians are now losing pride in their language, preferring to use a kind of lazy English-Indonesian that obfuscates rather than challenges.

Finally, some words on the selection of essays presented here. I made the selection with input from Goenawan and also from New York-based writer/producer Terence Ward, who has been connected to Indonesia for over twenty years and has written an foreword for this book. In making the selection, I wanted to find those that showcase Goenawan's writing. I looked for essays that have remained fresh and pertinent, and those that engage a foreign reader. I chose essays that I find most reveal Goenawan's unique vision and voice, and his range of style. Of course, the choice cannot help but reveal my own preference for those essays that show connecting threads between the local and the international, Goenawan's mastery of the Indonesian language, and his quicksilver thinking.

The selection is presented in three groupings reflecting three major overall themes of his writing over the years: faith, religion, spirituality and belief; world issues broadly; and the vexing topic of Indonesia and being Indonesian. The short essays in this book are merely 100 of the 2000 or so he has written – and merely 100 out of the 1000 or so I have translated into English. They are just a taste – an introduction to show the vitality of the essay form in Indonesia and Goenawan's mastery of it, the rich potential of the Indonesian language, and the unique thinking of an Indonesian intellectual whose voice the world needs to hear in our troubled times.

Jennifer Lindsay

In Other Words

Books
(a preface)

Books can fuse with trauma, at least in my experience.

When I was about six years old, the occupying Dutch army arrested my father and ransacked our house. That day, after they had bound my father's hands and put him on a truck, our family sat terrified. I still remember one thing clearly: two soldiers took some books from my father's study and threw them down the well.

I did not know what books they threw, or why. The only thing important to me was this: a soldier broke my wooden toy gun and threw that down the well too.

Books and a toy gun: signs of enmity? Decades later, my older brother who had been close to my father (I was not so close to him), remembered that in my father's study there was a book with a picture of Karl Marx on the cover. Probably it was such a tome that had to be eliminated. And guns – real or not.

Because some books were not touched. Among them was a 1939 Webster's dictionary with a black cover (inscribed in fountain pen by my father on the front page) and a book about English history.

In the big dictionary I found an illustration: four people carrying a box. Because I didn't know what a dictionary was for, I thought this was a picture of people who had to carry corpses. Only later did I learn that the picture was illustrating the word 'palanquin'.

Another book had an olive green cover. It had many colored pictures. I never forgot two of them.

The first picture was a detailed illustration, like a photo. It depicted a man sleeping, fully clothed, while two other men standing in red coats looked at his exhausted face. At the time, I thought it was a picture of someone unconscious, visited by two ghosts. Later when I could read English I learnt that it was a scene from 17th century English history: King Charles 1st, the night before he was taken to be beheaded. One of the 'ghosts' in the picture was probably the prison guard.

The second picture: a man sprawled on his back in a deserted field. A woman sits at his side: one of her hands stops the blood flowing from his wound, her other hand makes a fist of anger. Red drops of blood can be seen. Later I knew that this was a painting of the slaughter of the Scots by the English at Glen Coe on 13 February 1692. The woman was yelling for revenge.

Slaughter, anger, people visited by ghosts, four pallbearers, books thrown into wells while my father was bound…. I did not realize just how deep and lasting this trauma was. Maybe it took on a different expression: my excitement for books with thick covers.

My brother and I also discovered books with sturdy covers by Karl May about Winnetou. We never knew who they belonged to, because our father preferred Karl Marx to Karl May. But inside were illustrations of Apache deep in the magical and idyllic jungle.

Moved by the impressive form of this book, the contents of which we could not understand, we began to order Indonesian translations like *Winetou Gugur* (The Death of Winnetou) and James Fennimore Coopers' *The Last of the Mohicans,* translated as *Suku Mohawk Tumpas*, from Noordoff Kolff in Jakarta, a branch of the publishing house in Groningen, Holland.

We waited anxiously for the day the books would arrive by post, and would nearly always fight over who got to read them first.

As with other children, books to me were magical vehicles: living in a small town with no movie theatre, books were the only things that led me into another world in reality never crossed. And every time I was led there, that world changed, was different, moved on, and yet always felt close.

I could never fully imagine the character of Winnetou, but I cried when, towards the final battle, he knew he was going to the 'eternal hunting grounds'. I cried when Jamin and Johan were tortured in some corner of far-flung Batavia. I was sad for Dul, who lived in Jakarta and who I had never met, when his father, a driver, was killed in an accident and when Dul was ridiculed mercilessly by his grandfather for wearing his scout's uniform complete with hat and shoes for the Muslim Lebaran holiday, and not a sarong and the fez-like *songkok*. My tears fell for Sampek and Engtai who died in the story that I heard some of the workers at the cigarette factory beside our house reading aloud in turn from a book written in Javanese.

When I grew up, I could link this childhood trauma with my subsequent experience with books. I could draw the conclusion: books die because they are stopped in their journey into our lives, as happened when they were thrown down the well. But stories do not end.

In 1958, President Sukarno turned Indonesia into a 'Guided Democracy' and 'Guided Economy'. In the name of 'Revolution' (that seductive word), the State was taking over the world of publishing, particularly that linked to foreign capital. In October 1962, publishing houses like Noordoff Kolff were nationalized. Noordoff Kolff was replaced with a state enterprise called 'Noor Komala' headed by a bureaucrat. Balai Pustaka, which until then had competed well with foreign publishers, was now run by a general. When paper, printing, transportation and almost all economic life became 'guided', many things ground to a halt. The most prominent Indonesian publishing houses such as Djambatan, which published a monumental atlas, were utterly shaken and never recovered.

The flow of books was chaotic. There were no longer any books with warm covers and whose paper smelt authoritative but inviting. Books became increasingly uniform. 'Guided Democracy' also issued in the history of power which, with one blow, could ban a whole row of books – a history that continues to this day.

At that time, the only entertainment left was the thick books published by the Soviet Union and sold cheaply in shops owned by the Indonesian Communist Party (PKI). There was still Dostoyevsky, Turgenev and Tolstoy – in English translation and published by the Moscow Foreign Publishing House – but incomplete. I could not get *The Brothers Karamazov* and *Fathers and Sons*. Moscow had its own censors.

I remember that morning in 1947: two soldiers of the occupying forces throwing a few books down the well. But I can also never forget those cigarette factory workers taking turns at reading from a book. Books die, but not everything dies. They have their own trauma and nostalgia. They have stories that always reappear.

Goenawan Mohamad
'Buku' *Tempo* 11 May 2010, CP IX: 601-4

I

Indonesia on my Mind

Naming

The term Indonesia was first used by a British anthropologist in 1850, to designate islands of the Indian Archipelago. It is however believed that it was a ship's doctor who gave a name to Indonesia. In 1861, Adolf Bastian, from the city of Bremen in Germany, was sailing in Southeast Asia. Later he wrote a few books. One of them became widely read: *Indonesien oder die Inseln des Malayischen Archipels, 1884-1894*. And it was from this book that 'Indonesia' began to be widely used to name the archipelago.

Bastian was influential because he was not merely a ship's doctor. He was a graduate of law and biology, and he was interested in the science that in his day was called 'ethnology'; but he was also a doctor. The fact that he became a ship's doctor shows that he wanted to explore other parts of the world. In 1873, he helped establish the Museum für Völkerkunde in Berlin, with its huge collection of man-made artifacts from all corners of the globe.

This ship's doctor who constantly traveled the seas traversing the world – he died while on a voyage at the age of 80 – was convinced there was something that physically united all mankind: 'elementary ideas' or *Elementergedanken*.

'Humankind,' Bastian wrote, possesses 'a store of ideas inborn in every individual.' These ideas appear in myriad forms from Babylonia to the South Seas.

But humans also display *Volkergedanken,* or 'folk ideas' that are conditioned by the different locations where they live. Bastian used the word *Volk,* or '*ethnos*' in Greek to refer to a group of people connected by race, customs, language and values.

Today, Bastian's theory is no longer surprising. And in fact, understandings of 'ethnos' as well as 'race', which are the backbone of his theory, are today no longer sound. But we can imagine just how powerful the impact of these ideas was in a century when imperialism shaped the globe.

Imperialism, like the explorations of 'ethnology' (or 'anthropology') puts together people from various origins, but at the same time points out a distance – even an imbalance and subjugation. In imperialism, as also in ethnographic works, 'Westerners' not only encounter (*menemui*), but also discover (*menemukan*) other worlds, as though those 'things' exist only after being seen by 'the West'. At that moment, the 'thing' is frozen. It is changed into 'the different', just as in the Greek legend; people turn to stone after Medusa turns her gaze on them.

The change from 'the other' into 'the different', solid as stone, is the primary principle of imperialism. Imperialism etches something bad into consciousness: 'in its fetters,' Edward Said said, 'people become convinced that they are nothing but exclusively 'white' or exclusively 'colored'. Imperialism makes people unaware that people are not just one identity, but have histories that make them not completely stable, whole, and single.'

In those histories too there is a dialectic going on between encounter and subjugation. People are within one location, but in a position where one is subjected, the other subjecting. The meeting is no longer a meeting, but a subjugation. Within the same political space they greet one another – and even within daily life.

In *A Certain Age*, the historian Rudolf Mrazek's fascinating collection of notes from interviews with the old generation in Indonesia, we know that formerly, in our towns, the Dutch population did appear, but at a distance.

'As a child', Mrs Surono relates, 'I never met a Dutch person in the street.' Mr Mewengkang talks about his childhood in North

Sulawesi. 'I grew up in a village, and there were no Dutch people. Only, on some Sundays . . . a Dutch priest came.' The journalist Rosihan Anwar's experience was almost the same. In his childhood in Agam, West Sumatra, his father knew a Dutchman: a *controleur* who used to visit the house every Lebaran. Only at Lebaran. The boy was allowed to observe from a distance. Pak Oey, who grew up in Surabaya and Batavia, saw Dutch people only at the swimming pool.

Wertheim, a Dutch academic well known as an intellectual of anticolonialism, also experienced that distance. He began to realize that something was not right around him only when his maid said that her baby had died because there was no one to treat its illness.

This was the time when what was universal in mankind was disregarded; Bastian's *Elementergedanken* were gradually forgotten. 'Others' no longer meant 'fellows'.

This is why the poison of imperialism stings when its context shifts. We are reminded of the biography of Soewardi Soerjaningrat. In July 1913 he wrote a newspaper piece criticizing the colonial government that wanted to commemorate the centennial of Dutch independence from French rule. Soewardi wrote an essay 'supposing' he was a Dutch person with a conscience, and in that voice cried, 'I would not celebrate an independence ceremony in the country where we ourselves deny people's rights to freedom.'

Actually, Soewardi was affirming what is universal among fellows: all want freedom, especially the colonized. But the colonial government would not acknowledge this. Soewardi was arrested. Aged 24, he was exiled to Holland.

But it was over there in that country with its democratic life that he became even more aware that 'others' were 'fellows' and that 'fellows' could mean 'equals'. The dialectic between meeting and subjugating shifted: whereas in the colonial country 'meeting' was submerged by 'subjugating', in independent Europe, 'subjugating'

---

was eliminated by 'meeting'. Soewardi's rebellion intensified. Application of the law equally in Dutch society strengthened his conviction that people like him were not servants. They came from an archipelago that did not want to submit to being the 'Netherlands Indies'.

In April 1917, on a page in the magazine *Hindia Poetra*, Soewardi chose for the land of his birth the name that Bastian had used. Indonesia: the land built by the universal, for all, and at the same time by those who differ.

August 2015

Native Land

Can you stop thinking about Indonesia for a while? Yesterday, this question came to my head. I wanted to say, 'yes, sure, why not?' For I sometimes want to lose myself in forgetting, hide in a corner far away. I want to pull the curtains, sleep, dream perhaps, and not think again.

But Indonesia always comes. Indonesia always knocks. And precisely when we don't want to care. Uncertainty makes us wary. The moment that hope becomes hard, despair is terrifying. I cannot run from this. A country, a history, a name. What does all this mean to you and me – what is the meaning of a native land?

I am writing this question in a waiting room at a foreign airport. It is crowded. People come and go past the thirty gates. In a few days, they, just like me, will forget the name of this city. All they will remember is this waiting room with its bookshop, news agency, shops selling bright shirts, sandwiches, souvenirs, duty-free liquor, advertisments for Visa and Amex – things always everywhere.

I, like them, am just a passer-by, someone who will give a hotel as an address. There are those who are looking for the excitement of another country, and there are those who are looking for solace from bitterness in their own. I am one of that crowd: transit man.

But Indonesia is always knocking at my head. I see the airline companies in Asia with their businesses flourishing, and I am reminded of Garuda, left behind. I glance at the exchange rates listed at the foreign exchange booth, and I recall Indonesia's fragile rupiah. Proud or ashamed, fascinated or scathing, it turns out that I cannot stop thinking about Indonesia.

Who knows whether native land is not just the name of a country that we write on an immigration form, or a territory on a map. And native land seems not to be an origin, either: it does not come from the past. So, what is it then?

Today I can only answer like this: native land is a project that we are undertaking together, you and I. It is a possibility that reveals itself, an ideal that is strived for generation by generation, a dream through which we travel, often with aching legs and with faltering awareness. Native land is a present space that we traverse because there are hopes for us all in the future. Native land is an *engagement*. We are all engaged in it, we all wrestle with it, in a relationship that began who knows where – it can never be explained completely. You might call this 'patriotism' – a worn-out word, or you might call it 'love', a word whose interpretation is never clear, except when we feel its pain.

These days, this pain is there, or, to be less dramatic, depression at least. Time is spent in anxiety – maybe with a little hope that only makes the anxiety even more nagging. What is happening to and will become of Indonesia, while other parts of Asia have freed themselves from the crisis? Not much is happening, and it is not clear what will happen. The economy moves as though in sleep, a sleepwalker who doesn't know what he is doing. The government has no program, only good intention. The President talks a lot, and little can be believed. The leaders do not demonstrate any quality. The political parties are like looters. People of various religions are killing each other. There is no end to violence.

I wish I could stop reading newspapers. I am not interested in following television. And yet at the same time I know that I cannot stop thinking about Indonesia, just as I cannot stop thinking about my own body – whether it is still fit, attractive, able to savor enjoyable things, exciting things.

Native land, body: the two can be separated by thought, but not experience. And I find that as time goes on, more and more I cannot deny either of them as a representation of me, whatever 'me' means. Of course I could go and live in some cave in Lebanon, or an apartment in the old city of Prague, change my passport and eating habits. But what would I do with the accumulation of reminiscences, memories of experience both beautiful and bad, that together help form a native land, an engagement?

Memory, experience, engagement: these words all show that when we think about Indonesia, we don't only know and draw conclusions, but we stand, with joy and sadness, with anxiety and hope.

Who knows, maybe we do love our native land, after all. A difficult love, it is true, but a love, nonetheless, that is more like a process of 'exchanging captivity for freedom', to use the words of Amir Hamzah when he was describing a different kind of love. Maybe the words of Ibu Sud's song are right, after all: 'native land, my native land, you cannot be forgot.'

'Tanah Air' *Tempo* 20 May 2000, CP V: 485-7

Becoming

It was as though I was witnessing a becoming. Tens of thousands of people gathered in a semi-open space one unexpected afternoon: layer upon layer of enthusiasm, pile upon pile of hope, and anxiety, line upon line of faces that were not just watching with fixed and passive gaze. Each one of them becoming a mountain of motion. A mass of movement. Booming something one could not name.

The Gelora Bung Karno stadium, Jakarta, 5 July 2014: the two-hour long concert for Jokowi. No one would say this just musical entertainment. But nor was it just one part of a political campaign. It might have been the actualization of the political itself: I was witnessing close up a transformation. I felt the sudden joy of becoming an 'us' – an 'us' that was ready. An 'I' that believed. A subject that from one moment to the next, was making itself complete. 'I am large. I contain multitudes', the line of Walt Whitman's poem flashed through my head.

Yes, maybe I was witnessing an event.

I think the Indonesian word '*kejadian*', 'becoming', from the root '*jadi*' 'to become', is better than Badiou's term 'event', '*l'événement*'. What began as unformed was suddenly manifest – without being mobilized by a system, and without being formulated and named. Something 'happened', or more precisely, something 'became'. Something extremely rare, something that cannot be analyzed with a single cause and effect, something whose ties to the situation that is whole, one and coherent suddenly break. 'Released to the stars', Badiou says.

But unlike Badiou, I do not want to give the impression that in politics '*l'événement*' is so extraordinary that is appears to be completely separate from the present situation. What I witnessed, what I experienced that afternoon, showed that yes, something is separated, but there is also something connected.

While in today's politics all kinds of things can be bought and sold – support in parliament, demonstrations on the street, opinion in the mass media – at the Gelora Bung Karno stadium it was the opposite: tens of thousands of people, hundreds of musicians and singers, all came and were active without receiving any payment or promise of any kind. Whereas usually thousands of people gather to protest against something, on that afternoon, there on the dias and on the grassy arena of the stadium in Senayan, there was no note of anger. 'It was almost like a miracle' Abee Negara, the leader of the music group Slank said to me, after witnessing what he and his friends performed that fasting-month afternoon. 'It was almost like a miracle: there was no fighting in that pushing throng'

An important phenomenon in the 2014 presidential election was the throng of thousands of volunteers. And a new word – '*relawan*' for volunteer (with new emphasis on '*rela*' meaning willingly or freely) – entered Indonesian political vocabulary. This has never happened before in our history, and is probably something that is going to change the future networks of power.

But it was not only that. Another phenomenon was important: the creativity and humor that appeared so quickly and with such agility from various corners. The simple, apt song '*Salam dua jari*' (two finger greeting) composed by the singer Opie Andariksa and arranged by Slank, which went viral; the artists who produced cartoons (the most notable being Jokowi as Tintin); the stickers, posters and t-shirt designs in an almost endless variety; film makers and audiovisual artists producing witty, funny short films on YouTube.

There was a kind of fascinating anarchy at large. There was no center. There was no command. But there was something in the air everywhere: hope.

Even now, I still do not really understand why Joko Widodo, thin, and a poor public speaker – he is no naval officer Ali Sadikin, so charismatic and full of energy; or serious, scary Soeharto – could become the focus of hope of so many people. An Australian political researcher once asked me 'What is the mystique?' and I could not answer. He then said that among the people in Papua there is a belief that everywhere Jokowi goes he has six Papuans with him. In Ambon, the story is different. Jokowi is thin because he always shares his breakfast with his staff. It is not clear where these stories come from and how they spread. But at the very least it seems they convey a desired image: Jokowi appears as a leader close to ordinary people, sharing with them and walking alongside them. He is someone always working, without much posturing, simple and clean. He is a new face when Indonesia's politics are so disappointing.

Perhaps Jokowi has filled a symbol that has long been empty: without becoming a saint, he has become the symbol of the 'good' leader, who, precisely, is not an extraordinary person.

And what is 'good'? It cannot be formulated. It can never be formulated. But I know this: 'good' is actually manifest every day. 'Good' breathes life to human relations, in selfless giving and helping, even in a smile that is sincere, a sign of greeting or friendly conversation between people who do not know each other.

In other words, 'good' is no miracle. However, when at a certain time one senses that 'good' is lost, and people become suspicious of one another, then it changes into intense hope. And something universal.

That afternoon in the Gelora Bung Karno stadium, in the enthusiasm of those thousands of people, the universal dropped by momentarily. Not from the sky, but from the dust on the streets that stuck to the sweat of people with hope. An 'Us' was born. But at that moment it was not just the exclusive 'you and me' type us of the Indonesian word '*kami*', but also the inclusive 'all of us' of *kita*'.

That afternoon I saw that politics does not have only one face. Politics is not just a tension with 'Them'. It is also a project of 'Us/All-of-Us', of '*Kami-Kita*'.

And the concert ended with the sunset. Dozens of volunteers – with no commander – came together to break the fast, with whatever was to hand, and then they cleaned up the stadium.

Communal celebration is always transient. But the concert was a get-together, and those ties last longer than celebration and enjoyment of a few hours. Weeks afterwards I said to one of the organizers: music really does bring together all kinds of surprises. He agreed.

'Kejadian' *Tempo* 27 July 2014

Coconut Juice

Something interesting is going on when power starts with a story about words and coconut juice. We find this in the Javanese tale about the founder of the Mataram kingdom.

One morning, the story goes, a farmer called Ki Ageng Giring shinned a coconut palm in his yard to pick a coconut. He wanted to make coconut cream. But at the top of the palm tree he heard a voice: 'Whoever drinks the juice of the coconut you now hold in your hands will sire descendants who will rule the future kingdom'.

Trembling, Ki Ageng Giring picked the coconut, climbed down the tree, and went home. But it was still early; he was not thirsty. So he pierced the coconut to prepare it for drinking later and left it on the kitchen shelf. He went back to hoe his garden.

Without warning, his neighbor and close friend Ki Ageng Pemanahan, who had been clearing some undergrowth, dropped by. Thirsty after his work, when he saw the prepared young coconut in the kitchen he picked it up and drank the juice.

And so it came to pass: Ki Ageng Pemanahan was the progenitor of the Mataram kingdom. His son, an intelligent and brave young man called Sutawijaya, became a trusted soldier in the Pajang Kingdom. He defeated Arya Penangsang, a noble who refused to pay homage to Pajang. For his service, Sutawijaya was given the title of Panembahan Senapati and some territory. Over time, he developed this territory into a kingdom he called 'Mataram', taking the name of the Javanese kingdom from the golden age before Islam. Panembahan Senapati ruled from 1584 until 1601.

To me, the important thing in this story is the first word in the phrase Ki Ageng Giring hears: 'Whoever....'. No name is mentioned. Power is essentially open to fate. There is no door closed to a certain person or group. When it is Ki Ageng Pemanahan who gets this reward, it means that the origins of power begin with destiny that is not explicit, and with chance. Magical words and coconut juice – as part of the opening of the story about the fame and failures of Javanese kings – seem to serve as a reminder that power holds both mystery and ordinary things.

In other words, there is no firm, lasting foundation that determines who will be on the throne and who beneath it. The source of the legitimation of power seems to come from an old, empty mine shaft, full of fog. The history of power is the history of anxiety.

This is why power needs to have aura, and aura needs myth. There has to be something to provide rationale that it is valid, that it is fitting to be received by anyone, at any time. This means, in its anxiety, power cannot be merely a monolog. It needs the Other to acknowledge it. In this way it actually acknowledges that there is another party considered to be equal, or even more exalted, who has the power to acknowledge or to reject it.

In the era of democracy, this Other is 'the people': the group that cannot be completely present except symbolically. Back in the 16th century the Other was symbolized in another way: a magical queen from the south seas. One of the famous tales about Panembahan Senapati is his relationship with the Queen of the South Seas, Nyai Roro Kidul. It is told how one day this queen from the other world comes to the King. They make love. But at the same time it also says that Nyai Roro Kidul surrenders to the powerful aura of the ruler of Mataram, '*sor prabawa lan wong agung ngeksiganda*'.

Senapati's power and his aura, throne, and legitimacy are strengthened in this story. But also evident is this: a ruler has to struggle in complicated and subtle ways to obtain hegemony.

This story might also be interpreted as challenging the thesis that the struggle for hegemony is entirely marked by antagonism. For what happens is the tense interweaving of competition and connection. There is indeed disguised conflict, but hegemony cannot be achieved only with bloody daggers.

We know what transpired. The rule of Panembahan Senapati's descendant in the Mataram dynasty, Amangkurat I (1646-1677) was a rule of bloodshed. The Javanese Chronicles (*Babad Tanah Jawi*) describe a terrifying and dark mood in the kingdom, which soon came to a dramatic end. The story of the kingdom of Mataram ends with the Trunajaya rebellion. Legitimacy is lost, hegemony collapses.

The storytellers then relate how Amangkurat I, while escaping from his palace, died from drinking poisoned coconut juice. Probably this is a parable: the thirst for power at the correct time is productive; the thirst for power at the wrong time brings ruin – and people do not always know when that wrong time is.

'Air Kelapa' *Tempo* 15 June 2014

Crush!

1965 – before the story of massacre, extermination, exile and enmity, there was something else, often forgotten: language. Language that facilitated all this. Language that had been developing since 1958 when Indonesia was ruled with 'Guided Democracy', and 'Revolutionary' spirit was being fanned once more, with continuous mobilization of the masses. Language constructed with brawny, acrimonious statements in speeches, slogans, posters, indoctrination and briefings: 'Crush!' 'Grind!' 'Retool'! 'Wipe out!' Language determining whom was friend or foe, and giving them meaning that set solid, even absolute.

Language and violence. People often think of them as separate. Walter Benjamin, for instance, believed there was a realm that was 'wholly inaccessible to violence' – namely the realm of 'understanding', *Verständigung*. Language, in other words.

But he forgot: language can coerce. Language itself contains a kind of violence, even before grammar and dictionaries constrain it. From the outset, words and their utterance come and enclose us, from mother's lullabies, father's conversation, sounds in the street, rules at school, state regulations, religious teachings and the influence of the mass media – which, without our being aware of it, seep into our very selves and then emerge as though we ourselves produce them.

Think of how many clichés we hear and use every single day. At the same time, how difficult it is to express our deepest feelings in an expressive and communicative way, to reach others.

Probably this is what made Lacan call language not a product of *je parle* (I speak), but rather *ça parle* (it speaks). 'I' is as though unimportant in making language. 'I' is half submerged in language, becoming 'it', when the meaning of a sentence appears in a form that is shaped by others, by people at large, continuously, over years and years.

I say 'half submerged' because actually there is still an 'I', a subject, who, hesitatingly, wants to say something entirely new. But the subject will never entirely succeed in this – and if within the cage of power that controls language, he or she will fail.

This reminds us, of course, of George Orwell's classic novel, *1984,* which was beautifully translated into Indonesian by Barus Siregar. There is no other work of literature to compare with Orwell's work in depicting the prison of power when language is tightly tied to violence.

Maybe because *1984* is a hyperbolic fiction. The novel gives an exaggerated depiction of England that has changed into totalitarian 'Oceania'. People are watched every moment by the ruler who never appears but is mentioned constantly as 'Big Brother'. And at the same time they are drowned in language that has been deliberately constructed to make them acquiesce.

That language is called 'Newspeak'. It is made up of newly formed words and old words whose meanings have been changed: 'War' means 'peace', 'freedom' is 'slavery'. And acronyms are propagated, making it easy for people to memorize them with sounds that are effective and need no analysis.

'Newspeak' is spread via gigantic television screens all over the country, compiled in dictionaries, and used in Party newspapers. The people, bureaucrats and Party members must use it – with all its clichés and slogans – facilitating the extinction of the old language. People have become mass parrots, no longer subjects who speak. *Ça parle.*

In the midst of this, Winston Smith secretly tries to retain *je parle*. He does not want to be dragged into a language that, as his friend Syme says, has dictionaries that are getting thinner all the time. Synonyms are abolished. Every meaning can have only one word to represent it. Variations are forbidden. 'Don't you see that the whole aim of Newspeak is to narrow the range of thought?' Syme says.

Thought: it is evil. Under this totalitarian power – reminiscent of Germany under Hitler, Russia under Stalin, China under Mao, and Korea under Kim – language has become technology to stunt people.

But language does not stand alone. It is part of the life constructed by those in power – those virtually faceless, nameless people – with tension. It is proclaimed that there is an ongoing war, there are enemies, there are conspiracies.

Every living space is full of suspicion and hate. Every day there is mass observation of 'Two Minutes' Hate': national traitors who, strangely, are never arrested, and therefore must be continually denounced. At those moments, as though electrically charged, people's passion rages. They want to kill, torture, smash faces with hammers – even though the anger is sensed as abstract, because it can be quickly directed from one target to another.

In situations like this, words and violence fuse. Winston is arrested. At the beginning he is merely invited to speak. They try to persuade him with language in the realm of 'understanding', to use Benjamin's words. He holds out. But eventually he has to give in. He submits when threatened with a cage full of fierce rats – of which he has a phobia. At that moment, he can do nothing else. The novel ends with Winston loving Big Brother. Through the rats and words, he is finished.

1984: I remember 1965. When enmity, hatred and suspicion are bandied about continuously, with bold, vicious words – as happened in Indonesia leading up to 1965 – there is no more difference between rats and language. All is terror, extermination, violence.

'Ganyang!' *Tempo* 13 October 2013

Arrows

To shoot an arrow is to destroy with precision. At one moment.

One day Durna ordered his students to take aim at a bird on the branch of a tree.

'What do you see?' asked Durna, the Guru.

Suyudana: 'Master, I see a bird on the branch on the left'.

Arjuna: 'Master, I see nothing at all. There is no branch and there is no bird. I see only the eye.'

The master knew that Arjuna was right. Taking aim means to determine focus. To the champion archer, that target is everything. In other words, the archer obliterates – or does not notice – things outside the intended target; context, background, history must all be considered non-existent. In this way, destruction is surer. The object fixed yonder must be given no opportunity to move and change.

The analogy of archery is power, particularly in its aggressive nature; an unbending assertion. What is to be destroyed cannot be allowed to move. With the intention of conquering, power places the world in its aim, in a center of perception. From that center is determined what is close and what is distant, what should be included in the first circle, and what should be rejected.

At a different level, the State, religious institutions, and other powers such as capitalism do the same thing. From the center of perception of capitalism, there is classification about what can be assimilated because it brings 'profit', and what will inflict a 'loss'.

To religious institutions, there are those outside and those inside the line of 'faith'. The State has different classifications, but with the same intent of domination.

The Netherlands Indies was an example. *Divide et impera* presented the Indonesian people as divided, not in order to respect existing differences, but rather to keep a firm hand over them. With these divisions, the administration of power could be efficient and effective.

So categories were created. 'Foreign Easterner', 'native', 'Javanese', 'Dayak', 'Sundanese', 'Papuan' and so forth – identities that prior to colonialism had never been clear or stable. By establishing this identification, the colonizer took aim and threw his lasso into the jumble of people outside the government buildings, snaring them into groups of names and concepts.

And so 'groups' or 'ethnicities' were born. Anything ambiguous, vague, unstable, and that represented exceptions to these 'groups' or 'ethnicities', was discarded. And then theses, arguments, discourse, words, and entire symbolic orders had to be recruited to assert these identities – as though they had all been there since the time of Adam.

Colonialism ruled over classifications that ensnared 'the other' in a radical way. People in the colonies were ordained as units utterly clean of various 'others'; in the 'Foreign Easterner' group there could be no diversity that changed with history. They were considered fixed. They were secured as though they had a fixed essence. 'Chinese' were forever 'Chinese', 'Javanese' were considered to be one, even though people in Magelang cannot understand the language spoken in Tegal.

The noose of *divide et impera* required that all elements within these identities be considered fully visible. Nothing was vague, nothing unobserved or not understood, and nothing to make us doubtful. The arrow of power had to find its mark.

But is this possible? Arrows and the noose of power eventually have limits. Administration, control, the whole language of power, the reach of the Church and the ulama, the long arm of capital – all these are not operations run by the gods. Life, with its body and essence, has its own dynamics that oppose or hold out against any noose of classification. Or shun it.

There is an energy within life that does not enter the structure of the perception of power, an energy that moves unceasingly. And it is in this moment that what Deleuze calls *devenir-minorité*, becoming the minority, takes place. Here the 'minority' is marked not by numbers, but by its nature: it is the antithesis to the power of the 'majority' (from the word 'major', meaning 'large', 'important') that dictates structure. There, in what is blurred, unclear, unfixed, flowing – and in what is not within the aim of the conqueror – lie the seeds of opposition.

So colonial power was always in a fragile position. The common cliché says that Indonesia lived under colonialism for 350 years. In truth: Indonesia was a thorn in the side of colonialism for 400 years. From the first European efforts at power in Banda in 1529, to the Aceh wars that ended only in 1904, through to the war of independence from 1946-1949, there were hundreds of eruptions of 'minorities' that escaped the lasso of power. They were invisible.

And indeed there are always areas that are unseen, as too emperors. Maybe this is what Italo Calvino meant when he wrote in *Le città invisibili:* Marco Polo, the traveler from Venice, told the Kublai Khan of fifty-five strange cities: cities that were unnoticed, cities in eleven categories outside the classification of rulers.

'In the lives of emperors there is a moment which follows pride in the boundless extension of the territories we have conquered, and the melancholy and relief of knowing we shall soon give up any thought of knowing and understanding them. There is a sense of emptiness that comes over us at evening, with the odor of the elephants after the rain and the sandalwood ashes growing cold in the braziers …'.

From the outset, Marco Polo used the word 'odor' and not 'view'. When we do not take aim to dominate, then the world can be magical and not entirely visible.

'Panah' *Tempo* 9 October 2011, CP X: 163-6

Cradling

Javanese kings were the expression of an ideal. Primarily, the ideal of stability. Think of their names: *Amangkurat* and *Mangkubumi* mean 'cradling the earth'. *Hamengku Buwono* means 'cradling the world'. *Paku Buwono* is the 'spike' (*paku*) that keeps the world (*buwono*) steady, staked to stop it from shaking.

We often forget that these names are relatively new, appearing in the history of Javanese monarchy only in the 17th century. Before that, from the old Mataram kingdom through to the new Mataram, we find only personal names: Sanjaya, Syailendra, Mpu Sindok, Airlangga, Hayam Wuruk, Raden Patah, Trenggono, Hadiwijaya and Panembahan Senapati. Then, in 1641, the title 'Sultan Agung, Senapati ing Ngalaga Abdurrahman' appeared (Sultan Agung, commander-in-chief on the field of battle, servant of the Merciful): the transition from the personal to the symbolic. And then, Amangkurat the First.

Symbols, unlike signs, invoke a cluster of information that is neither precise nor fixed. The symbolic contains something unsaid. The names 'Amangkurat' and 'Paku Buwono' hold the sense of a different sense of geography: the ruler imagines territory that is not limited to the area under his direct rule. But the actual breadth of that territory is not marked by any precise line. It reminds us of the famous myth of the intimate and mysterious relationship between Panembahan Senapati, the founder of the Mataram kingdom, and the ruler of the 'South Sea' and 'Mount Merapi'. Hidden within this story is an unspoken expansive desire.

Perhaps this was just a sign of megalomania. But then again, it might be something else. When scrutinized more carefully, these names do not imply the desire to conquer. The word '*mangku*', to cradle, means both to hold and to nurse. Cradling is something intimate, calm and protective. And the word '*paku*' for nail or spike in the name 'Paku Buwono' is more associated with keeping guard.

But at the same time, there's another facet to this: what is cradled and guarded is also taken to be something stable, steady – something that is comfortable with what holds it where it is. In other words, it is expected that the country or society cradled in the king's lap has no antagonism either within it or between it and the king.

Of course, I repeat this is just an ideal. A symbol has another role: not as a representation of something, but rather as an attempt to achieve something that does not exist.

In the history of Mataram, what did not exist was precisely harmony between the cradler and those cradled. From the reign of Amangkurat I, violence was the rule of the day. Amangkurat I slaughtered 3000 Muslim clerics in the main square in the space of half an hour. It was he, too, who ended up causing Trunojoyo's rebellion: even his own son opposed him, so he had to escape from the palace and he died on the distant north coast.

The case of Amangkurat I shows that this attempt at symbolism arose precisely when the king was a divided figure. He was linked to something mythological; as one cradling the world, he was not part of that world. In that position he was expected (and he expected) to be the one unifying the earth. But at the same time, he was within the earth's confusion. Expectations of him being the 'unifier' were too high. A gap arose.

Amangkurat I demonstrates the extent to which the 'cradler' was actually not the foundation of stability at all. He himself had no support. He arose from the conflict and violence that shape history: from the fall of Majapahit, the vanishing of the Demak sultanate and the disappearance of Jipang. In fact, probably long before Ken Arok built Tumapel with blood and kris.

And so through to our times: we must admit that the ideal of stability is both good and futile. Every country, kingdom or republic, no matter what, is shaped through conflict, contestation and hegemonic wrangling. Antagonism is never ending. Ever since Kautilya wrote the *Arthasastra* in India in the 4th century BCE, or since Machiavelli wrote *Il Principe* in Italy in the 16th century, through to the democratic competition of the 21st century, political thinkers and actors have known: politics is a kind of war.

That is how it is. People create power for themselves, but they are unable to make that power identical with themselves: recall Amangkurat who escaped from the palace; or the deposed and decapitated kings; or the caliphs murdered and disgraced. What is important, of course, is not to acknowledge brutality as something valid. What is important is to eliminate the illusion that the world will cease shaking once it is cradled and fixed. Power keeps shifting. 'The creator', as Ernesto Laclau put it, 'will search in vain for the seventh day of rest.'

We in Indonesia easily slide into nostalgia for that seventh day: the achievement of consensus. I do not entirely agree with Laclau that antagonism is the one and only foundation shaping a society. But indeed we cannot assume that consensus will surely come. The various elements in political life will not automatically find 'rationality' and with it arrive at consensus. In Indonesian history, with or without democracy, there is no contest without opposition. Politics cannot merely chase coalition without confrontation.

In a 19th century Javanese manuscript it is written that possible future leaders should be patient, accommodating and all-embracing, like the ocean – *den ajembar, momot lan mengku, den kaya segara.* This advice appears to have been formulated by someone who felt himself safe from politics, and to have been directed to those inheriting a power currently at peace. But here in Indonesia, the ocean is no ripple-free lake. It has tempests and tsunamis.

'Memangku' *Tempo* 20 March 2011, CP X: 47-50

Names, or why Juliet was wrong

A cliché: What is in a name? Those words have been repeated in millions of conversations ever since *Romeo and Juliet* was first performed in 1597. Whenever people are bothered about names, Juliet (or, more rightly, Shakespeare) is quoted. Juliet Capulet and Romeo Montague can fall in love even though the other Capulets and Montagues are enemies.

> *What's Montague? It is nor hand, nor foot,*
> *Nor arm, nor face, nor any other part*
> *Belonging to a man.*

Names, to Juliet, are merely affixes. 'Romeo, doff thy name!' she says to her sweetheart. She is in love. To her, that love would be no less were Romeo Montague to call himself 'Johnny Puyol'.

But clichés come about through repetition, and in this case repetition comes about because it transpires that people are constantly bothered by names. *Romeo and Juliet* became a tragedy (replayed for almost 500 years) precisely because Juliet's theory was wrong; she did not realize that there are many things in a name.

Especially in Indonesia. Here, a lot is made of name giving. When he was a child, Bung Karno's name was changed from 'Kusno' to 'Sukarno'. His father hoped that a change of name would help his sickly son keep healthy. The new name, he hoped, would make him like the wayang hero, Karna. According to Bung Karno, his father thought of Karna as a patriot; he hoped his son would thus be imbued with this spirit. His father's decision shows how names are not merely affixes. They have performative power.

Yes, Juliet was wrong

Bung Karno, like his father Pak Sukemi, also gave great thought to the naming of his children. He called his sons 'Guntur', 'Guruh' (both meaning 'thunder) and 'Taufan' (typhoon), all words that have suggestive power about the majesty of nature. He called his daughters 'Mega' (cloud) and 'Sukma' (soul), both of which connote something soft and gentle. Of course, apart from the meaning and associative power, the sound factor was also important. The words 'guntur' and 'guruh' were chosen rather than other less resonant words with the same meaning, like 'gledek'. Bung Karno and the Indonesian people would have been embarrassed to have a boy at the palace called 'Gledek Sukarnoputra'.

But it seems that a child's name is more reflective of the wishes (and nature) of the parents than the fate of the child. 'Guntur', 'guruh', 'taufan' and 'mega' show Bung Karno's love of non-static sublime things that are linked to the sky.

The artist Djoko Pekik, a Lekra painter who came from a poor village in central Java, looked in another direction. He took the names of his children and grandchildren from ordinary daily things that people ignore and even discard: Pakuril (from *paku rel* or train-track nail), Lugut (the fine hairs on bamboo), Drejeg Lalang (the point of tall, coarse grass).

The writer Bur Rasuanto was different again. Aware of his position as a writer, he gave his children names from literary forms: Legendariya and Mitologenta.

Children do not choose their own names. Perhaps this is part of their colonization by their parents. Thus in Indonesia, children often change their names once they are adult and independent, if they feel their childhood name is no longer fitting for them. Yapi Panda Abdiel Tambajong became 'Remy Silado', the well-known writer. The late Budiman S. Hartojo was born as Munawir. This is especially true in central Java: people usually discard their childhood names and use an adult name, a *jeneng tuwa*: 'Harjowiryo, formerly Sukidi'.

In this way, a name is an affirmation of self and a sign of transition. But what is signified is not merely personal transition. Indonesia has witnessed the politics of naming shift on a grand scale – proof that language, which has power over us, is also part of the collisions of power within larger society. To strengthen Indonesian-ness, the political elite pushed Indonesians of Chinese descent to change their names so they would no longer seem 'Chinese'. This 'Indonesian-izing' applied to other areas. Bung Karno gave the film star Lientje Tambayong a new name, because the 'tje' ending on her name was Dutch. She became 'Rima Melati'.

The politics of naming can also take place in another way. In Java, names reveal class. 'Suryo Sumirat' is clearly an aristocratic name. 'Paidin' and 'Kromo' are usually farmers. The main figures in the Indonesian Communist Party, as part of their political stance, used names that were more lower-class: Njoto, Njono, and Rewang. Njoto and Njono did not use the prefix 'Su' before their names, because those who do so are usually more upper class.

But it would be wrong to then conclude that we always give political substance to a name. The Tapanuli often give their children names of ordinary things: 'Radio', 'Kantor' (office), and 'Sutradara' (director), for instance. In West Java, a father gave his children names taken from models of cars: 'Fia Fiati' or 'Honda Impalawati'.

Names are also used commemoratively. A Balinese artist called his daughter 'I Made Waikiki' after the famous beach in Honolulu because she was born while his father was exhibiting there. Then there was 'Amagapa' after the name of the ship on which the parents travelled to Manado. There was 'Delanov' who was born on the 8th (*dela*pan) of November. Another example from West Sumatra is 'Ampeno Herlino', an acronym from Ampek Nopember Hari Lahirnyo (Born on November 4, in the Minang language).

If you really look, you see that there is virtually no limit to the variety of naming in Indonesia. There can be military titles, 'Kapten' or 'Letnan', or historical figures, "Gandhi', 'Kennedy', and 'Mussolini'.

Then there are book titles. I named my first child 'Hidayat Jati'. A friend in America asked what this meant. I said that I did not know: I had merely taken the title of a book by Ronggowarsito, the 19th century Javanese writer. My friend retorted: 'You mean you named your child with a book!' (He would certainly never name his child 'Gone with the Wind'.)

But Indonesians are not so easily surprised in this naming matter. The late S. Prinka, a graphic designer at Tempo magazine, got his name through an acronym: 'Prinka' is from 'Perjuangan Republik Indonesia Merdeka' or 'the struggle for Indonesia's independence'. Understandable when one knows his father was a police officer during the revolution. My friend Choki Sapta Wanusi got his name through another acronym: 'Sapta' means 'seven' and 'Wanusi' is from 'pahlawan revolusi' (heroes of the revolution).

There is such variety in the sourcing of names that it is often difficult to trace the 'etymology' of an Indonesian name. There is someone with the name 'Marmorita-rita stell taurantia gutata'. I have no idea what this means or why it was chosen. It seems as though there is an idea that a name is more impressive the longer it is. For instance (and I swear this is a genuine example), 'Buyung Abdurahman Nanda Aria Megat Sambat Elang di Laut'. People are not fussed at all about what to call those with such names. Marmorita-rita stell taurantia gutata, for example, is just called 'Muning'.

But names can also be chosen without any urge to sound impressive, and without ornament. There is a child named 'Disiplin Pribadi' (self discipline) who is called 'Ipin'. The singer

Melly Goeslow and her husband Anto Hoed have a son whom they named simply 'Anakku Lelaki', (my son).

Funny? I find it charming. In this name-creating business, I think Indonesians are the most innovative and free in the world. And given the current bad feeling with Malaysia, I am sure Indonesians will be happy to hear that we are richer in naming. In Malaysia, Malay names do not stray far from the tried and trusted Anwar, Badawi, Harun, Muhammad, Musa…

Actually, Malaysia is not strange. In America, Europe, and the world as a whole, there are only so-so variations on common first names: John, Paul, Tom, James, William. In America you can compile lists of babies' names. In Indonesia, this would be impossible.

So to Americans and Europeans, Indonesian names are confusing. A German couple wanted to call their daughter 'Lilian Ayu'. When they went to the registry of births, the officials at first rejected it; 'Ayu' was not a name, they said. But the father did not give in. He pulled out the novel *Saman* with a photo of the author Ayu Utami on the cover and showed it to the bureaucrat. Only then did he see that 'Ayu' was not the name of a vegetable.

There is even more confusion over what people call surnames. In Indonesia, people commonly do not use a 'family name', or at least there is no accepted practice about this. When Ahmad Sahal registered his daughter Sri Mulyani at a school in England, he was called 'Mr Mulyani'. The English do not know that in Indonesia people do not usually take on the name of their husband or father. While this is often a nuisance for us, in fact we should be proud. Because implicit in this is the acknowledgement that each person's identity is not necessarily dependent on the head of the household.

Take Qori Sandioriva, for instance. She appears as herself, Miss Indonesia Universe 2010, and not as a member of a family 'Sandioriva' or 'Qori'. Not as a member of a clan. We cannot tell, from that name, what 'ethnicity' or religion she has. She represents Indonesia.

So too with Rima Melati. Bung Karno gave an example of Indonesian-ness in choosing that name, just as he called his daughter 'Megawati' and not 'Waljinah'. Bung Karno avoided names that were typically Javanese (or typical of any other ethnic group), and thus showed that this land of ours is not only multi-cultural, but also 'inter-cultural'.

While in Malaysia and Singapore there is a clear line between 'Harun' and 'Stephen', in Indonesia we can come across 'Stephen Harun' within the name of a single person. Whereas in Malaysia 'Muhammad Ali' is most certainly a Malay, here in Indonesia this is not necessarily the case. Thirty years ago a friend of mine had an acquaintance named Muhammad Islam. He was Christian.

Juliet was wrong, but her question was a good one: 'What is in a name?' Because it turns out that there are many stories in a name. Particularly when we consider names not as shackling identity markers, but as signs that people are individuals. Free. Not examples of a group. Not a number.

Gepeng's real name: Freddy Aris

Nadia Adeline: Papua Miss Friendship 2009

Elichon Christellgo Pentury, alias Igo: Indonesian Idol 2010

'Nama, Atau Mengapa Juliet Salah' *Tempo* 21 September 2010,
CP IX: 679-84

Darkness

That day I saw a woman wearing the headscarf sitting at work by a microscope in a laboratory. It reminded me of Kartini.

In her letter of 15 August 1902, Kartini included a short verse:

> *Door nacht tot licht*
> *Door storm tot rust*
> *Door strijd tot eer*
> *Door leed tot lust*

Many people have misquoted or misinterpreted these lines. The first collection of Kartini's letters was published in 1911 as *Door Duisternis Tot Licht* (Through Darkness to Light). J. H. Abendanon, the Netherlands East Indies official who supported the Regent of Jepara's daughter so enthusiastically, probably chose the phrase. It was Abendanon, too, who selected the young woman's letters and published them. Later, the poet Armijn Pane translated the book into Indonesian as *Habis Gelap Terbitlah Terang* (After Darkness Comes the Light).

People seem to find in this title a metaphor to depict Kartini's struggle to free herself from a world that was outdated, backward and constraining. 'Light' is a metaphor for enlightenment in attitude and thought: the sign of emancipation from all that constraint.

Joost Coté, the researcher who translated a more complete collection of Kartini's letters and published them in a book published by the Monash Asia Institute in 1992, was one who thought this. He wrote that the phrase 'reflects...[Kartini's] own sense of her historic struggle'.

But I don't think so. If we read the letter with that verse (which Kartini might have composed herself), we can see that the word 'light' indicates something completely different: 'light' is the moment Kartini finds her identity as a Muslim woman. She gets that 'light' through the guidance of her mother who came from an observant Muslim background. She did not get the 'light' from a Western-educated woman but from 'an old woman...from whom I have gathered many flowers that spring from the heart'.

The fact that Abendanon did not link his chosen phrase with the facts, expresses a perspective typical to an educated European of the early 20th century: to him, Kartini's struggle was a model of modernization. Modernization was the path to *Aufklärung*, 'enlightenment'. And this path was definitely not the path to religion, especially Islam. 'Enlightenment' was the coming of light that replaced the old darkness: irrationality, superstition and unquestioning observance.

To Abendanon, as also to Indonesian thinkers about modernity (Takdir Alisjahbana, Sjahrir, Tan Malaka, Sukarno), Kartini's place and time was a miniature of history, when rationality pounded at the door of a 'backward' society. And so they called Kartini a 'champion' (as the line goes in the song we Indonesians all learn by heart), specifically a champion for freedom for those like her: freedom from constraining tradition and mind-numbing belief.)

But to Kartini, the problem was more complex. She lived in the midst of the forward march of reason. However, and at the same time, she knew that religion – usually considered a set of frozen dogma – was not relegated to the past.

Probably this was why the headscarfed young woman by the microscope reminded me of Kartini: religion and rationality are not two opposing camps.

There was a time, particularly in Europe, when reason rejected faith. Science abandoned religion, or the two separated, while reason dominated life. But with this victory, something happened to reason. When the battle between reason and religion ended, religion declined, but as Hegel said, 'reason…. became mere intellect'.

In the French Revolution, reason was celebrated and religion expelled. From then on, faith has lived in inner spiritual life, not in social life or institutional bodies like the Church. Religion retreated from the arena, but faith found its new living space in the private world. Reason felt no need to expel faith – nor was it able to explain it. Thus reason was better busying itself with other matters: becoming intellect, or even wit (*akal*, which is where the word *mengakali* or 'outwit' comes from). And with this tool, mankind outwits nature and controls it. Man becomes Lord. Mankind produces something that did not previously exist.

Formerly, reason never ceased being stirred by wonders of the world; philosophy and science were even born from this. But eventually reason, as intelligence (*akal*), assisted the disenchantment of the world, and in Max Weber's depressing view, humanity was gradually pushed into an 'iron cage'.

So the story of the victory of reason is also the story of its defeat. Reason forgets that actually it is manifest as 'light' only because there is 'dark'. 'The dark' is not a state of light deficiency, but rather it is what makes light, light. When the dark is rejected and discarded, nothing of worth remains.

But it is then – in discarding the dark – that religion and intelligence (*akal*) often meet. It reminds me of the headscarfed woman with the microscope: it reminds me of Kartini. It might just be that Kartini was one of those who abandoned 'the night' (a transitory state of darkness), because to her religion and reason both desired this. After all, do not religion and the modern world both reject confused and unexpressed aspects of humanity – like the world of the subconscious?

But if this is so, then I fear that humankind will reach a dead end: it will cease understanding life. It reminds me of Chesterton's words about mysticism: 'the whole secret of mysticism is thus: that man can understand everything by the help of what he does not understand.'

But maybe that hand-held microscope is different. Maybe it is part of a re-emerging sense of wonder – not as a tool of intelligence to conquer life, without acknowledging the dark.

'Gelap' *Tempo* 23 May 2010, CP IX: 613-6

Indonesia

Sometimes I wonder what possibly could have crossed my father's mind in the few moments before he was executed. Sometimes I want to imagine that the name 'Indonesia' was on his lips, or 'Indonesian independence', but of course this imagined image is a cliché, and thus whenever it appears I quickly stop it. It is possible that my father was terrified before the Dutch army firing squad. Or resigned, perhaps? What is more or less certain is that for a few minutes or a few seconds afterwards, all fear (or resolve, or perhaps even the self dignity that looks like courage) vanished; the bullets pierced his forehead. Blood spurted, he collapsed, and would never come home again.

In deep mourning, and afraid, my whole family wept. Only mother remained strong; like a magic pillar. She cried, but she calmed the rest of us, and took over the urgent matter of the burial and ritual mourning preparations.

These days I try to understand what made mother so strong. Perhaps she already knew that her husband's life would end in such a way, or perhaps in a way a little better than being shot. Mother had seen Father go in and out of prison; she had even accompanied him into exile in far off Digul, Papua, further than anyone could imagine. Was she resigned to all this? Mother never spoke about her husband with the praise due a revolutionary fighter; only once or twice did she speak about his stubbornness: there were times when he sort of meditated in order to neutralize his enemies (I was never told who they were); there were times when he left home for some secret meeting on a boat somewhere; and there were times when he listened to the radio constantly. And all this time, mother never spoke about 'Indonesia'.

Probably this is because to the generation of political activists at this time – those who had been directly involved in the nationalist movement from the beginning of the 20th century – 'Indonesia' was something automatically present in their minds, so that there was no need for mouths to re-utter it. Or the word 'Indonesia' was automatically rebellion against the word 'Netherlands Indies'. Because every moment in political activity at that time was rebellion, the word 'Indonesia' was already implicit when someone was prepared to go to prison. Or go into exile. Or be executed.

Mother raised the rest of her young children in a practical way: they had to eat and go to school. It was almost no more than that. In our family conversation, there was never any instruction to love our homeland. But I was raised, and I think my brothers and sisters too, with the memory of our father – and together with that, quietly, 'Indonesia' hung about us, involved us. In the sense that it became intensely meaningful. At least I cannot imagine myself living without bonding with 'Indonesia'.

I am sure that I am not alone. Along with others, I cannot easily formulate what 'Indonesia' means to me. But I see my friends who, with no such formulation, stand and sing *'Padamu Negeri'* (For you, my country), prepared to do great deeds for people in their country – to oppose oppressors, for instance. I see Upik and Udin who, with the red and white flag on their backpacks, went to Aceh to help people struck by the tsunami. I know Tati and Toto who, even though they do not like anything to do with 'politics', go all glassy-eyed when they hear the Indonesian national anthem played solemnly.

What makes them like this? Perhaps it is because homeland is memory and hope that involves the body: remembered fragrance of rice, the aftertaste of spices, the swift current that cannot be forgotten, the sound of father's praise, mother's soothing song, grandfather's cough, and the children's stories that settle deep in consciousness. And hope: the house that will be built, the children whose schooling will be fine, the career that will be made. And the hope of doing something meaningful.

Of course there are those who reject all this – or who feel no bonding with any homeland. I think that those who remain loyal to the idea of 'Darul Islam' that has no map on this earth are a good example; they move from one area to another, but never bond anywhere. They have no homeland, for homeland is part of the earth and the body, whereas they are convinced that the law – which to them is everything – has no bonding with the earth, the body, space, and fixed time. It is not surprising that 'Indonesia' means nothing to them. Their geography is simple: a place is part of enemy territory or their own territory. There is nothing else.

We know that they are prepared to die, to be shot dead. But how different it is with those who feel bonded with a place of life and a place of death. Most probably, there in front of the firing squad my father never proudly uttered the word 'Indonesia'. Most probably too, my mother worked determinedly for her children and not for the future of this country. But to me, they are like most of us: part of a community of fellows, who live and die, at a time, in a place, and who can never be obliterated with law and weapons.

'Indonesia' *Tempo* 23 August 2009, CP IX: 201-4

That Name

In the mid 18th century, an explorer in this archipelago, seeing the brown-skinned inhabitants who resembled Polynesians, wondered: What are these people called? What is the name of these islands of theirs?

George Samuel Windsor Earl, this English explorer, decided: 'Indunesia'. But then he changed his mind, 'Malayanusia' would be better, he said. But this name did not last long. His colleague, James Logan, chose the name 'Indonesia'.

And 'Indonesia' then entered history. R.E. Elson, in his book *The Idea of Indonesia: A History* (published in 2008, and the most comprehensive document about the idea of our nation) tells how this name came to have its own saga.

Actually, names not only become signifiers. Names are not just made and constructed. Names also construct. Names also establish an identity. But names are not entirely born from the intention to make concepts. People say 'Indonesia' not only with a definition. Names are not abstract indexes. The robot in the film *Star Wars* was given the label 'R2D2' but we remember him as 'Artuditu'. The label became a name when the object bearing it lived, moved, displayed emotions and acted like a human being. The name suggests personification, just as sets of gamelan instruments are given names, like '*Kyai Tunggul*'. The name presents an image in our heads, arousing passion or fear, anxiety or hope.

The name 'Indonesia' is also like a person. It signifies not only a place. When Bung Karno used the name 'Indonesia' in his defence (*Indonesia Menggugat*) when he was tried before the colonial court (published in English translation as 'Indonesia Accuses!'), the name referred to something suffering through injustice, but also yearning for a free tomorrow. It was not very clear what that 'something' was, but the remarkable energy it held gave Bung Karno the courage to be imprisoned, and made young men prepared to offer their lives.

'Indonesia' had already become what Laclau calls an 'empty signifier'. Nothing existed that in itself was capable of completely and fully filling it with meaning. What happened was merely this: every person or party gave it meaning, through competition or conflict. Elson's book is the story of the filling of that 'empty signifier' that is sounded as 'Indonesia'.

To nineteenth century anthropologists from France, Britain, Germany and Holland, 'Indonesia' was a practical working concept. But the Dutch generally did not understand this. One of them in a parliamentary session said that the name 'Indonesia' would be better as a trade name for cigars.

It was quite another thing for the young men who came from the Dutch colony. In the foreign land of Holland, there arose among them a special sense of togetherness, whether they came from Aceh or Ambon, and whether they were of Chinese or Javanese descent. From this togetherness, the name 'Indonesia' became a series of sounds that unified, and with that unity these people demanded independence. Initially, they did not agree with the formation of a branch of Boedi Oetomo (because it was limited to 'Javanese'). They formed the *'Indische Verenging'* (IV), which later became the *'Indonesische Verbond van Studeerende'* (IVS).

Conservative colonial politicians like H. Colijn tried to point out that Indonesian unity was impossible because of the differences of peoples and race. People like him saw 'Indonesia' as merely an illusion. But this viewpoint did not last. A young man from Minahasa, G.S.S.J. Ratu Langie, stressed the need for 'brotherhood' of various peoples and races in 'Indonesia'. Elson's book notes that in a meeting of the IVS held in 1920, the son of the Sultan of Yogyakarta referred to himself as 'someone who within certain limits represents the Javanese, and thus also part of Indonesia'. He ended his speech with the cry, 'Long live Indonesia!'

History reveals, I think, that those who most succeeded in filling the meaning of 'Indonesia' were two figures from a radical party, the Indische Partij.

The first was Soerwardi Soerjaningrat, later known as Ki Hadjar Dewantara. In the magazine *Hindia Poetra* that was republished in 1919, Soerjaningrat the activist said: '…An Indonesian is anyone who considers Indonesia his or her homeland, whether they be pure Indonesian or those with Chinese, Dutch or other European blood running in their veins'.

The second was E. Douwes Dekker, later known as Setiabudi. An activist who was also of European blood, he wrote an open letter to Queen Wilhelmina on April 1913: 'No, Your Majesty. This is not Your Majesty's homeland. It is ours.'

And when his two comrades-in-arms, Tjipto Mangoenkoesoemo and Soewardi were captured and exiled by the colonial government, Douwes Dekker wrote sadly, but also with resolve: 'We stand not merely… side by side, but also *within* each other.'

Soewardi and Dekker's words are being proved true a century later, when these days Indonesia is not merely multi-cultural but also inter-cultural: every person becomes Indonesian because he or she takes another culture into him or herself. For Indonesia is not a partitioned diversity, as in apartheid. Indonesia is an eclectic process, freely mixing and fusing.

With this, Indonesia, this 'empty signifier', calls upon anyone and everyone to never cease moving the exclusive 'we' (*kami*) to become the inclusive 'we', or 'all of us' (*kita*). It is never narrow. It lives in space and time, but it feels infinite.

'Nama Itu' *Tempo* 27 September 2009, CP IX: 477-80

Debris

1945, 1966, 1998... These numbers are becoming names now. Each of them names a historical change: the first, the birth of the Republic of Indonesia; the second, the collapse of Sukarno's rule, and the third, the fall of the Soeharto regime.

In other words, each of these numbers no longer means merely a year. Each written figure refers to a grand event: events that made an era break with that which went before it: when a situation collapsed and all the hinges of life changed, and then came a totally new beginning. Even, to use Alain Badiou's rhetoric, 'a new truth'.

These names also point to mankind's attempts to preserve the process that occurs when the huge event explodes. For each event is indeed an explosion: fierce, terrifying and destructive, but quickly ebbing, fading, vanishing.

1945, 1966, 1998: each a metonymy. Each of them is a concise replacement for something more complex: '1945' for instance, is the signifier for the time when Sukarno and Hatta proclaimed Indonesia's independence. With metonymy we are really acknowledging that various things – many, many things, one could even say an infinite number – could be assembled in Jakarta on 17 August 1945.

Those many things made the words 'break with the past' and 'a totally new beginning' merely hyperbole. There is an exaggeration in 'break' and 'new'. For included in all the things that emerge as traces of huge events like '1945', are exceedingly small things. And besides what is 'broken' is what continues and what is even strengthened. Not all things are a 'beginning', and perhaps there is no beginning that is 'totally new'.

This is why every huge change always holds disappointments, and is accompanied by disillusionment.

Take '1945', for instance. The spirit that drove Indonesians to form an independent republic flared so strongly, and was so sacred. Thousands of young men defended the independent republic from attempts to recolonize it. They moved with pain and death, and with sincerity and courage. But then, swiftly or gradually, this sacred spirit turned bland.

We recall the scenes of heroism in Pramoedya Ananta Toer's novel, *Di Tepi Kali Bekasi* (On the banks of Bekasi River). Farid, a Jakarta youth, joins the revolutionary fight, initially merely because of his urge to 'join the army'. But eventually he becomes a guerilla commander who, without any heroic words, defends Kranji and Bekasi, then loses Kranji and Bekasi but fights on against an enemy force much stronger in weaponry.

This story, to use Pramoedya's own words is 'an epic about the revolution of spirit – from the colonized spirit to the independent spirit'. The transformation is astounding. For as Pramoedya writes, this 'change or Revolution of spirit was more successful in the entire history of Indonesia than all the armed Revolutions it ever undertook.'

But the Revolution, that huge explosion, swiftly ebbed, faded, and vanished. Only a few years after Farid's battle along the Bekasi River, Indonesia entered the 'revolutionary cramps'. Ramadhan K.H used the word *'royan'*, referring to the cramps of afterbirth, as a title and metaphor for the frustration-dogged 1950s. This was the time when things in the newly independent republic did not improve: people began putting their own personal interests first, and their loyalty to '1945' evaporated.

The same thing can be said of '1966'. The students overthrew the repressive 'Guided Democracy' of 1958-1965 – youths who were prepared to endure violence and were not afraid of death for a democratic Indonesia – and then gradually they became aware they had been cheated. The regime that replaced 'Guided Democracy' turned out to be merely another form of 'Guided Democracy' – issued in with slaughter that spread terror for three decades.

Yap Thiam Hien, that champion of human rights, tried to open a new era under the 'New Order'. But we know what then happened. The law was continuously brutally trampled upon; freedom was kicked to the corner of the cell; Indonesia was turned into a tamed buffalo, pierced at the nose.

Now it is 2008. Ten years after *Reformasi,* a time post Soeharto: and are the 'revolutionary cramps' being felt once more, and people complaining?

It seems that the fluctuation between 'event' and 'cramps' or between hope and disappointment has become a repetitive pattern. This might just mean that we need to look again at what '1945','1966' or '1998' mean.

It just might be that we give these names as a way to hold out against confusing attacks of darkness and chaos present in every political transformation. And isn't this a radical aspiration about history?

The aspiration is radical (Badiou calls it 'speculative leftism'), because of the desire to purify time, to order space. But space and time are forever tangled, and will always be encircled by chaos.

After 1945, 1966, and 1998, we found that the 'new truth' that appeared had traces from the past. These very traces appeared and inspired us once more. But along with them came the debris of the previous time, piling up.

I am reminded of the angel of history in Paul Klee's painting – but with a different narrative to Walter Benjamin's. The angel does indeed look backwards, while he flies forward. And he is accompanied by the remnants of the past he has destroyed – debris that keeps piling higher and becomes more urgent, pushing him to fly forward, overtaking one event after another.

I doubt whether the figures 1945, 1966 or 1998 are on his wings. Probably not; just a plain color that moves.

'Puing' *Tempo* 17 February 2008, CP IX: 129-32

From Ambon and Scorched Ruins

Ambon is still haunted by scorched ruins. On both sides of the streets: dismal rubble. People in this Moluccan town still talk in great detail about the long period of savagery that started early in 1999 and continued almost to 2005: their houses burned to the ground; churches, mosques and universities razed; bombs assembled and detonated, speed boats attacked, thugs and paramilitary from outside Ambon stirring up hatred, the military and police inciting people, some leaving probably never to return, hundreds of friends and family slaughtered. At the end of this conflict between Moluccan Muslims and Christians, around 13,000 were dead; how can people forget this?

Miraculous, though, is the fact that in July 2006 the city and its inhabitants appear back to their friendly, courteous and genial ways, for which Ambon is renowned. Life is on the mend and it seems now there is greeting where before there was silence: the airport looks brand new, better than the one in Solo, and cleaner than the one in Surabaya. In the lobby of 'Amans' hotel, where guests can connect to the world via wireless internet, people were welcoming some young Moluccan women participating in a beauty contest. And the roads are crowded and the market buzzing.

I was only briefly passing through, of course; I was just a guest. I could not possibly really know if there was trauma, revenge and ongoing suspicion lurking there in the alley-ways. Yet something seems convincing when popular Moluccan songs blare out from roadside CD stalls, when women both with and without headscarves sit chatting in the seafront *rujak* stalls run by Christians, and on the day the ship *Lambelu* berthed, the harborfront thronged with people from all walks of life. Among the street-carts across from the offices of Firma Abudullah Alie (the Alie family are one of the Chinese Muslim families who have lived in the Moluccas since the nineteenth century) is a newspaper vendor; the latest issue of *Playboy* magazine is clearly on display. A little further off, the Mardika market is full of color: rows of bright red tomatoes, vivid green limes, yellow sago in plastic bags, cinnamon-brown smoked fish.

Driving along the bay I heard a driver say: 'We here are stupid people, wanting a thriller made of us.' He was speaking of that dreadful civil war, of course.

He seemed to realize, as the world realized, that here God was invoked by both sides, with blood-smeared beliefs, for unclear causes; perhaps part of the jockeying for position by people in upper echelons, perhaps some thugs fighting over their zones of extortion. I wasn't sure whether that driver was speaking with sadness or ridicule. But the awareness was there, or perhaps just fatigue, with no energy left to turn into anger. People here are returning to life from congregating on the footpaths: in small trade, in small conversation, in practical actions, and in friendships that can still be salvaged. They patch and darn life, they build houses from ruins, rub balm into their wounds.

I fell in love with this town. And not just because of its adornment of green trees, its nestling by the bay, all rounded off nicely with the hills.

> ...*no one exists alone;*
> *Hunger allows no choice*
> *To the citizen or the police;*
> *We must love one another or die.*
>
>   *W.H. Auden*

Something finally speaks from within that tragedy, 'We must love one another or die.' 'Love' is maybe too inflated a word. But what is the option besides death?

Auden's poem, *September 1, 1939*, was written on a corner of 42nd Street in New York when the world was haunted by a great war. But let us imagine that the poet was not in New York, but in Ambon – or in some corner of Indonesia – with the Republic on the brink of being torn apart by local civil war, like the tragedy in the Moluccas. Auden probably would also have felt '...the clever hopes expire', and 'a low dishonest decade' when waves of anger and fear whirl, and when 'the unmentionable odour of death offends the .. night'.

However, as in Ambon, life can redeem itself: an alternative can always be constructed when 'clever hopes expire'. At the end of his poem, Auden asks whether he, who is also made of 'Eros and dust', and 'beleaguered by the same negation and despair, can show an affirming flame.' The question seems tentative or modest. But hope is not something impossible. The poem mentions the 'ironic points of light' flashing in the dark, when the night offers no protection.

The word 'ironic' is important here. It is supposed to come from the Greek *eirōneia,* meaning 'feigned ignorance'. It comprises distance, even a step back or turning away from sure 'I-know'ing.

Auden wrote this poem at a time when:

> ...*blind skyscrapers use*
> *Their full height to proclaim*
> *The strength of Collective Man*

This was the time when various forms of totalitarianism were on full parade. This was the time when each language spewed out twisted slogans of pride and one-upmanship. Just like our times: when 'collective man' is incited by blaring loudspeakers on minarets, when religions that should foster humility actually become pretexts for the 'I-the-knowing-and-right-and-pure' attitude, when faith slowly changes into social identity, and the 'ummah' – one form of that collective man – becomes so important, even more important than truth.

Irony reveals that actually there is something jarring in such positions. In taking distance, we discover that no social identity can ever be completely formulated. The Muslim or Christian 'ummah' can mean many things, for each one comprises unacknowledged differences. And actually, within any formation of social identity even when we speak of the 'ummah', there is repression.

The seeds of violence are sown with that repression: over time, those who are not in line with the collective 'us' will be eliminated. In Ambon on 27 April 2001, the local radio station *Suara Perjuangan Muslim Maluku* (The Voice of the Moluccan Muslim Struggle) was quoted broadcasting this warning: 'If among the Muslims there are those who still talk of reconciliation, kill them!' In the area of Kudamati, fighting broke out between two Christian groups who attacked each other and burned down each other's houses.

Maybe this is why within every social identity there are wounds, and thus fractures. And attempts are made to shape that identity precisely because of those fractures. At the same time, that identity formulates itself or is formulated, names itself or is named, by a language – language, what is more, not created uniquely by that identity. It enters a convention. It links into a system; really, it is just a sign. There is nothing there completely and permanently as something that it signifies (what, actually, does 'ummah' refer to?). Its meaning appears only when it is aligned with different social identities and is then delineated by those other identities. It differs, of course, from the-other, but because it exists in a system of meaning-making, it is not entirely closed; it is not radically different from the-other. How could it possibly deny the-other?

'We must love one another, or die', Auden wrote.

Probably 'love' is not an inflated word. 'To love' means to be enchanted by the-different, to touch what is limited within oneself at the moment of meeting the-other, and to be aware that language cannot capture what exists in oneself or that other. As Auden said, *'Each language pours its vain, competitive excuse.'*

'Loving' is a simple thing to do.

In 1969 I crossed the sea from Buru Island to Ambon on a small boat called a 'Landing Craft Material'. For nearly eleven hours the waves washed over the narrow deck that stank of eucalyptus oil. In late July 2006 I repeated this journey, but this time by speedboat that got me there in around three hours.

The other shore is almost never beyond reach. To be in the Moluccas is to be aware of this, and the meaning of 'abroad': a place far from one's home, yet not completely foreign. In Malay, another country is referred to as 'across the water'.

So the sea has two sides that are in opposition, and yet fused: the sea both divides and connects, it is a thing between but a locus unto itself. It is full of suspense, it fascinates.

Chairil Anwar, in one of his most famous poems, *Cerita Buat Dien Tamaela* (Story for Dien Tamaela) presents the voice of a mythological figure from the Moluccas – it is not clear where exactly – calling himself 'Beta Pattirajawane'. He has a voice of thunder; when he is born he proudly proclaims that people should bring him 'boat and oars'. And he calls:

> *Mari menari!* Come, let's dance
> *Mari beria!* Come, be merry!
> *Mari berlupa!* Come, forget!

In other words, the sea signifies exciting adventure, the freedom to forget, travel away from home. Sometimes the sea is the zone between home and abroad, a transit. Sometimes it is abroad. The sea is never empty: it is the source of life and connects trade, war, migration, and civilizations.

And in this way it becomes a new home, a home that is not the closed place of origin, but rather one that grows because of the meeting between the-different and the-unpredicted. I am reminded of Heidegger's words (speaking of the flow of the Danube in Hölderlin's poem *der Ister*): 'Homecoming is...a transit through otherness'. Perhaps that is Indonesia, that is its fate: the place of our homecoming, but also a series of 'abroads', a place to which one pays respect, yet also the home that is at once merry and complex in diversity.

'Dari Ambon dan Gedung Hangus' *Tempo* 21 August 2006

Etc.

The historical text is a set of hasty words. Not long. And all recorded on half a sheet of folio paper. Every 17 August we recall it, because on almost every Independence Day, newspapers and magazines reprint a photo of that short document, or people reproduce it enlarged on parade banners: 'We, the Indonesian people, hereby declare the independence of Indonesia....'

The lettering is clearly Bung Karno's handwriting, with which we are familiar from other documents. The phrases were probably written with a cheap pen. There are scratches out and corrections here and there.

Was he nervous when he wrote it? We do not know. We can imagine only this: a tense atmosphere. One area of the city was still under Japanese control. Bung Karno and Bung Hatta were surrounded by impatient youths. They had all heard on secret radio that three days earlier, on August 14 1945, the Empire of Japan had lost the war. Emperor Hirohito had surrendered to the United States and its allies. It was all over for the Japanese, who now no longer had the power, let alone the right, to claim sovereignty in Indonesia. With Japan's surrender, this was the best moment to take over. Power had to change hands. When would there be another chance? 'Come on, Bung, move! Our independence is now!

And Bung Karno wrote. Time was short. The situation was pressing. The youths were putting the pressure on. The momentum could not be lost.

But then, what? After power was in the hands of 'the Indonesian people', what would be done? The text had no time to explain. '.... Matters concerning the transfer of power etc., will be carried out in a conscientious manner and as speedily as possible.'

On that night, and 61 years later, we knew that this nation had to be independent; for decades it had been longing for liberty from colonization. But it seems that no one knew precisely how to implement various matters 'in a conscientious manner' and 'as speedily as possible'. And what was actually meant by the 'etc.' in that sentence? What were all those 'other things' grouped under 'et cetera'?

There is no answer. Perhaps there was no need yet for an answer. The decision that night to become independent did not assume that everything had to be precisely spelled out, merely awaiting implementation. The decision was aware, anxiously perhaps, that all was in a state of multi possibility – and aware of how impossible it is to avoid moments in life that are open not only to all kinds of opportunity, but also to all kinds of disaster. That night, the decision was not the application of a program.

In that sense, it reflects freedom of action, courage, and also humility. For the founders of the Republic – who were not one hundred per cent sure of what was going to happen – acknowledged that uncertainty while making the leap into history. If there were some Hamlets amongst them, hesitant and endlessly thinking, like him they too eventually came to the conclusion that 'thinking too precisely on the event/..... hath but one part wisdom/And ever three parts coward'.

In that 'etc.' we see that Indonesia's revolution was no Leninist revolution. It did not spring from theory. Nor was it like the Iranian revolution, which sprang from the teachings and sayings of Ayatollah Khomeini. Indeed, if the Indonesian proclamation of independence can be seen as an important part of our revolution, it is an expression of pragmatism much more radical than the American Revolution. On 17 August 1945, the founders of our Republic rejected the 'spectator theory' of knowledge.

The 'spectator theory', according to Dewey, the pioneer of modern pragmatism, privileges this illusion: that mankind, from its position on high, can determine eternal truth about its affairs. Whereas the 'true' cannot be separated from deed. To the pragmatists, it is only through deed that we can discover the tread of knowledge about the world

That 'etc.' is an acknowledgement that while 'independence' is a discourse, it is an unfinished one. But more important still, the entire proclamation text indicates that there is no discourse that can be finished and satisfactorily encompass things.

We note: there is no actor in the sentence 'will be carried out in a conscientious manner'. Who will do the carrying out? Could it be Sukarno-Hatta, as the two people who wrote the text in the name of 'the people of Indonesia'? But how could that be, when 'the people of Indonesia' had not yet elected them? And on that tense night and morning, when the world was changing radically as World War II ended, how could people formulate what 'the people of Indonesia' was?

In the beginning was the word, the Bible says. But not on that day: it was not *logos*, not 'truth', but rather action. This did not mean that the proclamation was a death leap from a complete vacuum, with absolutely no idea of direction.

Over the previous months there had already been meetings of the committee for the preparation of independence. On June 1st, Bung Karno summarized the deliberations of those who had taken part in the meeting in one word: '*Pancasila*'. But even Pancasila, as a product of deliberation, contained what was later implied by the 'etc.': no one principle is fit to negate other principles, for in a freer and more just communal life, there is always the 'et cetera', all the rest that appears, unpredictably, and sometimes awkwardly. There is no discourse unchallenged by those whom it does not accommodate.

The proclamation text is a set of hasty words. But the critical situation that produced it reminds us: life, including the life of a nation, is made of moments that are never perfect. Life always comprises the 'etc.' which is not yet written out. And because of this, we must be open, we must shout to this Republic of ours, in the words of our national anthem, 'Arise then, its spirit'.

'Dll' *Tempo* 27 August 2006, CP VIII: 245-8

Not

I ndonesia began with a void. Indonesia began with the word 'not'.

On that morning of August 17 1945, what happened was a dislocation. Suddenly, the image of collectivity (more often called a 'country' or 'nation') that had been presented to the masses was overturned: an image that had been shaped and nurtured by colonialism. Dutch rule collapsed with ease under Japanese attack, and the Japanese took over. But then, suddenly the Japanese lost. Suddenly, there was a gaping void.

People were worried, hopeful, longing, excited and nervous all at the same time – and in Jakarta that day, they thronged to the Ikada Square, jostling for space. And there Bung Karno and Bung Hatta – in the name of the 'Indonesian nation' or *'bangsa Indonesia'*– read out a short hand-written text, with scribbles here and there, declaring 'Indonesia's independence...'

'Indonesia': actually, it wasn't at all clear what the word meant. The word was first used in 1925 by a group of young men who were impatient with life under colonialism; and it was reinstated in 1928 in a declaration called the *'Sumpah Pemuda'* or 'Youth Pledge'. But at that time, there was no agreement on 'Indonesia' as a geographical entity. Nor was there yet any definition of what named someone as a member of the 'Indonesian nation'.

It was only towards June 1945 that there were attempts for a more 'official' formulation. The venue: a building in the suburb of Menteng, Jakarta, during the discussions of a committee formed to prepare for Indonesia's independence.

We know that this committee was not representative of all groups in society. We know too that all formulations are limited in their very nature. They are only a means, always unsatisfactory, to define what is in a name.

But what is in a name? For years, people had relied upon the word 'not'. Even so, this gave meaning to vagueness. 'Indonesia' was *not* the colony of the Dutch East Indies. 'Indonesia' was *not* the Japanese colony. And it was from here that the shout '*Merdeka!*', 'Independence!' was heard.

Carl Schmitt is probably right: all political concepts, images and terms contain polemic meaning. The word 'sovereignty', even the words 'Indonesian independence', could not have been understood had people not known what those words opposed, contradicted or rejected. Politics, in the broad sense, is a process of shaping antagonism – the emergence of 'friends' and 'foes' – via action and rhetoric.

So one can say that on that morning of 17 August 1945, Indonesia was a product of antagonism. As I said above, it started with 'not'.

This does not mean that after 17 August 1945 there were no more stories of 'not'. Politics did not cease. Collectivity can never be complete; society cannot possibly fuse like the nodes on bamboo. The word 'not' shapes rhetoric. Some formulated Indonesia as a country that is *not* capitalist – and they longed for socialism or communism. Some considered Indonesia as *not* a secular country – and they yearned for the implementation of Islamic law. Some defined Indonesia as *not* an Islamic state – and they wanted equality for all citizens regardless of faith and religion.

History tells of the antagonism that has taken place between all these 'nots'. And often bloodshed. The 'Darul Islam' movement that aimed to make Indonesia an 'Islamic State' raged as a brutal guerrilla war during the early years of the Republic. For almost twenty years, areas in West Java became battlefields of murder and destruction. Ramadhan K.H's famous poem *Priangan Si Jelita* ('Beautiful Priangan') addresses the Priangan area with deep sadness.

But the misery did not stop there. In 1965, those yearning for Indonesia to be a communist country bellowed their presence, and the Indonesian Communist Party (PKI) became the third largest communist party in the world after the Soviet Union and China. Those they considered 'foes' were often afraid. Violence was sitting there ready, right at the door, and this is what eventually happened: mass killings, silencing, and when the army – which wanted Indonesia as *not* an 'Islamic State' but also *not* a 'communist State' – took power, then never-ending violence.

The problem probably began when people forgot that Indonesia began with a void. Nothing is eternal or must necessarily rule to fill that void.

A void can make people nervous. Yet this nervousness can make us see there is something in communal life that allows us to fill it. With this proviso: no political force is ever able to fill it completely – for there will always be disagreements, as the saying goes 'there is no ivory without flaw'. Voids and flaws are indications of promise, but also impossibility.

The experience of Indonesian history, tragic and yet valuable, is this – the experience of impossibility: every regime tries to give a final formulation to what 'Indonesia' is, but never succeeds.

This is why democracy is important in this country. It reminds me of a sentence from Claude Lefort: 'democracy is instituted and sustained by the dissolution of the markers of certainty.'

Democracy indeed starts with the acknowledgement of the non-existence of certainty: a flaw that shapes it, in fact. So socialism, which claims itself 'scientific', and thinks it can establish fixed markers – will renounce democracy and impossibility. Just as politics motivated by religious doctrine, which considers itself absolute and eternal in building 'God's realm' on earth, will reject democracy and human failing.

They are both forms of arrogance, the first step towards destruction.

'Bukan' *Tempo* 25 July 2006, CP VIII: 213-6

Azahari

They are foreigners, but they are not strangers. But nor are they locals. Azahari and Noor Din Top entered Indonesia secretly from Malaysia, recruited Indonesian locals for training in explosives, and murdered innocent people, and Indonesia has been in an upheaval ever since. From then on, this country, which schoolchildren used to laud in song as 'safe and strong', has become a place unsafe and insecure for everyone. Azahari and co. say they oppose the United States and Zionism. Of course they would say their jihad is part of the current global war. But eventually it comes down to this: the country that is hurting is not the United States, not even Israel, but Indonesia – a country which to those two Malaysians has no meaning at all.

No, they are not locals. The word 'local' implies a boundary between 'inside' and 'outside'. Of course that boundary does not come from God or nature, but from a political process in history. Nor is that boundary something everlasting. But does the non-everlasting have any meaning and particular power of its own?

Azahari and those of his ilk – who dream of establishing an Islamic caliphate that surmounts the 'nation-state' – are motivated by the spirit of 'de-localization', transcending the locality they consider self-confining. They have no desire to be loyal to any 'native land', Indonesia included.

To them, Islam is universal, operating at all times and all places. Moreover, this is an era that delights in assaulting national borders, driven by science, technology, and fully-fledged capitalism. 'Religion today allies itself with tele-technoscience, to which it reacts with all its forces', Derrida said at a symposium in Capri in 1994 – a phrase that still has resonance a decade later.

But religion too, as promulgated by Azahari, contains contradictions. It claims to be universal, yet the more it becomes the banner of group identity, the more it opposes its own universal nature – even though television, the Internet, and the technical expertise of weaponry and killing that come from 'tele-technoscience' support its move of de-localization.

But a peculiar trend perhaps, is that 'de-localization' endorses religion as group identity. It is as though religion is cut off even from the meaning of 'place' itself.

But can religious truth operate without place? Has it ever done so? Caliph Abdul Karim, a former member of the Ikhwanul Muslimin movement in Egypt, in his book titled *The Quraish Hegemony* postulated that Islamic history from the time before and immediately following the Prophet Mohammed cannot be separated from the political position of the Quraish tribe around Mecca.

At least, it is difficult to imagine Islam outside the history of a place and time. The Caliph Usmani who was based in Turkey and is said to have overcome 'nation-state' borders, was fundamentally part of the experience and sovereign interests of the Turks themselves.

'De-localization' will forever be impossible: Islam practiced on earth will be limited by the map of that earth. Something 'non-global' will continue to exist: an area and a group of people whose self identity is named with a country or nation.

And that is 'native land'. Native land is the place where a person is flung. There she chooses to accept that position, actively or passively, with enthusiasm or resignation. Native land, as Indonesia experienced when it emerged from colonialism through revolution, is an event, something that shakes life and stirs the heart.

But native land is also an experience: a process of growing roots. This is not the same as origins, the *Blut and Boden* of German nationalism. Roots are not things to be sanctified, and the place where we live and from whence we come is no sacred place. Native lands are shaped continuously by history, by our work, and this is why, with blood and sweat, they have meaning to us. The native land is not merely space, but time.

Indonesia, our native land, was born in a time, through revolution – something Malaysians like Azahari did not experience. The Indonesian revolution involved many people who suffered under Dutch colonial rule. That revolution was an event of solidarity, with sacrifice and pride. And Indonesia grew from this, and eventually became a common project. But once Indonesia emerged, it was not something to be praised, something eternal. Indonesia is a limited project, because it is aware of human limitation.

But increasingly we became aware that this project was not perfect. This is why Indonesia was born in 1945 with hopes and also fears, full of both ardor and anxiety. And in this it differs from an 'Islamic state' that bears the name of something everlasting, with no possibility of mistake.

The 'Islamic state', particularly as Azahari dreams it, is arrogance towards history. 'Indonesia' is the opposite: it neither denies nor fears that it will be wrong, even sin. This is why it needs democracy: a mechanism to forever correct itself, and to minimize wrong steps.

All this is something that Azahari and his friends, who have no links to Indonesian revolutionary history, do not understand. They detonate bombs, over and again, destroy this country over and again, and yet what do they achieve other than giving a vision of an express lane to Heaven for a chosen few, an instant paradise, like things offered on the ever-impatient world market.

And meanwhile, America stands strong and Zionism is not extinct. This is why Azahari and his friends are prepared to die with the hope of quick Heaven for themselves alone, and not the hope of winning victory for those they defend in the world.

'Azahari' *Tempo* 27 November 2005, CP VIII: 89-92

1965

And have we ever been able to speak cool-headedly about the killings, about those hundreds of thousands of Indonesians murdered over 1965-1966? Maybe not. And maybe we never will. It's not easy to say when the story should start. Some would begin with the night of 30 September and 1 October, when a few top ranking officers were captured by some army troops and then murdered in a rubber plantation just outside Jakarta. Some might say that the violence spread from there. The Indonesian Communist Party was seen as the initiator of these early murders. And so, as Hermawan Sulistyo describes in his book *Palu Arit di Ladang Tebu: Sejarah Pembantaian Massal yang Terlupakan (1965-1966)* (Hammer and Sickle in the Sugarcane: A History of the Forgotten Mass Killings of 1965-1966), both military and civilians, acting out of revenge and fear, massacred thousands upon thousands of Communist Party members or suspected members. Terror was rampant – and a new government was established.

How could all this have happened? One can easily counter this question with another: why not? Savagery is nothing strange in history, particularly the history of this archipelago. In 17th-century Mataram, it is recorded that in just half an hour Amangkurat 1st exterminated three thousand Muslim scholars he had gathered in the town square.

Nor is it because Indonesians are incapable of restraining their cruelty, as some fly-by-night analysts applying the Malay phrase 'to run amok' would have us believe. Indonesians too are creatures crawling along in history, and that history is a frightening journey. The violence of 1965-66 did not come out of the blue.

We can trace its beginnings to deep in the preceding period. Perhaps from 1945: Indonesia was trying to establish itself as an independent republic, but the postcolonial world was no friendly environment. Only one year after Indonesia's declaration of independence, the Dutch, not wishing to cede power, commenced their military action. A war to safeguard independence was then inevitable. And at almost the same time, the Darul Islam guerrillas emerged out of the forests of West Java with their fight. From abroad, the tension of the Cold War between the 'capitalist blok' and the 'communist blok' was spreading. And at the same time, the spirited voices and cries of pain of the newly independent and the nearly independent countries of Asia and Africa were reverberating.

The convergence of all this brought about a decade that ended in 1958, which was apparently 'normal' and yet contained something 'abnormal'. This was the time when Indonesia, with a parliamentary democracy, aimed to control conflict and competition through political parties, bodies for people's representation, and the judiciary. In other words, a system that set out to be at once ordered and open, when the press was free, parties were free, and the judges independent.

But the army was not happy with this, particularly because this democracy placed the army under civilian authority. Moreover, it was always easy to see this system as a commotion that fractured unity, a mechanism that was not working effectively, a structure that was 'aping the West'.

One of those who opposed 'Western' democracy was President Sukarno. So when parliamentary democracy was incapable of bringing under control the armed insubordination of a group of colonels (assisted by the CIA), Indonesia chose a radical path. Bung Karno dismissed the parliament that the people had chosen with such optimism in 1955. He also outlawed political parties that he thought opposed him: the press was censored.

In 1958, 'Guided Democracy' came into effect, with Sukarno at the head. 'Guided Economy' was also introduced; foreign businesses were taken over and led by the army and bureaucrats, who ended up running all kinds of businesses (and do so to this day). Everywhere, the spirit of 'revolution' was proclaimed in order to achieve the lofty ideals of 'Indonesian socialism'. And as is normal with 'revolution', enmity became doctrine: there were 'friends' and 'foes', there were the 'revolutionary progressives' and the 'counter-revolutionaries'. As the Cold War heated up in Asia, as the United States became cornered in Vietnam and 'communist phobia' infiltrated all quarters, this atmosphere of enmity sowed acute mutual suspicion in Indonesia.

And from that point on, in fact, the seed of violence thrived. All kinds of organizations were forbidden, dozens of newspapers were banned, and people were jailed without trial. Anything considered 'counter-revolutionary' was hunted down. Rhetoric was given a fierce imperative accent, and violence became the primary signifier. *Ganyang!* or Crush! was the word of the day. Anything with political power, particularly the Indonesian Communist Party, fanned the revolutionary flame. Fiery propaganda echoed all around, and almost every political group mobilized youths wearing uniforms, kitted out on battle alert.

And in the end, an eruption. This is what happened on 30 September, 1965. People still argue about who first pulled the trigger: The CIA? The People's Republic of China? What seems not yet to be recognized is that it was the 'revolutionary' fire that could eventually be put to any use, to wipe out anyone. The generals killed that night were all accused of being 'counter-revolutionaries'. But when, in early October 1965, Major General Soeharto retaliated, he accused the murderers as also being 'counter-revolutionaries'.

With or without the CIA and China, the Indonesian 'revolution' was fully prepared to devour its own children.

This is not to say that the sin of forty years ago is a communal curse. There were henchmen who slaughtered, tortured, and incarcerated innocent people for years: they were responsible for great evil. But that evil became something seemingly trivial, once 'cleansing' was condoned in the attainment of grand ideals, communist or not.

And so those who controlled language and position at the time also wronged when they did not pose the question, 'have our ideals been wrong? Aren't there limits? And aren't those limits implied in worthy daily life?

'1965' *Tempo* 10 October 2004, CP VII: 273-6

Papua

I don't know how I should see this part of the globe: expansive, unfamiliar, with jungles and sheer tall mountains and its sturdy people, silent. This territory has been on the map of Indonesia – the country that is so important in my life – since I was a child. I sang *From Sabang to Merauke*. But I sang it not with a sense of pride about this huge geographic spread, possibly useless. I sang it with a sense of gratitude that exclaimed, 'We also have brothers and sisters way over there'. The song was a greeting.

But I don't know whether that greeting was reciprocated. This part of the globe has been called in turn 'Papua', 'West Irian', 'Irian Jaya', and 'Papua'. A territory, it seems, that has never chosen its own name. The ones doing the choosing are the big shots who love rhetoric, and the cartographers who don't want errors. Perhaps the naming is a part of listing – an administrative matter – or a project of victory and power. Naming is limiting. And beyond that – silence.

History, which gathers stories of various events, also often proceeds from a name, a limiting. And so, concerning that part of the globe way over there in the east, perhaps I can speak of it only within limits already formed by history – although through a particular experience: one day in 1927, my older brother was born there in Tanah Merah, when my parents were exiled to Digul by the Dutch colonial government.

So, when I write with sadness now about Papua, it is because there is a personal historical tie between Papua and me. But this tie is not separate from the group history: the government that made a colony in the east, the place where my brother was born, was the same government that controlled in the west, where I grew up.

Distant, of course. Different, of course. Yet the history that I know seems able to cross all that distance and difference. But is it only the past that so determines? No. Michael Richardson wrote in the *International Herald Tribune* (1 December, 2000): '[West Papua] has few historical, ethnic, linguistic or religious links with the Indonesian archipelago'. He is right. But the same thing could be said – and perhaps even more forcefully – of the weakness of the historical, ethnic, linguistic and religious links between Hawai'i and Connecticut.

In other words, Indonesia, like the United States, stands because of a force that Ernest Renan called 'forgetting'. What is 'forgotten' is the weakness of the ties between the various components of nationality. What is 'forgotten' is the breadth of the diverse differences of background. What is desired is togetherness. The nationalists call it 'unity'.

But nationalism at the beginning of the 21st century turns sterile when this 'unity' ends up as merely a matter of force. Take the broom made of reeds, every nationalist says. If the reeds are separated, each one can be easily snapped. But when they are held tight in a bundle, unified they are strong. But what is strength for, when war, troops, and borders are becoming increasingly irrelevant? The biggest change in the world over the last two decades has been the expansion of the realization that a country's might is not through its terrifying army or expansive map, but through trade – and free trade at that.

Nationalism these days, particularly in Indonesia, is even turning poisonous as it loses its own ethical moment. In the past, when we 'forgot', we were actually becoming more open. When the Youth Pledge (*Sumpah Pemuda*) was made in 1928 – when the youth who came from various different and distant regions wanted to 'forget' their regionalism and become 'one nation' – at that time there was willingness from each 'I' to greet something that was 'not-I', the other, the different. At that moment too, 'I' was not something final and defined. The handshake took place because the difference between 'I' and 'not-I' was not absolute. That difference was not everlasting, nor stagnant, nor stable – and maybe we should not use the word 'difference' here, but rather (if we may follow Derrida), *différance*.

Indonesian nationalism forgot that *différance*, once difference and unity were maintained as something stable. Taman Mini Indonesia is a symbol of that tendency: there, 'difference' is declared with various models of 'typical' buildings, one from each province. And 'unity' is symbolized by a clear (and arrogant) vision from above of an extensive mapped-out territory. Within this whole, change is not possible; conflicted lives and hybridity are out of the question. What we witness is violence towards a process that in fact goes on continuously – a process of movement between unity and difference.

This violence, we know, takes place not only in the world of symbols. It is also expressed with terror. In 1975, East Timor was absorbed into Indonesian territory through military force, and the ethical moment of nationalism of the 1920s became extinct. Suddenly, those holding the guns told us that Indonesia was not born through handshakes and openness. Suddenly Indonesia appeared as a construction built with money and weapons.

Until when? I don't know. Right now, from Sabang to Merauke there are people shooting and being shot dead. Whether or not there is any echo or reply, tomorrow someone must have the courage to call out, once again, that greeting of old.

'Papua' *Tempo* 10 December 2000, CP V: 593-5

Dur *)

A rude historian once said that Indonesia has two categories of heads of state. The first is presidents who like living things. The second is those who like dead things imagined to be living.

In the first category are Sukarno (he liked women who were living) and Soeharto (he liked pre-dead cattle). In the second category is Habibie: he liked metal planes that could fly like dragonflies. And Abdurrahman Wahid: he likes graves, or more precisely, their inhabitants. Graves, we know, are places for people no longer living, yet it is said they can summon a president to come and visit.

Now that historian who made those categories insulted many things, including presidents, women, the saints, (and perhaps too agriculture and technology). But maybe he was right about Gus Dur. I have heard that *The Guinness Book of Records* is going to list Gus Dur as the Head of State who, in the history of the United Nations, has done the most graveyard visits. If true, then the good name of Indonesia will be restored.

But not without problems. Just recently a wise Islamic teacher advised the President of the Republic of Indonesia: 'Don't go only to graves, meeting with the dead', he said, 'go more frequently to meet those who are living.'

It seems that the teacher knew that Gus Dur had neglected the obligation of a president who is not chosen directly by the people:

---

*) Gus Dur was the popular name of Abdurrahman Wahid, Indonesia's fourth president from 22 October 1999 to 23 July 2001.

the obligation to strive in a serious and careful way to build strong support in parliament, which is made up of still-living politicians. But rather than going there, Gus Dur keeps going on pilgrimages to various saints' graves, or those thought of as saints. Why? We hear the answer only in passing from the President himself: when he goes to grave X, he says, it is because the inhabitant of grave X has 'called' him.

Don't rush to surprise or mockery. Who is to say that a dead person does not have words? We often receive them as a memory, something from an obituary, written or not. What Gus Dur does with his pilgrimages is make a composition on that memory. But certainly, as the poet W.H. Auden said:

The words of a dead man
Are modified in the guts of the living

So anything that enters Gus Dur's awareness – or anyone's awareness – as a message from the departed, is finally a message that has been modified by anyone still using language.

Lies or not? When one morning after a deep sleep, an ordinary man – let's call him Durakhim, or Dur for short – says that the spirit of Old Father Bimbim told him, via a dream, to move to the north side of the market so that he will be chosen village head, then it cannot be ascertained whether we are speaking of lies. Maybe Old Father Bimbim was not speaking the truth, or Dur interpreted him incorrectly, or the whole thing was a fantasy. The business of lies and non-lies becomes unclear; for death distances people from the expectation that communication via language is to speak the truth. One does not hear the dead bringing any assumptions about the meaning of communication with words.

Maybe this is why Gus Dur likes to visit graveyards. Before the silent grave, there is not what Nietzsche calls '*Wahrheitstreib*', that mysterious impulse towards truth. Particularly when truth and the prohibition against lying are regarded as something upheld within history, not outside of it; something underscored because humans need a jointly-held precept, and do not want to be continuously at war, all against all. In other words, truth is a kind of 'peace treaty', formed at one moment in the process of life. And there, before the grave, there is no life, there is no negotiation: and actually there is also no peace or consensus.

Maybe Gus Dur is secretly apprehensive about accepting that truth is born from peace after a long fight. He wants to see truth as something originating from outside of history – from eternity, like those spirits. In this way, it is as though truth appears within us without any struggle, and without any interaction with others; it appears, moreover, in a form seemingly already final.

Yet of course we recall Auden's poem: the words of a dead man are modified in the guts of the living. And the living never make a monologue. In the end, we must ask whether it is impossible to have consensus with our fellows; whether it is impossible for truth to develop and be experienced through a communal process in history; and whether the advice of that Islamic teacher – that a person should spend more time communicating with the living than the dead, with those within history rather than with something outside of it – is just futile advice.

Gus Dur never answers this. Maybe he never even worries about it. But any democracy will sooner or later come up against this question. For democracy is finally a way of viewing history: not as part of an eternal and finished nature symbolized by a cemetery and silence, but rather as the commotion of we who are living, shifting, differing, and frequently making mistakes, while acknowledging imperfect humanity.

'Dur' *Tempo* 8 July 2001, CP VI: 39-42

Han Sui

Where do rights come from? Who knows? But here is a story of a journalist's experience sixteen years ago in Jakarta.

That day three young children came to see me. Their eyes were red. They showed me some photos. 'These are photos of our father', one of them said.

What I saw was the sprawled, naked body of a man, dead. His middle-aged face was disfigured. You could see blue bruises around his waist and on his back; swellings; dried blood. Terrifying. One of the kids explained to me: 'our father died in detention. His whole body was covered with torture wounds.' Then she added, 'Father was arrested one night as he walked past the Grand cinema. He was accused of distributing pornographic films'. She explained that the people who detained her father were from a security post in the Senen area.

'We are asking your help to write something about this', said the eldest (let's call him Han Sui). We don't know how to take legal action.'

I was silent. I knew that I lacked the courage to write up this story. I was not even brave enough to check all the evidence. It appeared that there had indeed been torture, no matter what his father's wrongdoing had been. If I started checking, I would certainly have to deal with the powers that be – you know what I mean – and my own safety would be at risk. I was afraid. That night I could not sleep. 'I am a coward and I refused to help a family that cannot appeal to the law.'

Today that journalist is able to sleep, but the problem is not solved. I always ask why it was that Han Sui seemed to have no right to make an issue of the death of his father – and why I felt that I had no right to tell it.

Rights? Where are they from?

From God, one opinion would say. Man is God's caretaker on earth. Rights are not given by those in power. They have existed since the beginning of our existence and therefore cannot be taken away by anyone.

However, no one in history has ever witnessed an angel coming to save the rights of man. In history, the experts say, these things have developed through the tussle of needs in society. In this process there will be certain rights for which the need is felt clearly, and once a group has won, these rights will come to be codified.

Problems arise here because it seems that this kind of historical process has not yet gathered momentum in Indonesia. Europeans often point out that the concept of society as something formed from free individuals (namely, not slaves and therefore possessing certain rights) is indeed a product of 'Western' history.

Writers in ancient Greece already stated that in the great war between Greece and Persia, the superiority of the Greeks ('Westerners') was because they fought as free men and were not enslaved by any ruler. In Persia (the 'East') the opposite was true. If the Greeks won in the end, then it was because they had a motivation to fight to the death: they were afraid of losing their status as free men.

The ancient Greeks knew precisely the difference it made to be a free man: they knew the fate of their own slaves at their feet. A Harvard historian, Orlando Patterson, wrote recently that the concept of a citizen's 'personal liberty' can only emerge in a society like that of the Greeks which also has a dark side: slavery, with its real shackles. And so in the beginning it was only in Greece – not in Asia, where slavery appeared with different shackles – that ideas about 'personal liberty' could become a pivot of socio-political life. This concept was strengthened by developments in European history.

Could such a process happen in the 'non-Western' world? Some would say it could not. Authorities in the 'East' say this because they are afraid that if the societies they control are infected by an awareness of rights, then it will be easy for people to make demands.

But it is not only these people in power who say this. Anthropologists also say that the 'non-Western' world is indeed different. In 1947, when the Universal Declaration of Human Rights was being drawn up, the executive board of the American Association of Anthropology warned against a 'statement of rights conceived only in terms of the values prevalent in Western Europe and America. What are held to be human rights in one society may be regarded as anti-social by another people.'

And so, 'West' is indeed 'West' and 'East' is 'East'? How complicated. To Han Sui whose father was tortured or to those who have husbands and children who have been arrested and never heard of since, the matter is not abstract: they have been tortured.

'Han Sui' *Tempo* 15 February 1992, CP IV: 267-9

La Patrie

In an anxious, clandestine room, in German-occupied Paris, Albert Camus was writing for an underground magazine: 'I should like to be able to love my country and still love justice.'

The fighting between the occupying forces and French Resistance was still raging. The magazine *Combat* was still being published, to communicate news and opposition ideas to its limited readership. Camus kept on writing his unique editorials. He presented a series of letters to his friend, a German, who was of course on 'the other side'.

We don't know where that German was from. Maybe he was an imaginary friend. Or maybe he was an intellectual who really existed and who could state what 'German' meant to him at that time of fervid nationalism. 'The greatness of my country is beyond price', is what he said. 'And in a world where everything has lost its meaning, those who, like us young Germans, are lucky enough to find a meaning in the destiny of our nation must sacrifice everything else.'

There is something stirring in words like this. But to Camus, there was something terrifying. 'No', he said, 'I cannot believe that everything must be subordinated to a single end'.

What we find here is an argument against the twentieth century spirit of totalitarianism. This argument admits that there is indeed something sensed as glorious when we are prepared to follow an idea, a belief, a fervor, or a group of humanity that is larger than any single one of us standing alone. But the question is whether, with such rationale, it is right that people lose the furthest reach of their souls. The thundering totalitarianism of Hitler's Germany or Mao's China says, 'Yes, it must be like that'. But then, what? Eventually we need a belief that one day, at a certain moment, mankind will be whole once more, not merely part of a grand sacrifice. Without that, there is only a ritual of destruction.

A friend of mine has an interesting idea about *Pancasila* (Indonesia's state doctrine, The Five Principles) and patriotism. According to him, what is important in *Pancasila* is not each individual principle, or the grouping of the five of them as one cluster. What is important is precisely how each principle can act as a balance of another. And so, if someone tends to be overly fervent in upholding the spirit of nationalism, then at the same time people must be reminded that they have to observe the spirit of 'just and civilized humanity'. If people tend to overstep the mark in their practice of faith in 'the One and Only God', simultaneously people have to be requested to view whether, at the same time, this is also observing 'democratic values'.

I don't know whether this way of looking at *Pancasila* is acceptable to those upgrading-course leaders in their safari suits who often bore people silly. But this kind of interpretation at least propounds something: 'native land' is something important, but it must first be questioned as to how important it is, for whom, and at what moment. In other words, there is a relationship that must be viewed at that moment. When, during Soeharto's New Order, members of the theatre group *Teater Buruh* (Workers Theatre) whose self-expression was constantly banned, met in a locked room, and weeping, one by one kissed the Indonesian red and white flag, then we sort of understand that the 'native land' symbolized by that simple flag is a land of oppressed people, the Indonesia of the tortured.

Now, of course the map, the name, the latitude and longitude
of this country are probably the same as those in the head of Mr
X. But the 'Indonesia' of the place where those workers shed their
tears is not the native land of Mr X, who feels that he, or his
friends, or his acquaintances, or his group, should be grateful to
the Government for their special position so they can now enjoy
so many things. Probably this is why what Camus says has more
resonance to us, rather than to Mr X. 'I should like to be able to
love my country and still love justice.'

That anonymous German, Albert Camus's friend beyond the
demarcation line, thought that if this is the case, then Camus did
not love his native country. Our love of fatherland, the German
more or less said, has to be unconditional. But I am sceptical
whether this can still operate these days. How easy it would be if
a country were continuously present as a mythological creature.
But we can imagine that to Marsinah, who was murdered with a
pistol barrel probably fired into her vagina, her 'country' had been
invaded by the 'state', and the 'state' had been invaded by those
pistol-toting officials. If Marsinah were still alive, she would say; 'If
the country meant for me is like this, then I am better off far away
from it.'

What is saddening is that people like Marsinah actually have
only one country, the place where they are born, grow up, and
die. They don't have the money to go to another country, to buy
real estate over there, or to become professionals in the world of
multinational corporations. They have no other land, while over
and around them people debate the meaning of 'native land' and
'Indonesia' with rituals, with mile-upon-mile of safari jaunts,
parades, television broadcasts, or with the thrust of all those guns.

'La Patrie' *Suara Independen*, 1 June 1995. (*Kata Waktu*: 1120-2)

Imogiri

On the dry hills of Imogiri, the young trees fight for life against the weather. The branches of the old tree trunks still manage to stand straight and their leaves give shade, but the huge 350-year-old graveyard of Imogiri, with its stained stone walls, has to keep up its battle against the thing that has claimed so much of the Mataram heritage: climate. In this area above Yogyakarta the air is humid and the sun beats hot. And now there is something else particular to our time of change – pollution.

And what should be saved from these giant carved stones here – if indeed there is anything to be saved at all?

Memories, perhaps – those things that seem to be of profound importance. For humans are special creatures – they remember. Death lies before them as a paradox: death means the road to eternity, yet also the threat of the destruction of memories. And we do not wish to forget or to be forgotten. People write history.

In the imaginary city of Macondo in Gabriel Garcia Marquez's novel *One Hundred Years of Solitude*, the people once worked too much. So busy were they that they did not sleep, and as this insomnia spread, another symptom emerged: people began to lose their memories. They seemed to forget the names of objects and reality until finally they lived in an 'imaginary reality' where 'a father was remembered faintly as the dark man who had arrived at the beginning of April, and a mother was remembered only as the dark woman who wore a gold ring on her left hand.'

A sad story, indeed. We do not wish to live in Macondo and suffer amnesia. In *One Hundred Years of Solitude*, Jose Arcadio

Buendia tries to combat this amnesia. He writes down the names of objects just as we write down history. For history, after all, is an attempt to fight our forgetting. Yet we rarely realize that this attempt is in fact feeble, limited and incomplete.

What do we know, for example, about the story of the hill and the Imogiri graveyard and all the dead kings? We do not know why the people wanted to build the extravagance to the glory of their kings. We don't know how they lived and thought, how they were oppressed or how they were free.

The writers of history, just like journalists, tend to prefer dramatic events and extraordinary people. The readers of history on the whole, like the readers of newspapers, also prefer such things: wars and defeat, cruelty and conflict, destruction and wrongdoing.

People say that in this way history easily becomes mixed with legend, and historical figures become myth. Napoleon even regarded history as merely commonly accepted fable. Certainly the *Babad Tanah Jawi* or Chronicle of Java 'from Adam to 1647', recounts two worlds of reality, one factual and the other fantasy. So we are required to believe in the magic power of Panembahan Senopati, the founder of the Mataram dynasty who is described in another Javanese text, the *Wedatama* as the most exemplary Javanese. What is not told is that in fact Senopati was just a common man who was ambitious and lucky, a smooth adventurer who was able to defeat a bunch of opponents.

A chronicle like the *Babad Tanah Jawi* is produced in a situation where there is not a strong tradition of open, critical, honest writing. Such a chronicle might be written in a state of semi-amnesia when the writer, like the people of Macondo, lives in a world of 'imaginary reality'. At times like this we tend to believe in only what we wish to believe. We do not need memories as memories. What we need is perhaps only a cult of heroes.

This is true not only of Mataram. Just last month a friend of mine met a taxi driver who did not want to believe that Bung Karno was dead.

'Why do you think he is not dead?'

'Because none of his wives has remarried', he replied.

The taxi driver thought that Bung Karno was still hiding somewhere 'preparing a weapon that will be more deadly than the atom bomb'.

Myth may be something that does not die easily. It is born from a different need to the need for history. It can even be born from lost memories. But how can one distinguish what is myth and what is history if one is not used to saying what is right is right and what is wrong is wrong?

On the dry hills of Imogiri, the trees try to fend off both the weather and change. We are probably like that, trying to put our roots down deep in the past. But right now perhaps we don't know if we are doing this for memory or for legend, to comprehend continuity or to strengthen cults.

'Sejarah' *Tempo* 15 October 1988, CP III: 443-5

The Death of Sukardal

Sukardal hanged himself, aged fifty-three. This old *becak* (trishaw) driver had lost his *becak* on 2 July 1986 at a crossroad in the city of Bandung. The local security police had confiscated it, following new government instructions.

'Poor man!' some people said. 'To think it came to that!' said others. 'But to despair is sin', said the sermon-givers (and the medicine advertisements). 'Extreme', said one official. 'There must have been a third party', said another.

But Sukardal would not have known who was a third party, a first party or a second party. He had just tried to keep his *becak* from confiscation by the authorities. He had been dragged along beside the ditch, he had kicked, and he had been dragged again and put inside a car. He had struggled and managed to get out of the car. But he saw his *becak* picked up and thrown on a truck – seen the source of his livelihood in mid-air – and he had run and jumped in front of the moving security vehicle, hung on to it and screamed, 'I'll kill myself... I'll kill myself...'.

And, sure enough, Sukardal hanged himself on a *tanjung* tree in front of a house on Ternate Street.

'Such a shame', some people said. 'To think he'd go that far', said others. 'We were only carrying out orders', said the security officials. 'The press had better not blow this up to something big', said an official.

But what really is 'big'? What is 'small'? One *becak* out of eighteen thousand in the city of Bandung is small. One person out of hundreds of thousands who have lost their livelihood in Indonesia is small. Moreover, the moment one Sukardal dies in one corner of Indonesia, in another corner may be born a genius as brilliant as the Minister for Technology and Research, Habibie. Human suffering is a wave that the history of one nation can avoid...

Human suffering?

A short time before he died, Sukardal wrote a testament. He spoke to his eldest child. 'Yani, send your brothers and sisters back to Central Java. Your father can no longer live. Please bury my body beside your mother's.' Yani, twenty-two years old, who lived together with her brothers and sisters in a rented four-by-four meter shack, could not fulfill this last request. It was beyond her. To send a body to Majalengka from Bandung was no small matter to her.

So where is the 'small' and where is the 'big'?

A father who had brought up his children alone and who rarely showed any anger was a big thing to those children. A *becak* that cost 50,000 rupiah and had just been paid off, this was a big thing to that family,

One and a half meters from the tree where Sukardal died there is a wall. On the wall was written a message (later scrubbed off by the police): 'I have hanged myself because my *becak* was taken by those security dogs.'

My *becak*, Sukardal said. There is pride in ownership. There is anger that his right has been taken from him. There is insult: these words at once express protest and despair. In other words, a big matter precisely because they emerged from someone 'small', an ordinary man,

An ordinary man is someone who voices protest with little certainty that his voice will be heard, and because of this, his cry resounds to the grave.

It is like a poem written by an inhabitant of Chichibu, to the
west of Tokyo, at the end of the last century when the Japanese
were not yet wealthy. The poem was written after an uprising by
poor farmers in 1884 that was quelled and is quoted by Mikiso
Hane in *Peasants, Rebels, Women and Outcastes: The Underside of
Modern Japan*:

> *The wind blows*
> *The rain falls*
> *Young men die.*
> *The groans of poverty*
> *Flutter like flags in the wind.*
> *When life makes no sense*
> *Even the old people quarrel.*
> *The words on our tombstones,*
> *Buried in the snowstorms of 1884,*
> *Are not visible to the authorities.*
> *In these times*
> *We must cry loudly.*

Sukardal also tried to scream loudly. 'If this is indeed a nation
with justice, then the security police must be investigated', the
becak driver wrote on the wall before he died. 'If indeed', he wrote.
He did not write, 'Because this is a nation with justice'. Sukardal
asks for this, with his neck in the noose and his soul far away (who
can ask more strongly than that!) – because he is truly unsure.

And how could he be sure? He certainly knew that he was not
counted among the winners. He was probably not even among
those who have *ever* won. Ordinary men are those who, in the
end, lose too often. Sukardal was over half a century old – too
old to choose any different life, too old to fight. Yet he, who had
completed his junior high schooling, who had come from a small

compound in the city of Yogyakarta and had been a petty trader in Jakarta, still felt the need to write his message. He died, and he was not silent. And our lives, as a wise person once said, are made from the deaths of others who do not remain silent.

'The Death of Sukardal' *Tempo* 19 July 1986, CP III: 99-101

The Believer

W hy do you reject communism? These days, this question can be answered fluently, easily and safely. But twenty years ago – in the years leading up to 1965 – circumstances were very different. The Indonesian Communist Party (PKI) was still strong. Almost every official, bureaucrat, politician, journalist and so-called intellectual would try as hard as possible not to make an issue of 'rejecting communism' – especially in front of more than two or three other people. They were afraid.

But fear is only part of the explanation. It was not only fear that was at the heart of it, but the preoccupation with learning a different dogma, the dogma of revolution. There were those who were genuinely impressed and who would scorn those they thought did not understand. There were those who were just like coffee-grinding machines: they could not think for themselves, but just ground up and refined any ideas poured into their heads. And their heads were ninety per cent empty.

I remember Amir, for example. I think he was one of those coffee grinder types. He was not a communist, but when the PKI campaigned for confrontation with Malaysia, he joined in. When the PKI attacked those who formulated the Cultural Manifesto, he joined in. When the PKI thrashed the group that was set up by anti-communist newspapers to defend Sukarnoist ideology, once again he was in full support.

Now in 1985, twenty years after the PKI became cursed, Amir is of course quite different. Now he can speak at length about the danger of communism, about how the nation's five guiding principles, Pancasila, must be safeguarded, and how we should be 'wary' of 'issues'. He tries to find out if, for example, I am aware of the need to be on the lookout against any extreme leftist ideology. More astounding is the fact that Amir can even suspect my friend Arifin. The reason: Arifin has discussed the gap between rich and poor.

No, Amir is not like he used to be – and yet I feel that basically he has not changed at all. I can remember the day – around July 1965 when the two of us were walking down Kramat Street and walked past the central office of the PKI. On top of the building – which was being extended at the time – was a huge emblem of the hammer and sickle.

There were red banners with some message that I cannot recall. But I do remember that I turned to Amir and asked him something that had often bothered me: 'If the PKI wins, what will happen then?'

Amir kept on walking and laughed. 'One thing is for certain. The counter-revolutionaries will be wiped out. People just like you.'

I was silent. I had to admit that this prospect was indeed frightening – and twenty years ago, it did not seem to be improbable. But then I just smiled (sourly, most probably) as I in turn asked, 'And what about people like you?'

Amir's expression was serious. 'I am different from you, brother. I stand in the ranks of the committed. You don't. You are never able to distinguish between friend and foe. That is subversive, brother. You suffer from communist phobia. You must know that.'

The traces of my smile disappeared from my face. I knew that Amir was half confusing and half judging me. He was accusing me with his sacred lore: a stock phrase quoted from the holy writ of the Revolution – and this is what made so many people unable to think for themselves any more. This indeed was the first sign of communism's success: the ability to hypnotize, to bewitch thought and to shackle it into categories: friends and foes, revolution and counter-revolution, etc., etc.

A few years later I was reading the memoirs of Nadezhda Mandelstam, the widow of Osip Mandelstam, a revolutionary Russian poet who, like many others of the intelligentsia, was captured, exiled and murdered by Stalin. She describes what took place at that time in the Soviet Union, something similar to what happened in Indonesia just before 1965: the word 'revolution' made the entire population so submissive, acquiescent and obedient 'that it was a wonder that our authorities still needed prisons and the death penalty.'

But not the entire population was submissive, in fact. There were always people like Mandelstam. There are always poets. For poetry is indeed bewitched by a different spell, no matter how amazing is the hypnotic power of the sign 'revolution' – the spell of beauty, and of wonder perhaps, which beckons from the reality that surrounds us. That reality trembles, is richer, more alive, more unpredictable in its colors, and is so recalcitrant that it refuses to be caught by a trap of any ideology at all. It is not surprising that communist parties everywhere have failed to control the poets.

So, if I am asked why I reject communism, I will probably quote an experience such as this. And Amir's answer? It would be different, perhaps. For he, as before (although then standing in a different line) is clever only with categories. He doesn't know that communism is now bankrupt everywhere just because it only memorizes categories – just like him, both then and now.

'PKI' *Tempo* 5 October 1985, CP III: 37-9

Ruins

Nine of the stupas at Borobudur temple are smashed, and the palace at Surakarta is burnt down. Each time an historic artefact is ruined, we are probably shocked, feeling that a trace of the past is lost – has become further lost. But then perhaps you ask, as I and my neighbors asked, whose history is lost?

When I was seven years old, I went with my family on a picnic to Borobudur. There were hardly any visitors at the temple. The area around Borobudur was not yet crowded. I remember a tree that gave some shade in the grounds around that ancient, still monument. Here we sat and met the old caretaker.

It was the revolutionary time of Indonesia's independence. Even now I do not know if that caretaker was working voluntarily, whether he earned his living from the rare passing tourists (not foreign tourists of course), or whether he was being paid by the young Republican government – at that stage still not yet one corn harvest old. 'Please do not eat when you are on the temple, for the people who built this temple had to fast while they were working here putting these stones together and carving the reliefs.'

His voice was convincing: at least we children, the youngest in the party, took note. We did not eat the rice and fried noodles and whatever else we had brought with us. But it wasn't just this that was important. The caretaker, who seemed to really love the temple and who was probably not receiving any pay from the Republican government, with a little story made up to discourage children from throwing rubbish around, succeeded in linking my body in the present to a huge task that took place in the ancient past. He connected a single history between those builders of Borobudur and me, a little snotty-nosed kid. The story held in those hills of Kedu was my own past.

Not all heritage is like Borobudur. There is not always a clear link between a historic edifice and us. What is the relevance of Versailles Palace to me? And what is the relevance of the palace in Surakarta, Central Java, to a child from the coastal towns of Cilacap or Weleri, even though these two towns are also in Central Java, like the kingdom of Paku Buwana and his palace in Surakarta?

The sense of proximity or distance of historic artefacts is not determined by a map, nor even will it always be determined by chronology.

Take, for example, a photo album: who do we see there, in a 1930s-style white-collared shirt, in a large garden decorated with oleander bushes? The child of the servant is not going to see any part of himself in this old yellowing photograph – he is not part of that particular sense of pride. He instead sees something bitter and painful: a record of his status as offspring of a servant, lasting proof of his misery as part of a low stratum of society. Or perhaps he will view the photograph with neutral eyes: as a curiosity because it is antique – something that could be sent to the 'Stories and Photos from Times Past' section of *Femina* magazine as an important document for future historians.

So this could be why many physical remains of Dutch history in Jakarta – the buildings in Weltevreden and other structures from old Batavia – were destroyed to make way for a new Republican city that wanted a new history, a new pride. Those who read the sad stories of the 1980s, '*Si Jamin dan Si Johan*' (Jamin and Johan) by Merari Siregar, and '*Si Dul Anak Betawi*' (Dul, a Betawi child) by Aman, will get the sense of a landscape that indeed can offer a particular kind of enjoyment, but which cannot really be glorified.

We know that in life, no matter how short, there is always something that we must let go – not always to become something better, but sometimes to become something worse. And there has never been agreement about what is 'better' or 'worse' in any period.

We do not always have the energy to save things, just as we cannot save all remains of our other 'histories' that are destroyed – the house where our children were born, for example.

On 18 February 1950, a group of artists and intellectuals prepared a statement that used to be very well known but is now virtually forgotten. They called this manifesto the '*Surat Kepercayaan Gelanggang*' or Gelanggang Testimonial of Beliefs. Its contents were passionate, for according to them 'the revolution in our country is not yet over'. To them, the revolution consisted of 'replacing with new values the old worn-out values that must be destroyed.' When they spoke of 'Indonesian culture' they did not mean 'the polishing up of old culture until it shines and becomes an object of pride.' According to them, what they thought of was 'a new, healthy culture.'

There is a certain arrogance in the tone of this statement. It is a gross error to think we are a test-tube baby with no connection to any past. However, the nine stupas of Borobudur temple are smashed, and the Surakarta palace is burnt down, and perhaps it is true that what is important is not to adopt the defensive attitude of conservation, but rather to create. For in the end, the sign of civilization is our actual behavior, our respect for everything that emerges from life.

'Puing' *Tempo* 9 February 1985, CP II: 637-9

The Violent

'I was familiar with violence even before I learned to utter the word "no".' This is the kind of sentence an Indonesian writes in his autobiography. I myself experienced it – and other Indonesians, no doubt. We share the same life story: the history of a country that is not naturally quiet, peaceful and calm like the 'Sarangan Lake' of the popular *keroncong* song. Our country is a land of spilt blood.

My earliest childhood memory is a vague recollection of a dark room. Mother had the youngest child on her lap in the rocking chair. Almost the entire family was there – but no one said a word.

It was only when I was adult that I realized what was happening in that memory: we were all hiding in a big hole that Father had made in the yard. It was during the Japanese occupation. The words that were frightening, although interesting and familiar, were 'bomb' and 'war'. And at that time we just had to get used to it.

Bombs and wars – they happened and continued to happen. The Japanese occupation ended and the adults spoke of independence. Father, his eyes damp, raised the new Indonesian red and white flag. Then the Dutch forces returned. One of the villagers was shot in the leg. On the first night that these foreign forces took over our town, a brave youth threw a grenade into their camp. He was shot dead, his forehead blown to smithereens.

How many people died in this way? Two young men were sent sprawling in the rice fields not far from where we played, when some Dutch troops – for some unknown reason – showered bullets in their direction. My father was executed. My uncle was executed,

The father of my friend Dowo, the neighbor's kid, according to people who witnessed the event, was thrown from a truck with his hands bound one afternoon – then soldiers (rash young men from Assen or Zuidbeierland, who knows?) pulled their triggers, almost without even bothering to take aim. I know that Dowo and his brothers and sisters have been bereft ever since.

We were as familiar with violence as we were with our grandfathers, our fathers and our uncles. We knew its progression, and we were aware of its proximity. The maid at home, Eni, used to tell us with trembling voice about how it was to live in a West Javanese village that was surrounded by Islamic extremist (*Dar-ul-Islam*) guerillas. She had seen houses burnt, people shot dead at close range and children screaming. When there was fear and suspicion, when there was sickness and anger – how were we supposed to distance ourselves from all this? We didn't know. Perhaps we could not until we met some foreigner, someone with a more peaceful history, someone who had seen a much tidier transition between eras.

One day I was telling part of my life story to V.S. Naipaul. I was surprised to find that this famous writer was surprised. In his book *Among the Believers* he wrote: 'Indonesians have lived through so much' – as though this were some revelation.

Indeed, we have gone through a lot. Gunfire and blood, daggers and bullets, scythes and fire – all of these have a place in our consciousness. Violence even finds expression in our political language. In speaking of attacking enemies, President Sukarno introduced words like 'crush' (*ganyang*) and 'devour' (*kremus*). Pramoedya Ananta Toer introduced the term 'cut down' (*babat*). The first words give an image of a force that pulverizes everything in utter destruction through the power of jaws and teeth: the second suggests an attack with a knife or sword that scythes clean through the long grass or jungle.

Our fate is not unique, but it is not every country that has such a stream of devastating experience within one generation. Violence and savagery exist in every era, but at a particular time they can fade and become transformed into legend. At other times they become real stories and shock us – or like a kind of pornography that is cursed before being hidden under the pillow.

However, we are not merely storytellers. Whether we like it or not, we are actors, and we can also be victims and targets.

You may have seen the recent Indonesian film about the 1965 coup, *The Treachery of the 30 September Movement/Indonesian Communist Party* that was made almost twenty years after the event itself. You might have been shocked to see the sadism depicted there. But our shock is not the same as watching a film of Nazi killings during World War II, for we, even as audience, do not yet feel free from the savage events before and after 1 October 1965. For we are not visitors. We are not foreigners. We bear this burden of history – a burden that others do not have; the burden not only as trauma, but also of hope. Impatience, even.

And so, in late October 1965, one dusk on a cold street in Paris, a young Indonesian man stood open-mouthed. Above the St. Lazare station the news of the day was written in lights. One of the items was a concise sentence about the cruelty and murder that was going on at that time in the island of Java.

The young man knew what was going on. But his friend, a foreigner, asked him: 'Why do they let these things happen?' Of course the young man did not reply.

'Yang Keras' *Tempo* 6 October 1984, CP II: 567-9

Cities

I have a friend who is very much like your friends: he lives in this city of Jakarta, he earns his living here, and he curses this city. Curses wildly.

One night I met him outside a restaurant in the area of Pecenongan. He looked as though he had just had a good meal, but he was hurling abuse. 'Jakarta', he moaned, 'is like a foreign town with no one to take care of you'. Then he sauntered over to the corner in the dark, stood up against a wall, unzipped his fly and had a pee.

When he returned, he put his hand on my shoulder. 'Remember', he said, as he brought his shiny moustache close to my face, 'that we are all foreigners here. We are passers by. We buy and sell everything here: our things, our bodies, our spirits – and then we want to go home'

And he did go home – to his house in Matraman, a suburb of Jakarta. To someone like him (and even perhaps to me), 'going home' has two meanings. People go home to their houses in Jakarta, or they take the train and return to their village, as hundreds of thousands of people do at Idul Fitri holiday time.

How can such a person feel like 'a Jakartan'? How can he or she feel affection for the parks of this city, its trees, its street stalls, its buildings and even its little windy streets? I don't know how.

To them it is as though Jakarta were lacking some kind of emblem or tie with the people that live there – a tie for the people in Menteng, Mester, Kota or Kampung Melayu. Jakarta indeed

offers many things, but is there any one thing that makes it unique
– any one thing that must be retained, must not be lost?

My friend (just like your friends, perhaps) shakes his head.
'Nothing', he replies. And every morning off he goes to earn his
living in this city. He is a type of person – just like us – who still
has the unsettledness of one who has not yet set down anchor:
someone who does not love his place of origin enough to stay there,
but yet cannot tie his heart to his new place. Jakarta merely catches
people like us and holds us – it doesn't shape us. And as for our
side of the deal – we merely accommodate the demands of this city
without ever really assimilating into it.

An expert once said that in a city like Jakarta one can witness not
only a process of urbanization, but also a process of 'ruralization':
there is a constant flow of people with their rural lifestyle entering
the city, and in the process making the city more like a village – in
the number of infant births and deaths, in superstition and in lack
of freedom.

But how else could it be with a Third World city in the twentieth
century? The Dutch-style fortress built by Jan Peiterszoon Coen has
lost – and it was defeated not by the forces of the Javanese Mataram
kingdom, but by something else, something stronger than that. This
fortress-style city was defeated by the reality that a city in Indonesia
cannot stand alone. It is surrounded and finally controlled by the
economic and political forces around it. It cannot become a place
that has its own particular character and energy – something that
historically, particularly in Europe, made cities become a source of
freedom and a force for change and development.

The case of Europe is indeed different. Cities there emerged
and became strong before territorial nations arose and became
established. In this more-or-less exclusive environment, the city
dwellers could organize their own lives. They were free from the
clutches of the feudal lords who lived in their castles far away in

the interior. Even the farmers who managed to escape from their serf existence in the fields could become freemen once they passed through the city gates and were registered as citizens.

The story of a city can tell many things. 'Cities, like dreams, emerge through hopes and fears', said Marco Polo to Kublai Khan in one of Italo Calvino's magic stories. But I am always reminded of my friend: his hopes and fears are probably hopes and fears of a different kind, so that he does not feel part of the creation of the city of Jakarta.

'Kota' *Tempo* 23 June 1984, CP II: 511-3

Twilight in Jakarta

The drizzle hastens the twilight, even along the boulevard. Traffic rushes by. The roads become slippery. The traffic lights are hard at work. And beneath a small shelter is a traffic policeman on duty wearing a white coat, a sign of loyalty beneath a stupid slogan: TRAFFIC DISCIPLINE SHOWS NATIONAL DISCIPLINE.

Weird. Who cares about 'nation'? This is a boulevard that never sleeps. The lights in the windows at the top of the hotel on the western side now begin to flicker on. The colored neon lights glow like the women with painted lips who ply their trade on the street corners. But this is a busyness that feels like stillness.

Who wants to make a show of national discipline at this place, at this time? The sociologist Daniel Bell lamented the loss of *civitas* in Western society. As for us, we do not know if we have ever had any such 'spontaneous desire to follow the law' or 'respect for the rights of others', or whether we have bowed down before a 'state' to which, as members, we willingly ally ourselves.

Civitas. The word itself is foreign. It is more foreign than the various words flashing in the neon signs above the hotels. It is probably as idiotic as the slogan asking all those drivers in their cars to behave as good citizens of a single community or society.

Not all roadside slogans are so stupid. Like any place, Jakarta has its share of both stupid and smart ones. An example of the former reads: 'To join the Family Planning Program is to support the success of the National Five Year Plan.' An example of the latter reads: 'Get rid of you hemorrhoids by using ...'. A smart slogan speaks to us as individuals who first and foremost think of ourselves. A not-so-smart slogan is one with the idea that 'national discipline' or 'the national plan' is already part of people's inner consciousness, while in fact I doubt that such an internalization of the meaning of these words has occurred.

The drizzle hastens the twilight, and hastens people's rushing. Twilight means the end of the day's work for most people – the time for themselves, their families, and their own enjoyment. At twilight, Aristotle's *polis* does not exist – meaning a city as an entity that represents a social unity enveloping and gathering all individuals within it.

There is no sure answer as to whether some social duties are being quietly fulfilled – like the policeman in the white raincoat at the shelter.

For, who knows, perhaps there is no 'state'. The government offices are closed. The office cars are now cruising movie houses and the foreshore. Maybe at twilights like these, what happens is not merely corruption and laziness, but a more developed kind of civic privatism. The state has grown swollen with new functions and duties that barge into new areas of people's lives. But, as a political scientist commented, the state has become less like a state. It does not really exist as a focus of service and loyalty.

What has really happened? Is this selfishness, because of the dynamics of social development based on the economic wellbeing of the individual? Or is it that members of society, for various reasons, become distanced from the desire to come together with a single communal focus?

The answer to this question, like the traffic lights, flashes on and off, alternately obstructing us and letting us through. Sometimes people stop and gauge whether it is dangerous to go forward. Sometimes it as though we are being pushed to speed ahead.

'Senja di Jakarta' *Tempo* 10 April 1982, CP II: 119-20

The Closing of the Newspapers, 1978

Every time in history, it seems, has a moment when it is not easy to speak, but when it is not easy to remain silent. We do not know precisely how our words will be valued, or if a gesture will be noticed. At times like this, there is only cloud, rain, or silence – even indifference – outside the door. All is a puzzle.

Nevertheless we still need to talk to ourselves. We do not only act. Every action demands approval. At the very moment we tell others to be silent, in fact deep in our hearts we want those others to approve our action. We wish to place our capacity to conquer alongside our capacity to convince.

Certainly, it cannot always be like this. But it is understandable that in our actions we seek approval for ourselves so as to be seen as 'good people' and our actions as 'successful'. In short, people around us are something we cannot ignore – they are something we need.

Perhaps this is why there is a type of unwritten law within any power structure: no matter how authoritarian the rule, it will still need someone else who is free of it. The great king all alone on the little planet, in the tale *Le Petit Prince* by Antoine de Saint-Exupéry, eventually had to find another person to come and be his subject. He could not rule over nothing but the silent sky.

When the Republic of Indonesia was established, it was not intended to be just forest, ocean and mute tropical islands. 'Order, peace, safety and prosperity'; these were the ideals. But a nation must always be prepared for reality – and reality, which often appears as confusion, can often bring with it a certain blessing.

On June 1 1945, when Bung Karno gave his first speech about the Five Guiding Principles or *Pancasila*, he spoke of this blessing:

No country can be considered alive if it does not contain conflict. Do not think that there is no conflict in Turkey – or no difference of opinion in Japan. Almighty God gave us thought so that in our daily social interaction there would always be some friction, and from this friction the raw rice would emerge and be husked to become the finest Indonesian rice.

Bung Karno then proposed the third of the five principles of *Pancasila*, namely *musyawarah*. We are often in a dilemma resolving conflict. Sometimes there is unforeseen risk. Our entire history since 1945 could be seen as a crusade to find the best method of *musyawarah* – with the way often blocked by bitterness.

The Indonesian Communist Party, for instance, offered 'proletarian dictatorship'; Kartosuwirjo mobilized people for an 'Islamic state', but until now something within the body of Indonesia has rejected both.

People may debate what this force causing rejection is. Clearly, it is not just a matter of weapons. It may be something quite simple – the reality of the huge diversity of Indonesia which itself created Pancasila, thus stipulating that there is no single force that can monopolize the whole country.

This is the very essence and aim of democracy. At times, this aim may get stuck – but it cannot disappear without trace. In a field mushy with snow, when the Germans were murdering their enemies, there was still someone who could stand and write, 'If our lot is complete annihilation, let us not behave in such a way that it seems like justice.'

'Ketika Koran-Koran Ditutup, 1978' *Tempo* 28 January 1978,
CP I: 241-3

Malay

We were sitting on the verandah of the old Raffles Hotel. He ordered a Campari and soda and then asked me, 'So, you are a Malay?'

I couldn't give a quick answer. He was Canadian and had been in Singapore for only a few days. We had just met and started chatting, and I realized that to him, as to many other Westerners, Southeast Asia was Singapore, together with some ill-defined region around it: a world known only through Paul Theroux's travel books.

So I couldn't give him a quick answer. Was I Malay? What do we mean by this word? To an Indonesian, 'Malay' means an ethnic group. To a Malaysian or Singaporean it is a racial label. To others it may even be a type of insult, as in Jakarta when people tease others as 'Malay spies', or 'having the mentality of a Malay'.

At last I answered using the annoying manner of a geography teacher. 'I am an Indonesian, born a Javanese, and my race is indeed Malay.'

He smiled. 'You're too serious for a Malay', he said.

I knew then that he hadn't just been reading novels. He had also listened to people talking. He must have heard how people frequently describe 'the Malays' (at least this is the description of the popular tourist-bus anthropologists): the Malays are a friendly race of people, always smiling and laughing, people who enjoy an easy life and who are unfamiliar with hard work; basically inefficient people who have no spirit of perseverance, creatures who are easily swept away by sudden emotion. Just remember that the English word 'amok' is of Malay origin – for the Malays can suddenly draw their kris and start stabbing wildly...

The tourist-bus anthropology could go on and on, for people finally believe only what they want to believe. Eric Hoffer's comment is right: 'There is a tendency to judge a race, a nation or any distinct group by its least worthy members.' If the least worthy members of a race are lazy, then the entire race appears lazy. If they are corrupt, then the entire nation is corrupt. If there are a few who have no love for their native land, then the whole group will be judged accordingly. And if there are some who are unable to work according to the demands of modern life, then people will say, as they sip their drinks, 'It's just a matter of mentality, brother'. They will not stop to ask where this mentality springs from.

The *Hikayat Abdullah* tells that one day in 1823 Thomas Stamford Raffles invited the ruling Sultan of Singapore and his Minister (Tumenggung) to his residence. Raffles, the British civil servant who founded Singapore, wanted to convey a strong wish. As the drinks were served, Raffles assured his visitors of the need for an education for their children in English language and basic arithmetic. The children would be sent to school in India, and the cost of their five years' education would be borne by Raffles himself. In this way, Raffles explained, the future successors of the Sultan and his Minister would be 'wise rulers'.

'Look at Singapore', Raffles said, 'so many different nationalities living from trade: but do you see any Malay traders? The Malays are not capable of taking part in more serious enterprise, primarily because they have no knowledge of how to keep accounts or how to write. If Your Majesties' children study arithmetic and other subjects, then the benefit of education will quickly become evident to other Malays.'

But the fate of the Malays was sealed the moment that the Sultan and the Tumenggung refused. Abdullah bin Abdul Kadir

Munsyi, who recorded this event so well, regretted the action of the two Malay figures. And yet, after all, what was the point at that time of arithmetic for the sons of kings? Kings and princes could enjoy life merely through their own power, and from power came leisure.

This could be where the attitude towards Malays originated. The *Hikayat Abdullah* is a record that tells how the complacency of the Malay rulers (some would call it their lack of responsibility) brought about a nation that remained stuck, with no vision of the future. Its people had no courage of original thought. They were afraid of flashy dress, of grand houses. The wealthy were afraid. No one could refuse the rulers' demands, and if anything was 'borrowed' from the people in the name of the ruler, there was no hope of it being returned.

Abdullah and Raffles speak of a time over one and a half centuries ago, but their voices are as clear as yesterday: the trace of exploitation stretches wide – wider even than we sometimes know.

'Melayu' *Tempo* 4 April 1987, CP III: 221-3

II
Wider Worlds

Douch

What can one say about an executioner? We have seen Anwar Congo in Joshua Oppenheimer's documentary, *The Act of Killing*: the thug from Medan proudly admitting that he killed many 'communists' in the mid 1960s, but the last scene is almost completely silent; all you can hear is him coughing in the former execution house, just an old man exhausted from going down the stairs....

When the film ends, there is no story about what happened to Anwar Congo right then, or afterwards. In the end, people cannot be fully documented, I think. There is not just one Anwar Congo.

Maybe this is also true of Douch. His real name is Kaing Guek Eav. In the bloody history of Cambodia in the 1970s, he was a Khmer Rouge official, the chief of Tuol Seng prison, also known as 'S-21'. He is a figure of brutality no less terrifying.

During the four years that the Communist Party ruled in Cambodia, thousands were held in this place whose name means 'Hill of the Poisonous Trees'.

Douch, from 1975 the prison chief of 'S-21', was a killer. When the Khmer Rouge was defeated and he was arrested and tried, evidence was produced: his written orders, for instance, to 'smash to pieces' seventeen prisoners (eight teenagers and nine children). On the list of twenty female prisoners, he wrote instructions beneath each name: 'for execution'; 'continue the interrogation'; 'for medical experiments'.

Douch also admitted that his men snatched babies from their mothers and smashed them against trees until they died.

From a total of around 17,000 prisoners, only seven survived.

Douch, a former mathematics teacher, appears to have been fastidious. Almost every victim was documented and photographed. When the Khmer Rouge left Phnom Penh, escaping from the invading Vietnamese forces that set up a new socialist government, Douch did not have time to burn this documentation – and this was his downfall.

Why would one record such cruelty? A butcher's sadistic expression? Or part of the design for the future for which proof of massacre is thought necessary – a future that will vindicate it?

Douch believed this is what would happen: the future would prove him right. He considered cruelty to be unavoidable in the mobilization of history. After all, were not hundreds decapitated in the French revolution? 'The scale of the sacrifice does not matter', Douch explained. 'What is important is the grandeur of the final goal.' (*'Peu importe l'ampleur du sacrifice; ce qui compte, c'est la grandeur du but que l'on s'assigne.'*)

He said this one night in some corner of the jungle to a person who had been captured and accused of being a 'CIA spy': François Bizot.

Bizot, a young anthropologist from Paris, was studying Buddhism in the interior of Cambodia. This was 1971: a period dangerous for everyone. The local communists, the 'Khmer Rouge', had formed and were gaining in power precisely because of the American bombing. Bizot, who was in the area of Angkor Wat that was now under Khmer Rouge control, was captured. He was tied up in a small prison camp in the jungle.

His two Cambodian friends were also captured (and later killed). Bizot was allowed to live. After being held for three months, he was set free. Around thirty years later, after a long period of silence, he wrote a book titled *Le Portail* (translated into English as The Gate) about his experience, a book he says he wrote with 'bitterness which knows no limit.'

That 'bitterness' seems not to have come from Douch. The 'torturer' left Bizot free to bathe in the river and roam around the camp. Bizot could speak Khmer, and Douch spoke French, Gradually, a kind of understanding arose between the two of them.

One night not long before Bizot was released, Douch held a party: speeches, songs and food, slaughtering thirteen chickens. And the prisoner and executioner sat until dawn, chatting before the fading campfire.

What can be said of Douch? He was a man with total conviction about the future, and at 29 was prepared to become a killer. But at the same time, he was prepared to put his own head on the line when he proposed to his iron-fisted supervisors to let Bizot go free.

When Douch was later arrested and taken before the courts, the question arose: would Bizot take the stand as a witness? To the *Libération* newspaper, he replied, 'yes, if the prosecution asks me to. Yes if the defense asks me to.' (*Oui, si l'accusation me le demande. Oui, si la défense me le demande.*')

An ambiguous position, certainly. To him, the butcher of 'S-21' camp was a tragic figure. 'He was a child venturing among wolves: to survive, he had drunk their milk, and learned to howl like them, and let instinct take over. Terror, from that moment, became all-powerful. It seduced him by putting on the face of morality and order.'

'Morality' meant conviction of the purest-of-pure communism; 'order' meant wiping out everything considered flawed. Douch lived with the ecology of violence in Cambodian modern history: colonialism, the Cold War, American intervention with its bombardments, the Vietnam War, the Cultural Revolution in China, the brutality of rulers, and suffering in the interior.

From all this came desire with ideology to change the world, with absolute, seething faith. The world was divided: the 'old' and the 'new'; 'patriots' and 'traitors'; 'proletariats' and 'bourgeois'.

History was the story of two tribes attacking each other to become Red or Black.

With this point of view, someone like Douch will not flinch when they realize that during the Khmer Rouge rule around two million Cambodians were killed. And we recall all the cruelty since 1914, and the words of Elias Canetti: 'It is a mark of fundamental human decency to feel ashamed of living in the 20th century.'

This, is seems, is the basis of the 'bitterness which knows no limit' that haunted Bizot in his writing.

'Douch' *Tempo* 16 February 2014

Dirt

How can one pass judgment, when there is no one left who has not sinned? When the measurement of what is and what is not sin trades places? When the dirty and the pure become sheer possibility – and increasingly, people do not know what will happen with history?

We have witnessed – yes, we have gone through – murder both big and small. We keep on wrestling with what stance we should take. Secretly, we hope that eventually history will bring us to a decision acceptable to all, for all times.

But are we placing too much hope in history? 'Ha[s] not history always been an inhumane, unscrupulous builder, mixing its mortar of lies, blood and mud?'

This ominous question is from *Darkness at Noon* by Arthur Koestler, a novel that arose from experience different to ours here in Indonesia, but maybe not too far different. Koestler wrote it in late 1939 in Europe when history was a political upheaval that was furious, full of fervor, and brutal. Both Nazism (which wanted to build a *Neue Ordnung* or 'New Order', and communism (which wanted to build 'New Life') believed that history would move – with definite and oblivious steps – towards the achievement of their ideals, even though, as Marx said, 'At every bend she leaves the mud which she carries and the corpses of the drowned. History knows her way. She makes no mistakes.'

With conviction like this, violence and murder cannot be cursed.

Darkness at Noon does not say where the story takes place. But the reader knows that the protagonist, Nicholas Salmanovitch Rubashov, is a fictive character shaped by the true experience of revolutionary fighters in the October Revolution who were shot by their own comrade, Stalin, when he took over the top leadership. Rubashov had served the Party while it established its power, but was now considered by The Leader (called No. 1) to be a traitor. He was arrested, tortured, made to confess to things he never did, and shot.

But what if 'No. 1' was actually right? Rubashov himself becomes uncertain. With his faith in history, he cannot bring himself to suddenly say that 'No 1' is a tyrant. The people he kills maybe eventually have to admit – 'even with the bullet behind their necks' – that the ruler at the top has not sinned. He has merely acted as a tool of history to build a better world. He is brutal, but he cannot be judged with any convincing judgment.

'There was no certainty', Rubashov mumbles in his cell, helpless. We can only appeal before History (written with a capital 'H'). But what is tragic in human life is that the decisions of History are given 'only when the jaws of the appealer ha[ve] long since fallen to dust'.

The judge arrives too late, always too late.

But I don't think so. I think there is something wrong in this view. History is not the judge. It is not the sacred oracle that does the shooting. History is not outside ourselves, nor are we outside of it, and man is not merely its tool. We do not need to write it with a capital 'H'. Marx was right when he said that it is not history that uses man in pursuit of its ends. Rather, history 'is nothing but the activity of men in pursuit of their ends.'

Meaning, the judge is man.

But this also brings problems difficult to solve, when people say, as Napoleon is supposed to have said, that 'fate is politics'. Fate, which is seen as ineluctably coming from human life, is increasingly read as the product of human interaction, *zoon politikon*. There are no stipulations coming from the sky above. There are no values unsullied by wrangling on earth. There are no universal values that are determined just like that.

But if this is the case, then passing sentence is impossible. If it is assumed that the universal never occurs, then values are unstable. What in one situation is considered 'good' is, in another, considered 'bad'. There is no one without sin when the measure of what is sin and what is not keeps shifting.

But can we live without passing judgment? 'I must have justice, or I will destroy myself', Ivan Karamazov says in Dostoyevsky's famous novel. And to him, the justice he craves is not 'justice in some remote infinite time and place'. He wants the justice that exists on earth.

Ivan Karamazov reminds us that justice – a universal value – even though it is never complete and eternal within life that is limited, is utterly valuable. 'Or else I will kill myself'.

'Kotor' *Tempo* 29 June 2014

Laws

I often recall that strange story, Kafka's story, about a man from the country who wishes to be accepted by the law. But he only gets as far as a guarded door. The gatekeeper, in a fur coat, big nosed and with a black Tartar moustache, tells him the time is not yet right for him to be accepted.

And he keeps on saying this.

And the man from the country waits. Day upon day, month upon month, year upon year. Actually, the gatekeeper is not really obstructing him. He says that if the man wishes, he can enter without permission. But, he says, be aware that beyond the door there is another one, with another gatekeeper fiercer still, and so on and so forth.

The visitor eventually does not try to go inside. He just sits before the door. Day upon day, month upon month, year upon year. As time goes on, he weakens. In the end, he dies. He dies realizing that in all that time no one else asking to be received by the law had gone through that door. This door, the gatekeeper says, is indeed especially for you.

We do not know why. But, before the end comes, the visitor sees a bright shining light behind the door. Is that the law? What is that thing called the 'law' like? And why is it that he, who has been given a special entrance, is still not accepted?

This story has been interpreted in various ways. I tend to see that Kafka is teasing us to show just how huge the aura of the law was for that man: as though it has something transcendental within – even though it does not. That aura is connected to mystery, and people do not see, or analyze, its origins. The visitor is easily compliant.

His own story is not clear. It is not said whether he comes to accept a sentence or to protest. He merely obeys, and not because he is forced to do so. I think he comes because throughout his life he experiences a gulf between 'the law' and 'laws'.

In Kafka's German, the word for the law is *Gesetz*, from *setzen*, meaning 'to set, to arrange', which is not far from the English word *law* which comes from Old Norse meaning 'to lay down, to fix'. In Indonesian, the word for law, *hukum*, is not the same as the word for 'laws', *undang-undang*, from '*undang*' meaning to invite, call or summon. Laws are not merely a set of posted regulations, but are something 'made to call'.

So one could say that all regulations (*undang-undang*) hold within them the invitation to everyone within the territory where those regulations are in force: the invitation to know, to be involved, to support and to obey. There are concrete 'others' implicit here. There is inhabited space. There are inhabitants who live, listen, speak, and use language from time to time.

But 'the law' (*hukum*), in its usual interpretation – and also as used in physics (such as in 'Archimedes' law') – places itself outside the other, and unconnected to space and time. It claims a universal truth. It assumes that every thinking person will be in agreement with it.

But there is diametrical difference between the law in natural sciences and the law as the product of legislative processes. Archimedes' law was formulated after an experiment that can be scrutinized in any time and place – the result of a rational process within an isolated self, the product of the I-who-thinks taking distance from the instability of quotidian experience.

In legislation it is the opposite: legislation is not prepared in a laboratory. Legislation is the product of social relations and political processes. When legislation is called 'product of the law', it is projected as having an aura that surmounts the political process. State institutions then build an 'ideology' and the law appears with an extremely noble image. Even the state must obey the law, as is implicit in the phrase '*negara hukum*', state based on law, or constitutional state.

But actually what happens is a kind of fetishism. I am borrowing the word 'fetishism' from Marx, who showed how commodities, things produced by the workers which are traded, appear to be disconnected from the work process and move on their own, are worshipped and fetishized. In the history of legislation, it seems that it is in a stage like this that 'the law' moves away from its process of production and distribution.

The ideology is ancient. Plato, in his last work, *Nomos*, already differentiated between *nomothetēs*, the legislators who 'bestow the law' and the *politikos*, those who govern the country. From the former is expected wisdom and the ability to think rationally, combined with competence to convince others. Not much is expected of the latter: they should just work effectively.

But outside of Plato's work, and particularly in the era of democracy, *nomothetēs* and *politikos* are together in one body, in one space, in one process – even though one half does not like to be revealed. A veil is drawn. What is more, legislators, who in Indonesia are usually referred to as 'people's representatives', seem as a matter of course to have transparent relations with those who should rightly be 'regulated'.

Kafka's story Before the Law opens the veil: it is a story about a kind of fetishism so crazy that a man is fascinated to death by the law – the law with its aura and mystery.

But at the same time, Kafka makes us see: before the door stands a strong guard. He is polite and direct, but his words and bearing are threatening in their cold-heartedness. The aura of the law indeed is not born of justice from the skies, or from the brains of geniuses – but can come about through trauma.

'Undang' *Tempo* 11 May 2014

History

A writer once said that the past is a foreign country. Perpetually foreign. We, living now, can never really know its internal and external world, its streets and valleys, its inhabitants and instruments.

Of course, history is written. Not merely once and not merely by one person. Of course, historians often debate amongst themselves about a certain unforgettable period, the dramatic and probably also traumatic, as for example 1965 in Indonesia – a past that demands revisiting. Documents are gathered and analyzed, statistics are re-read, interviews are recorded. But to what extent can a reconstruction restore the past?

Memory comes from dark caves; it is like part of those caves. When we bring it into the spotlight, we should be aware that it has changed. Reconstruction involves metamorphosis. Particularly when we are aware that the past is like a text in another language that has to be translated, and every translation involves transformation, because it is done in a different time and also a different climate.

Also because we create.

About ten weeks before he died, in August 1941, Rabindranath Tagore gave a sharp, even bitter, criticism of historiography. '...I am nothing but a poet', Tagore wrote. 'I am there in the role of a creator all alone and free. There's little to enmesh me there in the net of external events. I find it difficult to put up with the pedantic historian when he tries to force me out of the centre of my creativity ...'

Tagore did not believe in historiography. Although, as Ranajit Guha in *History at the Limit of World-History* quotes him at the close of the paragraph above, he brings history back into the conversation. 'Let us go back', Tagore says, 'to the inaugural moment of my poetical career.'

What he then tells is an example of how the most authentic history (at least to Tagore) is the story of one's own experience of absorbing the world – as one's very first childhood observations: the sparkling dew on the coconut fronds at dawn, the thick clusters of dark blue clouds over his ancestral house at dusk, a buffalo licking its calf's back....

These are private experiences, and Tagore stresses this: history is not what is recorded from public figures and scenes. History is the story of *pratyahik sukhduhkha*, a person's 'everyday contentment and misery', which are conveyed creatively. World-History in the Hegelian sense is unable to capture this.

We know that Hegel, as his philosophy later developed, did not view history as the story of a person in solitude. History follows designs from on high – a grand overall narrative of humanity, the progression towards freedom, via dialectics and stages of progress. In the view Hegel held in his old age (which was also reflected in Marx's ideas), the old eschatological shadows of religion which the Enlightenment had tried to purge, stealthily return: human fate starts with origin, and there is destiny, struggle towards redemption, and heaven. With this proviso: to Hegel, 'The overall content of world history is rational, and indeed has to be rational.'

So the subject of history is not a person alone viewing the dew and a buffalo's back, clouds at dusk or the brightness of dawn. The actor of history is Spirit, *Geist*. The 'everyday contentment and misery' of a person – in a mortal body – is not the important story.

Often, in the movements of history that follow this design, the oddness of creativity is not recognized, because everything is predetermined. The fascinating, the amazing, has no place. Everything can be explained.

Hegel, just like religion and mythology, depicts humanity as what begins with origin. But this is not entirely correct. Humanity began its life with no awareness of origin. Man's first steps, first words, and initial desires were done with no clarity about what would follow and how things would end. Humanity was not determined from origins, but created its story from the beginning. Because basically, man is a creator.

This does not mean that we can only cling to Tagore's preference for the 'mysterious history of [the] inner soul'. Poetry like Tagore's can enrich our experience, but it is not enough for knowing the past. Humanity is not merely a private room. Man's life story – as creator – ineluctably holds political dimensions. Humans exist within a space and time along with other things – conversing, gathering, quarrelling, fighting – even when attempting to revisit that foreign country, the past.

And this is the process that will continue *ad infinitum*. The past, like a foreign country, will have pictures that are always different, and always undergoing metamorphosis. But this is also why the future is not as Hegel imagined it. It is always born of 'the production of novelty', to use Whitehead's words. It will not have a sure ending, but probably because of this, it thrills, fascinates and makes us anxious.

'Sejarah' *Tempo* 27 October 2013

Lies

'...in the end, everybody breaks, bro. It's biology.'

The CIA agent in the film *Zero Dark Thirty* has changed the person he is interrogating: the detainee has been turned into a biological construct. The body is tethered hands and feet. Every so often it is laid horizontally while the head is wrapped in cloth to be submerged in water until almost out of breath. The CIA wants this man to break and reveal Osama Bin Laden's hideout. So in the dingy torture chamber he has been formatted as a sack to be trampled upon until he spews out information.

A sack for trampling, a biological form, a life completely naked, *la vita nuda:* he is material without protection. When someone's sense of self respect, shame, guilt and convictions are eliminated, then there is no hope of holding out. Everybody breaks.

We know that the film is fiction, but the brutality is not. And a work of fiction, like a poem, is often charged with unintended interpretations. American rightists, Senators and the CIA accused *Zero Dark Thirty* of overdoing the role of torture in the hunt for Bin Laden and thus smearing America's reputation. Leftists, on the other hand, accused the director Kathryn Bigelow of acting like the filmmaker Leni Riefenstahl who glorified Nazism eight decades ago. One well-known writer warned Bigelow that she would be remembered as 'torture's handmaiden'.

The controversy is not over. But one thing has been achieved. *Zero Dark Thirty* – with its impressive realism – has exposed that the 'war against terrorism' holds intrinsic contradiction. Its initiators called it a 'just war' because terrorism is repugnant. But that same war actually marks the beginning of unjust and repugnant acts.

There was a time when a modern order in international relations took shape. That was in Europe after 1648. The Peace of Westphalia ended the war between the Protestants and the Catholics that had brought life to its knees. From then on, spatial orientation became more organized, and borders clearly marked. This was the beginning of a legal order. It was the birth of the unity of *Ordnung und Ortung*, order and orientation. A *nomos*, to use Carl Schmitt's term.

From then on, according to Schmitt, war became a state-protected monopoly. Conflict more resembled a duel: a 'war in form', *une guerre en forme*. It was motivated more by rational considerations, not moral; it was not holy war. With rationality there were also mutually accepted rules. Opponents were not considered 'absolute enemies'. The opponent was not the Devil, nor filth or barbarians that had to be wiped out or made to repent. They were still like 'us'.

Schmitt, a pro-Nazi German, gives an explanation that is of course Euro-centred and limited; he does not tell how colonial armies treated their opponents in Asia and Africa. Schmitt's statement was a criticism of what happened after Germany's defeat in World War I. Germany was not invited to the negotiations for the Treaty of Versailles. The nation was treated as a criminal.

It is not surprising that Schmitt presents only the aspects that strengthen his thesis. He wipes the fact that even with 'war-in-form' there are rules observed only momentarily. 'As if there were any rules for killing people', Leo Tolstoy wrote in his great novel, *War and Peace*, when he described Napoleon's complaint to Kutusov, the Russian officer, in the 1812 invasion: the French forces used rapiers while the Russians – a people's army – responded with cudgels, 'without consulting anyone's tastes or rules'.

The history of wars 'without consulting anyone's tastes or rules', usually popular rebellions, is as old as the story of *une guerre en forme*, wars between regular armies of two countries in conflict. From the American Revolution of the 18th century through to the war in Afghanistan this century, there has been no restriction on the kind of weapons used, nor has there been any boundary between the civil and the military. All can shoot. All can be shot. Violence is not only a State matter. Victims can be anywhere.

But that is not the problem. The problem is the pretext of this war – both the pretext of guerillas and that of their opponents in counter-insurgencies that are equally unlimited.

I think what is important in Schmitt's thesis is that he is not extolling the 'war in form' because it is not brutal. He praises it as war that began when the state became separate from religious precepts: it is not a holy war. The enemy is not some cursed creature. It is a dispute between fellow people.

But on 11 September 2002, two aircraft crashed into the twin towers of the World Trade Centre in New York and thousands of innocent people died. Bush prepared the 'war against terror'. And so war with no clear indicators of victory bloomed, because there would never be any representative of the opposing side to sign a surrender.

At that moment, angry Americans and their intellectuals screamed about and formulated 'just war' – a kind of war of vengeance from the innocent side, the side that was clean, God-faring. Moral arguments returned, as in the Crusades. The enemy became Satan. The world had to change. America aped the Taliban.

In its enthusiasm for 'just war' Taliban style, America felt it had the decisive right to consider anyone its enemy as inhuman. And very soon after, America also felt it had the right to ignore international law – and to promulgate an extraordinary lie and attack Iraq, which actually was then no threat to it at all.

This week, that lie is ten years old.

Rushdie

It was a bright Tuesday in London, 14 February to be exact, Valentine's Day, and Salman Rushdie answered a call from a BBC journalist. 'How does it feel, to know that you have just been sentenced to death by Ayatollah Khomeini?'

'It doesn't feel good', he replied. But in his heart he knew, 'I am a dead man'. He put down the phone, closed the shutters and locked the front door.

And from then, one year after his novel *The Satanic Verses* had been published and condemned by Islamic leaders the world over, Rushdie went into hiding for nine years – an experience he has just written about in his memoir, *Joseph Anton*. Rushdie attempts to recreate his memory of fear during that time, almost a decade, when he had to move from house to house, knowing that Khomeini's fatwa – authorizing his murder by any Muslim anywhere – could be carried out at any time. And during those nine years, as a British citizen, he was guarded night and day by Special Forces of the Metropolitan Police. Over that same time, he also had to assume another identity. He chose the name 'Joseph Anton', a combination of Joseph Conrad and Anton Chekhov, his two favorite writers. Rushdie became a new 'self'. This is why, in the memoir, he uses not 'I' but 'he'. As though he is talking about someone else. For what is self, actually? It is not any permanent 'I', nor an 'I' that is transparent and fully formed. He was no longer the 'Salman' that he was to his friends, but 'Rushdie', the author of *The Satanic Verses*. He even changed from being the author of the novel with that title, to the writer of 'satanic verses'. He was considered to be the secretary of the Devil.

Some say that *Joseph Anton* shows he was not merely a writer of fiction 'who invented characters for a living and had now turned himself into a sort of fictional character as well.' Rather, the opposite: Rushdie is typical of writers in that he never invented his characters alone, even less invent himself. Like Gibreel Farishta and Saladin Chamcha in his novel, Salman and Rushdie are names bestowed by others. The character is also the product of the interpretation of others – interpretation that can change and differ.

Again, there is no completely transparent 'I'. There was no (nor was there is need for) 'him' as such. When people burned his photograph in demonstrations, it was increasingly unclear what and who Salman Rushdie really were. There was only 'an effigy, an absence'.

As an effigy, as an absence, he could be projected in more than one way. *Joseph Anton* is the story of someone who views himself and his own flaws acutely, but also someone who puffs up the ego. Probably because every life story, like every novel, does not appear in a vacuum: there are always others watching, expected to applaud or be angry, because of their desires and traumas. Because of their histories.

Rushdie himself once talked about the strong role history plays in our attitudes viewing the world (and literature). 'We are all irradiated by history, we are radioactive with history and politics'. We live in a world 'without quiet corners', and there is no easy path to escape from the 'terrible, unquiet fuss'.

This is what happened in the story of *The Satanic Verses*. As a novel more often talked about than read, it could not be free of the 'irradiation of history'. It entered the world 'without quiet corners'.

Rushdie's self defence was that in his novel the bad image of the Prophet Mohammed appears not within a factual description, but rather in the fantasy of Gabriel Farishta, a schizophrenic. But all the novelist could do was explain. Despite everything, his novel reached corners unquiet and unliked, or unusual, with blending and paradox between the 'real' and the 'magic' in magic realism – a narrative style Rushdie also used brilliantly and amusingly in *Midnight's Children*.

One might doubt whether he really was unaware that his novel would be provocative. At the very least, he surely knew a premise that has been familiar in literary theory since the 1960s: in every text, in every conversation, there is always *aporia* or uncertainty of meaning. No novel can offer one complete and permanent purpose. 'To read' is something infinitely more complex than usually assumed. Within every process of reading is always implicit the process of misreading.

By choosing the title *The Satanic Verses*, Rushdie himself actually took on this issue of reading. What happens in 'reading' and in the text that is read? When determining a 'good' and a 'satanic' text, can we really say we are not influenced by our interests or shaped by our practical considerations in the world? Why do people not want to admit this? And is it wrong when we are influenced by practical 'worldly' considerations?

It seems that we are so intent on 'correct' interpretation that we forget about 'just' interpretation…

I am reminded of Althusser. He said that the word '*juste*' is an adjective not from *justice*, but *justesse*. And within it is an attitude of '*adjustement*' or adjusting, putting interpretation as praxis in the midst of the world that changes from one moment to the next, contingent. So 'just' interpretation contains wisdom about what happens in life.

This is why reading is not something done in a static situation. We, the readers of novels, the interpreters of Holy Books, are always on the move, shifting, although not always in secret.

'Rushdie' *Tempo* 16 December 2012, CP X: 415-8

Akhenaten

'O sole god, like whom there is no other...'

In the year 1380 BCE, in ancient Egypt, a king wrote a beautiful poem for the One. Probably this is the most ancient voice of praise of a monotheist, 700 years before Isaiah. But what experts more often write about is that he was a pharoah who changed the religion of his ancestors into a faith that became more like Abrahamic religions.

Akhenaten, the pharaoh, called that sole god Aten, the name of an older god that he retained to facilitate worship. But in a radical departure from earlier Egyptian religions, Akhenaten's faith forbade people to make statues of that god. According to the young king, the unimaginable god could not be represented in any form whatsoever.

Aten was god of all humankind, not only of the Egyptians – an entirely new conclusion and inspiration for those times. In the hymn to Aten, Egypt is even mentioned last in the series of lands under his protection.

God, or this god, is the god of love who, in sending forth his rays, 'the two lands of Egypt are in daily festivity, awake and stand upon their feet.' Aten is not the god in the midst of war and victory, but flowers and trees, where life grows. Aten is the joy that makes lambs 'dance on their feet' and birds 'flutter in the marshes.'

Can one say that actually Akhenaten was the first monotheist? It is impossible to answer this question without first knowing precisely the origins of Akhenaten's beliefs, and the history of the influence of religions those thousands of years ago.

In 1937, Sigmund Freud's book *Der Mann Moses und die monotheistische Religion,* which was published in English translation two years later as *Moses and Monotheism,* proposed a startling hypothesis. First, that in contradiction to Jewish belief, Moses was not a Jew, but an Egyptian noble. Secondly, that Moses' monotheism did not spring from revelation, but rather came from Akhenaten. Or even that Moses himself was actually Akhenaten.

According to Freud's reading of the Old Testament, Moses led a group of chosen followers out of Egypt. But along the way, they murdered him. They then joined another tribe that also practiced monotheism. Later, they regretted that they had murdered their leader, and from then on they longed for the return of Moses as the Messiah.

I am not readily convinced by Freud's interpretation. My own knowledge about ancient Egypt is minimal, but many experts have noticed similarity in tone between Akhenaten's hymn and the words of Psalm 104.

Psalm 104:
LORD my God, you are very great; you are clothed with splendor and majesty.
The LORD wraps himself in light as with a garment; he stretches out the heavens like a tent and lays the beams of his upper chambers on their waters.

Akhenaten's Hymn:
The barges sail upstream and downstream alike. Every highway is open because thou dawnest. The fish in the river leap before thee. Thy rays are in the midst of the great green sea.

But perhaps what went on between these two hymns of praise was not cause and effect. The relationship is not one of A being older and more dominant than B or vice versa. It could be that both were kindled by the creative élan that is always there in human history – the trembling that longs for God and makes poetry, from where prayers are born and songs composed. It is probably wrong to see that there is always a relationship of cause and effect in two different events, because every event is an actualization of its own. Just as a poem composed today is neither an echo nor is influenced by a poem from a previous time, even though they might both be love poems, for instance.

History repeats, but in fact it does not repeat. Every event is always new, even though the past is retained there in the traces of memory – and helps to shape history.

What is tragic is that in the story of humankind, history also contains the story of loss. Akhenaten could not hold out, and not only in his rule. His conviction of bringing a new gospel – an remarkable faith – made him aggressive.

He destroyed statues of the old gods. He eliminated from stone inscriptions words that mentioned 'gods' in the plural. He even destroyed parts of his father's palace, in order to wipe out the names of other gods that were linked to the name of his father, the late King. In Thebes, the capital city, he changed the name of the area of the old temple so the new name would contain 'Aten'. This of course infuriated the priests of the old religion, whose positions were important.

Conflict broke out. The King was backed into a corner and had to leave the city. His monotheistic faith was eliminated.

It was only centuries later that people rediscovered Ahkenaten's contribution. This was not to do with monotheism, but rather the belief in god the all-merciful. 'Aten' differed vastly from Yahwe, the god of the Israelites in the early period of their belief – the god of fiery mountains, Freud said, god the jealous, the vengeful, the wrathful.

But fortunately, like Ahkenaten, there is always someone or some people who liberate themselves without wanting to lose song, worship and the discovery of God who makes a single day, even though just a day, happy:

The barges sail upstream and downstream alike. Every highway is open because thou dawnest. The fish in the river leap before thee. Thy rays are in the midst of the great green sea.

'Ikhnaton' *Tempo* 8 April 2012, CP X: 271-4

And then

In Tahrir Square, even as the night cold descended on Cairo, they gathered once more, one year to the day after 24 January 2011. The Square was warmed by the rows of Egyptian flags and optimism. And along with this: nostalgia. A young woman calling herself Nia who had taken part in last year's protest that toppled President Mubarak said, in English, 'We were full of hope'.

She used the past tense: *were*. Last year.

It is no longer clear whether that hope is still full. Like thousands of other 2011 activists, Nia sees that the situation has not changed much: the military is still in control; the price of food and petrol is still high – as though these two things are linked. True, to many people a clear path is beginning to appear: the holding of free general elections, the first for sixty years. And the winner will be the legitimate voice of the people.

But then what?

An Indonesian older than Nia would answer with rather melancholy wisdom: Child, hope soon becomes a memory. Great changes in politics are usually heralded with widespread freedom for improvement of life (in Indonesia in 1945, 1958, 1966 and 1998...), but then, what remains is nostalgia – as you all are feeling now in Egypt. And dashed hopes.

There is a 1954 film by Usmar Ismail titled *Lewat Jam Malam* (After the Curfew). It is the story of Iskandar (superbly acted by A.N. Alcaff), an ex guerilla fighter from the independence struggle. In the 1950s, once war is over, he comes out of the jungle and enters city life. He works in an office managed by a friend from his guerilla days. But it turns out that he is not ready for routine, bland hours without the tension of guns and ideals – without 24 hour-long courage for self-sacrifice that is intertwined with the excitement of action. He is bored and frustrated. And at the same time, he sees his former fighting comrades getting fat and corrupt. In one instance, he confronts his friend and angrily demands that he confess his sins – but then his pistol fires accidentally and his friend is killed. Iskandar escapes while Bandung is under curfew.

He dies in the end – and we ask: what is the meaning of revolution? To him? To many others?

Every year we commemorate our independence day of 1945. And every commemoration is a symptom of *After the Curfew* in a version not quite as dramatic as the film: people talk as though they want to emphasize that the struggle of the past is unforgettably extraordinary and life these days merely undermines that. Thus all one finds in the newspapers or TV every 17 August is a ritual of complaint, nostalgia, and melancholy.

But is revolution no more than that? If we open the archives of the 1950s, we find sharp political debate. Some of the leaders were then saying that 'the revolution is unfinished'. Others were saying that 'revolution cannot be permanent'. Bung Karno uttered the first view. Bung Hatta the second.

From today's viewpoint, both were wrong. Bung Karno said the revolution was unfinished, as though that finishing point would be approached; but actually revolution is *never* finished. Bung Hatta said that 'revolution cannot be permanent', but – as an event capable of stirring and changing a world, revolution comprises moments that, although impermanent, can become perpetual inspiration.

This inspiration does not come from the souls of dead revolutionaries: it comes because the situation on one particular day, in one particular place, requires it. And situations will go on requiring it because thus far demands for justice have never been fulfilled. Justice has never had formulas. Justice is not from the world of ready ideas.

But then the demand for justice – through revolution or reformation – ends up making formulas, institutions and systems so that justice can be fulfilled. And democracy is born.

This does not mean that the demand for justice will end, as was proven in Indonesia after the 1945 Revolution and the 1998 Reformation – and might yet be proved in Egypt a few years after the Tahrir victory.

Because democracy has two meanings and two moves.

Democracy is often translated as institutions and procedures. Political parties. People's Assemblies. Legislation. Legal institutions. General elections to choose representatives.

In that process, the State happens. But the State, as Stuart Hall said, is 'the instance of the performance of a condensation'. Various interests, streams and social forces cannot be accommodated and channeled simultaneously. 'Condensation' is inevitable. So too the fact that at any particular moment and any particular instance there will be elements that 'do' and 'do not' count. Then the time comes when those who 'do' count are able to strengthen their position with the power and funds they get. An oligarchy is created. And at that time, inequality, which often means injustice, occurs. Particularly as sensed by those who Rancière called *les incomptés*, 'the uncounted'.

In identifying 'the uncounted', Rancière pointed out another meaning of democracy. Democracy is not form, but action. Or, more precisely, 'the action that constantly wrests the monopoly of public life from oligarchic governments'.

History notes that word 'constantly' to this day. And if we are mindful of this, we will not be surprised if flags fly once again in

Tahrir Square: not as signs of satisfied optimism, but as a summons for the return of revolutionary inspiration.

'Kemudian' *Tempo* 5 February 2012

Tintin

I discovered Tintin for the first time in a house in the village of Marly-le-Roi, a few kilometers from Paris, where I used to go when there was a break from lectures. It was 1965. One night, I saw a pile of illustrated storybooks in the corner of the room. I picked them up. And I couldn't stop reading them – and laughing over and over: humor is the first (and final) attraction of these comics.

My host in the dining room could hear me laughing away to myself. 'You poor thing', he said. 'You've only now got to know Tintin.'

He was right, of course. He was from Belgium, the native land of these comics: I was from Indonesia; from a time when reading material from the 'West' was almost impossible to find. But actually, when and how someone gets to know the fictive character created by George Prosper Remi is not important. Since 1929, when Remi, using the name Hergé ('R.G.'), began publishing them weekly in the pages of *Le Petit Vingtième,* through to 2011 when Steven Spielberg made *The Adventures of Tintin,* people have been discovering Tintin every day. And loving it.

Actually, the hero Tintin would not be attractive if he were to appear by himself outside of the story. He is neither tall nor well-built. His face is smooth; his cheeks look as soft as cream puffs. His skin is white as milk. With his blond hair with its tuft at the top, with his clothes as neat as a student from some church school, Tintin looks thoroughly clean to his very core. He never makes a nuisance of himself. He is polite. Bland. Boring. 'Every hero becomes a bore at last', Ralph Waldo Emerson said.

Heroes, the center of stories where good always prevails, are usually in the category of extraordinary people – but with ordinary norms of goodness. Superman, who has lived in the American imagination since the 1930s, is a marvelous creature and at the same time an immigrant from another planet. But actually, he upholds the values Clark Kent reflects in his everyday behavior: the attitude of the majority that feels complete wearing suit and tie. He is someone who will not attack his surroundings. He is a hero because he upholds what makes the majority feel secure.

Like Superman, Tintin is not strange. And he is certainly not an immigrant. Created to fill the youth page of *Le Vingtième Siècle* – a conservative Catholic newspaper in Belgium – Tintin is a kind of everyday saint: someone extremely good, but not from any extreme sacrifice. His age might be about 20. I don't know what his family background is (his name is just 'Tintin') but clearly it is close to the conformity of old Brussels. Meaning: he does not misbehave. There are no scenes showing Tintin drinking in bars amidst fights. There are no passionate kisses. In *Tintin*, the hero is depicted as celibate, a sexless body – because sex, as the Church warns, is dirty.

This is why he is not interesting – especially these days, when saints are not crucified, but laughed at.

But there is something valuable in Tintin: he invites us to escape these cynical times of ours for a moment. Tintin's straightness can, of course, make those who do not believe in selfless heroes laugh. But there is other laughing going on. The stories of his adventures stimulate a gentle laughter – a laughter that brings us closer to others, however funny they are. We do not remember Tintin for his heroism. What we remember are the funny things about his stubborn dog Snowy; or the silly things about the two stupid secret agents Thompson & Thomson; or the rudeness of Captain Haddock, the tempestuous drunkard.

And so it is that the boring hero gives space to characters that are different to him: delightful people. This is why Hergé's illustrations are made on two levels. The first level is the lines drawn with very little 'realistic' detail: Tintin's bland face. The second level: the background of a place, of a time, whether in Russia or India. Incredibly varied.

In the first level, we find the neat Tintin as though in a formula. In the second level: crazy difference. Here Captain Haddock hurls more than 200 different types of insults: or we hear the shrieks of the soprano Bianca Castafiore, or the annoying interruptions of the insurance agent Séraphin Lampion (alias Jolyon Wagg).

In the end, the humor in *Tintin* is created from openness to different others: to people we do not admire, but we love. It is not surprising that it can unite people who enjoy it via eighty languages.

But that's not easy. The history of Tintin is also the history of European myopia. *The Adventures in Congo* (published in 1930) reflects Hergé's view of the Africans as subordinate beings. The faces of the Congolese resemble monkeys. They are lazy and stupid. At one point, a Congolese woman says thank you and makes a respectful gesture. And Snowy the dog says arrogantly, 'We are on top, aren't we?'

Hergé later regretted this work. He changed.

In 1934 he met Chang, a Chinese student who was studying in Brussels. They became friends. And this was the source of *Tintin in Tibet*; the hero is determined to save Chang, his little friend who is trapped in the cave of the yeti, the mysterious creature of the Himalayas.

In the end Chang is saved, and the yeti, it turns out, is not an evil creature at all. He looks out longingly as Chang leaves him. Resigned. In that scene, the yeti seems to be the witness: man, that other creature with extraordinary love, prevails, but without subjugation.

'Tintin' *Tempo* 4 December 2011, CP X: 195-8

Ten years on

Ten years have passed. 11 September 2001. But I remember it well: that night, nine hours after two planes had crashed into the Twin Towers in New York and the entire world was in shock, I was standing on the sidewalk in Bleecker Street, Greenwich Village.

I was with the composer Tony Prabowo. We were stuck in New York. We were on our way to a small town in California for rehearsals for our opera, *Kali*, but could not go on because of the events of that day: no planes could fly in or out of New York.

The city felt strange. That night, not knowing what else to do, the two of us walked south. The subway was not running. There were no taxis. It was getting dark when, wanting just to fill the time and also driven by curiosity, we walked along Mercer Street to Wall Street, where the Twin Towers were still being ravished by fire and smoke.

The electricity was off in that area. A few dozen meters from Duane Street we could see the huge spotlights amidst the black shadows of the buildings. Some armed soldiers were on guard, in the middle of the thick smoke and ash. The whole place was like a war zone.

Near the closed Chambers Street subway station, a soldier stopped us. 'You can't go on. Entry to this area is forbidden'.

Rather disappointed, we set back, walking in the almost completely deserted streets. There was just one small bar open on the corner of Worth Street. We went in. There were four men inside. Whispering. We had a drink. Virtually silent.

Was New York changing? Two nights later, we walked along the streets of Manhattan. There were rows of candles placed on various corners. There were photos posted up and lines written like prayers – for those who had not returned from the Twin Towers, those lost, probably incinerated or crushed.

A few hours after 9/11, New York looked like an altar. On it, people offered everything for hope in their distress. Something unpredictable and inexplicable had attacked this powerful city. Daily life that yesterday was just banal, had been jolted by the sublime – the indescribable, the terrifying, the painful.

And from this mood Tony Prabowo wrote a composition for piano and chamber orchestra that he titled 'Psalms'.

But music capturing that atmosphere was no match for the rhetoric that then translated 11 September 2001. New York very quickly changed from an altar to a podium, where words give names and pretexts. And lies.

The name: '9/11'. Derrida called that naming *fait date*. People mention a date in history to mark an event felt as unprecedented. But, as Derrida reminds us, this 'feeling' is not entirely spontaneous. The feeling about that date, about that name, was also shaped and circulated via the media, via what he calls the 'techno-socio-political machine'. And with that name, various events, various reasons and various attitudes could be bound together as one – becoming a sign whose meaning was determined by the loudest voice, and, at that time, the narrowest one.

With that name, too, some television stations and media centers from the White House formulated an image that attempted to make an indescribable event into something comprehensible. 'America is under attack!' was heard repeatedly – with the explanation that this was the second attack on American territory since the Japanese bombs destroyed Pearl Harbor in 1941.

American rhetoric post 9/11 succeeded in giving shape to the chaos of fear, confusion, and anger at the time. The terror was tamed into a framework of explanation, so that anxiety could be mastered by reason. The rhetoric also presented the United States as a single harmonious unity, as a body not built out of conflict. And the rhetoric presented the United States as something unsullied by any history of foreign policy that made people in other parts of the world so full of hatred and so determined that they would crash two planes into the Twin Towers that day.

The post 9/11 rhetoric was a pretext. Then lies. Because '9/11' is not comparable to the Japanese attack on Pearl Harbor in 1941. It is actually comparable to the terrorist attack in Oklahoma of 19 April 1995. A bomb was detonated in a government building; 168 people were killed (including 16 children under 6) and 324 buildings were destroyed or damaged. But this terror was never mentioned in the post 9/11 rhetoric because it was carried out by Americans, namely Timothy McVeigh and his accomplices. These opponents of the American federal government were an indication that America is not a whole. On the other hand, the 9/11 terrorists (like the Japanese planes at Pearl Harbor) were 'outsiders' whose threat could shape the image of the United States as an intact tribe.

A few days after 9/11, the Stars and Stripes was flying everywhere. It was the only flag flown at Rockefeller Plaza on 50th Street, the flags of other nations that had flown there previously had all been taken down. The United States had changed victimhood, the mood of mourning, and universal fear into something entirely its own. In other words: an old expression of nationalism.

So it is strange when people state that 9/11 changed the world. What has changed? Al-Qaeda has still not conquered America, and America's wars that followed are still an old imperial violence. Robinson Jeffers' poem from the late 1930s still resounds sharply in the 21st century: 'Never weep, let them play/ Old violence is not too old to beget new values.'

'11/9' *Tempo* 18 September 2011, CP X: 151-4

Srebrenica

In a place that used to be unknown, around 8,000 Muslims were murdered. Since then, Srebrenica, a small town in the mountains in eastern Bosnia and Herzegovina, has become a terrifying name. Or repugnant. Or shameful.

It is there that for seven days in late July 1995, General Ratko Mladic, the Serbian commander, carried out his plans. Maybe this, to him, was the final solution for the future of Bosnia, just like Hitler's *endgültige Lösung* for the Jews: those Bosnians who were not Serbian, particularly the Muslims, had to be exterminated.

Mladic matches the stereotype of cheap novels of an executioner: heavily-built and rough, it is said that he once killed a man with his bare hands – after convincing the victim that nothing was going to happen to him, all the while flexing his fists before killing him. When Mladic's troops surrounded Sarajevo, he ordered them to increase the artillery fire 'rhythmically' so as to 'splinter' the minds of the inhabitants.

The Bosnian poet Abdullah Sidran in one of his poems called Mladic the 'monster with epaulets'. Others call him the 'butcher from Srebrenica'.

Srebrenica started out as a protected area: the Muslims found a safe haven there. There was a United Nations battalion that guarded those who were escaping the ethnic fighting in the fragmenting Yugoslavia. The refugees were mainly those escaping slaughter, knowing that the Serbian 'nationalists' would kill them.

But that July, the situation changed. From the first week of July, the Serbian forces surrounded the town. Gradually, Srebrenica ran out of petrol. Food supplies dwindled. Emic Suljagic in his book *Postcards from the Grave* tells of how, before the mist lifted, hundreds of people with ropes and axes used to climb over the city walls, to search in the forest for wood to burn.

The United Nations battalion, an unarmed Dutch contingent of around 600 men, tried to hold out. Their commander, Lieutenant Colonel Karremans, asked the Commander of the United Nations, General Bernard Janvier from France, for air support. But what happened then was a procedural mistake: Karremans' request for air support was written on the wrong form. It was eventually granted, but too late.

What Karremans did get was aid of a different kind. Two Dutch F-16 fighter planes dropped two bombs over the position of the surrounding Serbian forces. But by then Mladic had his own trump card: the Serbians had already attacked a United Nations post and had captured thirty Dutch soldiers. The Serbian General gave an ultimatum: if the bombing persisted, the captives would be killed.

Around two hours later, towards evening on the 11th of July, Mladic and his army entered Srebrenica. That night he summoned Karremans for a meeting to hear Mladic's demand: the Muslims had to surrender their weapons or they would be killed. As recorded by the Serbian cameraman, that night Karremans joined Mladic in a toast. He can be heard saying, 'I am a piano player. Don't shoot the piano player'. And Mladic answers, whether or not in jest is not clear: 'You are a lousy piano player.'

What one could say about this is that the Dutch officer was a bad battalion commander. His troops then left Srebrenica, leaving the Muslims to be slaughtered. On 13 July, the killing began at a building near the village of Kravia. On the same day, Karremans turned over five thousand Muslims to Mladic, in exchange for fifteen Dutch soldiers who were being held at Nova Kasaba. Three days later, reports of the slaughter began to emerge....

And Karremans did not report this to his superiors. A Dutch journalist, Frank Westerman, the author of the book *Srebrenica: Het zwartste scenario* writes that at the official leavetaking, Karremans even accepted a gift from Mladic. 'Is this for my wife?' he asked, smiling.

But the victims did not remain silent. Two Bosnian Muslims whose families Mladic murdered, brought the case to the court in The Hague. Exactly sixteen years after the savagery of Srebrenica, the Dutch judge decided: Holland indeed is responsible for the mistake of its army that left thousands of unarmed people to be killed.

Sixteen years later the world saw Mladic brought to The Hague to be tried by the International Court.

These days, a country feels ashamed and repents its wrongs of the past: the wrong of its own people towards those from a distant country, whose faith and history is distant too. At such moments 'the other' means not only those who are not-us, but also 'fellows' who are not different to us. In the faces of the powerless before the executioner, in the rows of heads with bulletholes, in the piles of bodies murdered merely because of awkward origins and different biographies, a Muslim in Srebrenica is like a Jew in Auschwitz.

Srebrenica ran with blood because people like Mladic do not want to acknowledge that the weakest among us, and those most tortured, are precisely those who remind us of what is astounding in mankind: a tie that is unseen.

'Srebenica' *Tempo* 31 July 2011, CP X: 123-6

Taking Sides

'The sad duty of politics is to establish justice in a sinful world', the theologian Reinhold Niebuhr said. While he made this as a general comment, I think it is particularly applicable to the public intellectual – meaning to those who with their writings and statements speak to the populace at large, setting forth what should and should not be done for communal life.

Niehbuhr used the word 'duty', and I follow his usage. It is an odd word to use, for this duty is not because of an edict of any party or power. This duty appears within us because of a wound. We feel we must do something because of it. The wound appears when, one day in our social life, an 'other' is tortured, when there are those who want to destroy a fellow who is different. The wound is injustice.

I call it a 'wound' because the problem of injustice is not something abstract, but rather concrete, involving the body and feelings, and arousing both empathy and anger: Munir, who was murdered but whose case still lies open; the thousands of people disappeared during the 'New Order' whose cases have never been prosecuted; Prita Mulyasari, the mother, sent to prison so casually by a judge; or Prabangsa, the journalist from *Radar Bali* who was brutally murdered because he criticized powerful people.

There is pain, and I exist: at that moment, I know what injustice feels like. Even though I cannot yet entirely formulate what is just, I am summoned.

The public intellectual here differs from what Julien Benda called a *clerc*. In English, '*clerc*' is usually translated as 'intellectual', but this is not exactly right. Benda used it to invoke the European Middle Ages, the monks who devoted themselves to universal values, living far from political intrigue. They were impartial; they safeguarded the purity of reason. In his book *La Trahison des Clercs* (translated into English as *The Betrayal of the Intellectuals*) Benda criticized the intellectuals who participate in the bustle of the market, take sides with a particular group, and fan 'political passion'.

It must be noted that Benda was a rationalist, through and through. He considered 'universal values' to be pre-soldered fast within oneself. He did not acknowledge that the 'universal' comes from the experience of human beings as creatures-on-earth, who have failings, are limited, who live with others, and are mortal. Benda separates rationality from the world, in the same way that he does not want anyone equal to the *clerc* to enter the arena of political intrigue where universal values are supposedly renounced.

Of course we must realize that when Benda was writing, as also today, political struggle existed that promoted only closed ideals: the Nazis wanted to make a new world only for the 'Aryan race', and the 'Islamists' want to establish supremacy only for their own *ummah*.

But we recall Nelson Mandela. He fought as the leader of the Blacks, but his achievements, in the end, were not only for the good of his own group. He won in order to destroy the power of *apartheid* that humiliated and discriminated on the basis of skin color. Mandela's victory would be true victory only if it meant that one kind of *apartheid* was not defeated by another. So in his government, Mandela did not discriminate against Whites. In the story of South Africa, the wound of injustice called for true justice: justice was only 'just' if it applied to all.

This universality is different to that of the rationalist. The universality in Mandela's politics grew from trauma. But not just this. The bitterness of trauma was acknowledged as an evil that must not be allowed to settle within a society if that society wished to live. In other words, politics, as pursued by Mandela, was the struggle towards something universal, coming from a particular situation.

This is where the public intellectual should be called to take a stand. In this way, she or he can view politics as a duty, not as an ambition. He or she does not just sit around twiddling thumbs, commanding prestige in the palace. The public intellectual is like a neighbor who helps to extinguish the flames when the house on the corner is on fire, not only to save the neighborhood (and his or her own house, of course), but also because she or he is called to save others from suffering.

But, as mentioned above, it is a sinful world. Suffering and wickedness will never disappear from within it. So struggle, or political wrangling, will always be haunted by failings. We cannot accept 'politics as the commander' when politics allows no freedom to acknowledge those failings, and when considerations of victory and defeat swallow completely all corners of our life, forever. Because every political struggle will come up against its own limitations.

So if today I choose A, I make this choice prepared for disappointment. I also make this choice as a temporary one. I choose A only as the medium that at this particular moment is the least flawed amongst the extremely flawed – as a temporary means to safeguard against further wounds, even though such safeguards are never guaranteed.

I said above: we are prepared for disappointment. But we do not give up. Because we will never forget Munir: we cannot condone injustice as something natural in life. The experience of history has shown that in the midst of our suffering of acute injustice, human beings always long for justice – which is somewhere, who knows where, and will come some time, who knows when.

From this perspective, the Just Ruler that the Javanese call the *Ratu Adil* is not mere superstition. The Just Ruler is an ideal that never appears. Politics is the duty to clear a path in the undergrowth, to open a gap for justice to come. Sometimes hands will be dirtied, hearts will be hardened – and this will cause its own distress.

Faced with the undergrowth, we gamble with the future. Those who demand complete certainty from history deceive themselves. There are always times to act and times to take sides – also times when we refuse to act and take sides.

But at the same time there are also times to stand a little apart. Sometimes with irony, sometimes with reproach, but always with loyalty: in this sinful world, the choice of words can be wrong, but duty never stops summoning and politics always begs. Maybe we will fail. Even so, there is still something worth fighting over.

'Memihak' *Tempo* 14 June 2009, CP IX: 413-6

Barbarians

The body of Saddam Hussein swings and his neck is strangled in the noose – we watch it on a video recording replaying that dramatic moment, and perhaps we whisper: a dictator dies in a cramped room, and a democracy is born.

But what can be said about democracy, really?

In Europe and America, decent people feel disgusted and revolted and say: 'Ah, the barbarism of Arab countries!' and they forget that the democracy they know began with a performance of a king having his head cut off. Charles Monnet depicted this important scene in the French Revolution, which he called *Journée du 21 Janvier*, and Isidore-Stanislas Helman later made a printing of it. The picture circulated widely. One can see there the bloody head of King Louis XVI clutched by his executioner after the king was guillotined, to be shown to the crowds gathered at the execution square.

At times like these, the head of the king seems unclean, without sanctity or authority, just like the head of Saddam Hussein dangling on his broken neck. Power, no matter how great, cannot give itself any guarantee of being free of filth or the threat of downfall. Ever since the French Revolution, people have been aware that when the one in power can be represented as the head, then a society must be prepared to be disillusioned.

Democracy proceeds from that principle: democracy is a system that has to continually seek ways for the body of the community to endure without a head that will fall one day.

To seek also means to find. And so acute political ideas are born, an unbridled press, a thriving market, and free expression in all kinds of fields of life. Scientific papers, journalistic reports, literary works that convey solitude or protest, knowledge that discovers new things and wards against the old – all of this starts from the awareness, perhaps too the frustration, that the chief is merely passing by and the one determining things will always lose his head.

In this way, democracy is a space of declaration of civilization. But whether one likes it or not, sometimes it is splattered with blood. Walter Benjamin's famous phrase is apt here: 'there is no document of civilization (the German is *Kultur*) that is not at the same time a document of barbarism.'

Benjamin reminds us of the need to acknowledge that the distance between civilization and barbarism is actually not very far. Didn't the miraculous progress in Europe under capitalism actually contain something disturbing – namely the exploitation of the workers – as was the case with the glory of the Pharaohs' pyramids, built with the capital of suffering of the slaves in Egypt?

Cultures that hide what is uncivilized within them – by showing as *scene* what does not acknowledge itself as also *ob-scene* – eventually provide opportunities for new barbarism.

The Nazis in Germany, among others, wielded such new barbarism. Nazism revered ancient Greek civilization, seeing itself as a continuation of that glorious history from the south. But just as the ancient Greeks created the category of 'barbarian' for those who were not part of them – an attempt to instate and affirm 'Greek' identity – so too did the Nazi rulers in Germany produce ideas about creatures who were 'non-Aryan' so as to underline and uphold the 'Aryan' nature of the German people. Just as Herodotus depicted the 'barbarians' as people who 'can neither think nor act rationally…driven by evil spirits, incapable of living according to written laws and only reluctantly tolerating kings' so did Hitler consider the Jews, the Slavs and the gypsies as filth to be exterminated.

The 'barbarians' are always merely those outside, not ourselves. This illusion, and probably also the hypocrisy – is not new, even when Saddam Hussein's body swings and his neck is strangled by the noose. A few moments before his death sentence was carried out, as Saddam stood brave, a whisper could be heard among those gathered in that crowded room: 'Moktada, Moktada...' It seemed that the Shiites mentioned the name of their leader to remind Saddam, just a second before his hanging, of the huge crimes he had committed against them.

The problem is the role of memory henceforth. We often hear that the law must be upheld, that dictators like Saddam must be hanged, for if not, this will be the death of civilization. But the voices in that execution room showed that the law holds something that is not usually acknowledged as a sign of civilization: revenge.

Actually, there is no wrong in people seeking revenge. But how can one ever decide upon an 'equivalent' revenge? In the Bible there is the *lex talionis* mentioned in Exodus 32:23-27: 'an eye for an eye, a tooth for a tooth...' As with the Hammurabi law engraved on a stone more than 1700 years before Christ, the Biblical doctrine is not merely an acknowledgement of vengeance, but rather laws for managing it. Without this management of vengeance, one life can be avenged with the lives of a thousand others – virtually without any clear limit.

Now a life has been taken – Saddam Hussein's neck is strangled in the noose – but is this punishment fair?

It is impossible to answer this. Barbarism is everywhere and cannot be compared. Eventually we know that there is uncertainty and unfairness behind every affirmation of law. There is barbarism behind every cry for 'justice'. There is a need to admit that the agencies of civilization, even including the Supreme Court, are always weak, and always sinning.

'Barbar' *Tempo* 14 January 2007, CP VIII: 327-30

Jeremiah

'I'm Jeremiah'—Kurt Vonnegut Jr.

Not all countries need a Jeremiah. But if there has to be such a prophet – who reminds mankind that God is angry and that the apocalypse will soon be here – then people will also need something else: moments to laugh.

Kurt Vonnegut Jr fulfilled both of these in today's America – but he died on April 11 in Manhattan, New York. So it goes…

He was 84. Vonnegut, the author of *Slaughterhouse-Five* who smoked Pall Mall cigarettes constantly for seventy years, was ready to die, yet his departure came too soon. Had he remained alive, his words of derision would continue to pierce holes in the soundproof space constructed by the Bush and Cheney administration, a construction made of lies and paranoia, ambition and myopia. An airless space that needs cracks to let in sounds of doubt and laughter.

'I'm Jeremiah', he said in an interview with Douglas Brinkley in *Rolling Stone*. But he was not talking of God. 'I'm talking about us killing the planet… with gasoline.' And he spelt out the pessimism with which we are familiar: the planet will become extinct through the effects of carbon dioxide.

And Vonnegut could be extreme. When asked his opinion about the actions of conservationists who have been getting more vocal recently since the documentary *An Inconvenient Truth,* Jeremiah answered: 'There is nothing they can do. It's over my friend. The game is lost.'

'The game is lost.' This was the same theme uttered by the first Jeremiah in 6th century BCE before Jerusalem fell to the hands of King Nebuchadnezzar of Babylon. Jeremiah saw that his people, the tribes of Israel, had no more hope. Not surprisingly, he was considered a traitor and was imprisoned by the Zedekiah rulers. But the prophet was right. Nebuchadnezzar occupied Jerusalem. The Temple of Solomon was destroyed, and the Jewish people were exiled. It is said that Jeremiah was later kidnapped, taken to Egypt and there killed by his own people.

'I'm Jeremiah', Vonnegut said, even though he was no exile. But his novel *Slaughterhouse-Five* was banned in a few schools in the early 1970s, and the book was burnt in one town in North Dakota.

But that act is already fault enough in a country whose constitution guarantees freedom of speech. It seems that the America of which the young Kurt was so proud has gone. And continues to go. One year after the United States attacked Iraq, Vonnegut came out with brutal words. 'I know now that there is not a chance in hell of America's becoming humane and reasonable.' He saw America's leaders as 'power-drunk chimpanzees'.

Vonnegut's prose was stylistically certainly right-between-the-eyes. His words seemed chosen from old anger. Yet he had no pretensions of bearing 'high' literature. In an interview published in the *Paris Review* of spring 1977, he said that he considered himself 'loaded with vulgarity'; this was because he used to write for magazines like *Cosmopolitan* and *The Saturday Evening Post.*

He would probably have found it hilarious to speak in respectful tones about the creative process. He regarded himself as 'such a barbarous technocrat' and treated his stories like Ford motor cars, 'to be tinkered with'. His aim was to give his readers 'pleasure'.

In other words, this American Jeremiah also wanted to entertain. In his old age, Vonnegut felt he could no longer do this, but he said, 'All I really wanted to do was give people the relief of laughing'. Humor is 'like an aspirin tablet', he said. And like his hero Mark Twain, he was skilled at dishing out that medicine. His words could be brilliant, biting, and funny.

The story *Harrison Bergeron*, for instance, begins with this sentence: 'The year was 2081, and everybody was finally equal. They weren't only equal before God and the law. They were equal every which way. Nobody was smarter than anybody else. Nobody was better looking than anybody else.'

This story is in many ways similar to Orwell's *1984*. One of the characters, George, 'had a little mental handicap radio in his ear. It was tuned to a government transmitter. Every twenty seconds or so, the transmitter would send out some sharp noise to keep people like George from taking unfair advantage of their brains.'

It is a depressing story, but it makes us laugh, at least when we come across an office of the 'United States Handicapper General' whose agents are 'unceasingly vigilant'.

With this funny-ghastly combination, life is depicted as absurd – probably a parody of American society that worships equality yet suspects that equality is the same as mediocrity. This is why people like Bush, Mr. Average himself, the epitome of mediocrity, can make it to the White House. 'If you actually are an educated, thinking person, you will not be welcome in Washington, DC' Vonnegut wrote in *A Man Without a Country, A Memoir of a Life in George W. Bush's America*.

But will life really follow the late Jeremiah's prophesies, from the Bush era to global warming? What will the antidotes be to make life worth living? Vonnegut himself, in his old age said that he had been awaiting fulfillment of the promise of the Brown & Williamson Tobacco Company that makes Pall Mall cigarettes. 'The lying bastards!' Brinkley quotes Vonnegut saying, 'On the package [they] promised to kill me. Instead, their cigarettes didn't work.'

His humor here is black, but it is a sign that Death is not the sole redeemer. Vonnegut still gives us aspirin. He also still had another antidote: music, particularly the blues, 'the only proof for the existence of God'. In other words, small-scale resistance against the looming apocalypse.

And if not, there is still the fantasy of the planet Tralfamadore, which helps Billy Pilgrim in the midst of the ferocity and futility of the destruction of Dresden in *Slaughterhouse-Five*. Tralfamadore: the alternative to the world of prophets of doom.

For Jeremiah does not see all things.

'Jeremiah' *Tempo* 22 April 2007, CP VIII: 383-6

Shanghai

S hanghai is a city on the move. Buildings soar to the sky, as though competing for space, or a name, or the future. Architecture seems to have been ordered as an afterthought; the rows of buildings look hard, loud, and often vulgar. From the boulevards along the Huangpu River in the Waitan district (which the English call 'The Bund'), people are startled, or laugh in amusement, to see the 'Pearl of the East' TV tower on the other side, sticking up 500 meters so full of ambition – stiff, sharp tipped and aggressive, like a syringe stretched to pierce the clouds.

Modernity is always seduced by speed, tempted by the desire to soar and to extend aggressively. But this does not mean that Shanghai, with its racy pace, has entered modernity only now. The story of this city, from the 11th century, differs from other Asian cities. When China was cornered after its defeat in the Opium Wars and then the Nanking Treaty of 1842, Western countries (and capital) obtained territory and special rights in this city. They brought both the good and bad of the 'modern', which had not existed since the Sung Dynasty.

The association of stockbrokers was formed in 1898. The Shanghai Stock Market in 1904. They say that today the stock market building is three times larger than the Tokyo stock market, and it is not surprising that it can be the epicenter of an earthquake in capitalism: on February 27 last, the Composite Index of the Shanghai market fell almost nine per cent, and all over the world, stock followed suit.

Shanghai is a force of its own, it seems: the grand history of hybridity. People used to live with the 'Yangjingbang culture', a word taken from the name of the creek that was filled in to make a street, a sign that the territory was now under foreign rule. In other words: mixed people live here. Those who despised this impurity often dubbed Shanghai 'the whore of Asia'.

But this is what shaped its dynamism and its tragedy.

In André Malraux's famous novel, *La Condition Humaine*, published in 1933 but set in Shanghai in 1926, this dynamism and tragedy are combined in the rebellion. The characters Chen and Kyo Gisors are revolutionaries (modern, in other words) who want to change Chinese society to become just, but they fail. Chen, the terrorist, dies when he tries to detonate a suicide bomb; Gisors, the rebel leader, does not want to surrender and swallows poison.

Malraux's novel depicts Shanghai as the background to 'humanity'. 'China' is part of the *humaine*. Along with Chen and Gisors, there is Baron de Clappique, a French gambler; and May, Kyo's German wife. In other words, the rebellion is the resistance of borderless 'children of all nations'. Or one could say this resistance does not take seriously human territory fenced with fake borders. This is what seems to make Malraux's novel claustrophobic: almost everything takes place in closed spaces. *La Condition Humaine* does not depict streets, rivers, parks, or other elements of the Shanghai landscape. All this – which should be shared space – is no longer relevant because it no longer bring people together.

Malraux's picture no longer applies today, of course, even though the foreigners still remain separate: the 'expats' live in the affluent Hongqiao and Gubei, the poor Chinese having been kicked out. But Shanghai of 2007 will not rebel; it has no political spirit. The city that in the 1960s fired the first salvo of the 'Cultural Revolution', which annihilated the 'capitalist roaders', has now gone back to inviting in capital from anywhere. You cannot miss the soaring IBM and Passat towers, and more than twenty-five other multinationals have opened branches in Shanghai (whereas there are only eleven in Beijing). The local population enthusiastically joins in gambling on the stock market, which they call the *du bo ji*, or slot machine.

When the 'Cultural Revolution' failed, and Mao became just a fixture on the wall like some distant god, the '*Yangjingbang*' culture was followed by '*Xingbake*' culture – the name of a local Shanghai coffee business that imitated Starbucks. But more than in times past, even this hybrid trade name was conquered by the original trade name that was truly foreign owned. Last year, Judge Lu in the People's Court decided that '*Xingbake*' had illegally copied Starbucks. The local businessman was fined $62,000.

These days, 'justice' indeed does not always benefit the weak; and 'justice' is not always the same as equality. And there lies the problem. Shanghai is being pushed by modernity yet haunted by its history, when 'equality' (the spirit of the Mao Revolution) was synonymous with 'justice'. And if all this does not cause large scale conflict, it is because people are not free to speak or politicize – all the while fully aware of another side of the past: protest and rebellion can be terribly destructive.

But the dilemma remains: any fast economic growth is accompanied by heavy social inequality. The China of 2007 contradicts Mahbub ul-Haq's conclusions. Three decades ago, this famous economist said that Mao's socialist development that prioritized 'equality' had proved better able to foster economic growth than India's 'bourgeois' method. Now, ever since Deng Xiao-ping said 'to be rich is glorious', the story has reversed. A report from the Academy of Social Sciences shows that 10% of China's wealthiest families own more than 40% of private assets, while the poorest 10% enjoy less than 2% of the total wealth. According to the World Bank, the Gini Coefficient in China in

2005 – which shows the gap between the rich and poor – was higher than in India. Higher too than Indonesia.

Maybe this is today's *condition humaine*: in the world that no longer wants to be poor, people must answer difficult questions of 'neo-liberalism': how can 'equality' be achieved without state intervention? But how too can state intervention not create corruption and despotism?

At the epicenter of the capitalist earthquake, where that question is still unanswered, I imagine a crater. Within, anxiety bubbles away, and who knows what it will become.

'Shanghai' *Tempo* 11 March 2007, CP VIII: 359-62

Cartoons

P uffy face. Heavy eyebrows. Bushy moustache. Black turban inscribed with sacred words in Arabic calligraphy. More interesting still: the turban is complete with a wick – it is a bomb. If this picture had been without words, we would not have known that it was a cartoon of the Prophet Mohammad. Yet we would still know this: for Muslims, it is insulting.

To me, this in itself is something that should be condemned. The *Jyllands-Posten* newspaper, with a circulation of 175,000, is the most popular newspaper in Denmark. Its office is outside Denmark's second largest city, Aarhus. The building looks like a neat factory, its interior painted white. Those who know, say that the newspaper is read by prosperous, law-abiding farmers and the rural middle class. Decent people, but it it is not surprising that they do not like to see crowds of people coming from the poor South, usually Muslim and 'not our kind'. Because for centuries they have been protected from things strange and frightening.

These days, they support a government that, like them, regards immigrants with caution, even enmity. 'We have gone to war against the multicultural ideology that says everything is equally valid', Brian Mikkelson said. Mikkelson, a 39-year-old politician who is now Minister of Culture, claims that the 'cultural war' now raging in Denmark is a 'war against the acceptance of Muslims' norms and ways of thought'. To him 'cultural heritage' (meaning 'original culture' or 'native') is a source of strength in confronting 'globalization' and the flow of migration.

Just how different is this voice from Hitler's ranting in 1937 when he raved about the 'characteristics of unity and homogeneity' in 'German' culture? Have they forgotten the consequences: the war or cleansing to wipe out cultures not of the Fatherland, then called 'Jewish'?

Maybe this is a sign of the depth of spiritual confusion today: the concentration camps are not yet forgotten, and yet voices calling for 'cultural war' against those who disturb 'unity' and 'homogeneity' gain respect.

One must admit that the cartoon published in the *Jyllands-Posten* on 30 September 2005 was indeed a cartoon. And all caricatures (from the Italian word *caricare*) ridicule by exaggerating one or more features of a figure. But the cartoonist had no idea about the face of this particular figure. What did the Prophet Muhammad's face look like? What were its special features? The article that accompanied the cartoon was titled *Muhammeds ansig* (The face of Muhammad) but actually the 'face' came from the cartoonist's image of 'Islam' – in a form not that far from what Danes in general imagine.

In other words, what was depicted was a stereotype. That day's drawing was something distilled from prejudice, excitement, fear, sneering at the other, at others; a feeling that has crept quietly into the heads of Danes in a time inflamed by suspicion towards Muslims, with various degrees of hatred.

It is not surprising that some of the cartoons are reminiscent of something horrific: the poster for the film *Jud Süss* in Germany in 1940 and the poster for the exhibition *Der Ewige Jude* in Austria in 1938: pictures made to villify Jews, reproductions of stereotypes born from hate and fear. In *Jud Süss:* a dark, bearded face, with a sharp, mysterious gaze. In *Der Ewige Jude*: a figure with crooked nose, with side whiskers and a droopy moustache. In his right hand is gold, and in his left, a whip.

Meaning, The Outsider, creeping around our neighborhood, so base, so stealthy, so frightening…

Jytte Klausen, professor of political science at Brandeis University in Boston (author of *The Islamic Challenge: Politics and Religion in*

Western Europe) shows how brutal the cries for cultural war shouted by the extreme right can be. Not long ago, two members of the Danish Peoples Party described Muslims as 'a cancer on Danish society'. Meaning: a tumor that must be cut out. Both these men are Lutheran pastors.

Like other right-wing extremists (the Indonesian Council of Clerics, for instance), these pastors oppose pluralism. Like others who hate (the Islamic Defenders Front here among us, for example), they both want to destroy the principle of multiculturalism and want society to be subjugated by one value system. And as is usual with people who see themselves as the center of the world, they use double standards. Even the *Jyllands-Posten* does this. Three years ago, the *Jyllands-Posten* rejected a cartoon that depicted Jesus, because it did not wish to offend its readers.

So what is disturbing is not just that there are people who insult the Prophet. What is disturbing is injustice and hate, and the failure of many parties, religious and no, secular or Muslim, the angry and the angered, to resist being infected by this festering sore.

It seems we cannot expect much from an era that suddenly amazes and alarms us at the same time. This is the era when technology – the Internet in particular – can make distances of time and space appear to vanish. A cartoonist in Aarhus makes an insult for the locals, but in actual fact he also faces an unknown community. An Islamic cleric in Ponorogo is angry because of something that happens in a fairy-tale land: nowadays the true and the untrue are sensed as free of situations that in actual fact are limited.

And what about us? Do we really become close? Or confused?

'Karikatur' *Tempo* 19 February 2006, CP VIII: 141-4

Amsterdam

Amsterdam: amid the winding alleys around the canals, in a corner where prostitutes are displayed in cramped shop windows, young women sit or stand like shopfront dummies, wearing transparent bras and skimpy skirts. They are waiting for customers under a dim red light. Some wear expressions of despair.

Amsterdam does not condemn the red-light area of Rossen Buurt, associated with illicit sex. For the past five hundred years, men of every hue (especially sailors) have been coming here to relieve their desires. These days, Rossen Buurt is nothing unusual. Situated not even one kilometer from the Royal Palace, one finds there rows of porno film shops and sex shows set between pizza houses and cafes, bars with beer posters, gay theaters and cheap hotels – a sign that after all, sin (which is nothing new) is not the City Hall's concern.

From the bridge that crosses one of the canals in the old part of the city you can see the Oude Kerk, like a gothic ghost. Built in the 13th century, it is no longer a place of worship, but a concert hall and space used for the World Press Photo exhibition: it also bears witness that this city, with or without religion, cannot wipe out obscenity. Amsterdam uses it in fact, markets it and gets taxes from it. In the end, the carnal cannot be completely bound by the spiritual. Amsterdam acknowledges how easily people have misconceptions about themselves.

Once, there was the fervor of Reformation. Along with anxiety and intolerance. Amsterdam in the 16th century was governed by the bourgeoisie who brought capitalism and prosperity. But also apprehension. For here people were living below sea level and always had the feeling that God's curse would come in the form of flood – a feeling that became all the more acute as they bathed in wealth. The 'moral geography' of the Dutch in the 17th century, Simon Schama writes in *The Embarrassment of Riches,* was '...adrift between the fear of the deluge and the hope of moral salvage, in the tidal ebb and flow between worldliness and homeliness, between the gratification of appetite and its denial, between the conditional consecration of wealth and perdition in its surfeit.'

Maybe this is why Calvin's teachings were so readily accepted. In the mid 17th century, Spinoza (who was born in Amsterdam) compared the Calvinists to the Pharisees in the history of the tribes of Israel: the Pharisees also insisted upon strict adherence to the purity of teachings. They wanted the norms of God's law used for political power. They were worried about the destiny and deeds of man. But, as Jesus chastized them, clearly they were hypocrites. When purity is unattainable and yet constantly demanded, hypocrisy is inevitable.

Amsterdam realized: it is impossible to pursue purity to the end. Every urban space, as Lefebvre says, is made up of the *scene* and the *obscene*: there is cleanliness, tidiness, and grandeur on exhibit, but there is also shameful obscenity. Amsterdam is an exercise in pragmatism: it manages the impure, the shameful, as something different and possibly useful.

Of course, the different used to be considered sin, particularly when the powers-that-be deluded themselves that once its citizens joined the 'true' faith, God's grace would come.

In Europe, this illusion of 'one faith' began in the 16th century. This was when the Holy Roman Empire and its ideology were crumbling. The continent was fragmented, and there was much bloodshed between Catholics and Protestants. Out of this rift, various nation-states grew, and the city as a power in itself. In these more confined political spaces, the idea arose that uniting a country and its people was an easy thing – something that of late those drawing up the regional regulations for decentralization in Indonesia also seem to think.

So it was that in France, people (meaning the Catholic majority) yelled the slogan *'une loi, un roi, une foi'*. There was no idea of including The Protestants (or Huguenots) in this principle of 'one law, one king, and one faith'. In 16th century Geneva, Calvin carried out a parallel idea of unity: being Catholic in that Protestant city meant the death sentence, and between 1542 and 1564, 58 people were executed because of their faith.

Geneva was even more fanatic in wiping out its diversity. In that city of 10,000 souls, a dozen elders and a dozen pastors scrutinized citizens' behavior. The city formulated itself with prohibitions. Gambling, playing cards, drinking and cursing were forbidden of course, but so were dancing, singing, painting, sculpture, and watching or performing theater. Wearing 'indecent' clothing, including jewelry and lipstick, was against the rules. Fornicators got the death sentence.

But history shows that Geneva changed, and did Calvinism. The city remained boring, but more humble, at least: in fact it could not follow a model of 'God's city', for life is not a monastery, but a night fair.

Amsterdam celebrates that night fair boisterously. Not merely with sex on the corner of Rossen Buurt, but also with concerts and theatre, history museums and visual art, works of literature and scientific discoveries, philosophical discussions and religion, sports and drinking – in short, by making a city that is comfortable in joy and boredom, faith and temptation, ambition and gratitude. There in that night fair, it is a city that does not baulk at accepting man.

'Amsterdam' *Tempo* 4 June 2006, CP VIII: 201-4

Sex

I once watched seven blue movies in a small cinema in some European city. It was a stinking hot summer's day. I decided to go in, along with my old university friend A, because we were curious, but also because we could get out of the heat and fill in some time while waiting for a meeting that was running late.

We handed over our change at the door, and went in.

The first film started. I was all eyes. The second film followed. I was less agog. The third film seemed just a repeat of the previous ones – and by the last film I was asleep. So was A.

Noel Coward was right 'I don't think pornography is very harmful, but it is terribly, terribly boring'.

Coward could say this because he knew how to create something that was not boring. He wrote *Blithe Spirit* in 1941, and the play was performed in West End over and over again until 1970. Meanwhile, in another corner of London, Soho, the sex shops couldn't keep attracting customers. Their appeal dropped, and these days they are being replaced by cafes and restaurants.

Pornography is easy to make, but just as easily trite. This is because it is virtually mere repetition. The focus stays the same: it is not people with different characters and changing dramas of spirit, but just body parts whose moves are totally predictable and limited in variation and possibility.

Yet people do indeed need something to satisfy their erotic desires, and they use pornography – just like fantasy – even if for a few minutes. This has a long history, and it is not merely a tale of lust and perversion.

In the ruins of Pompeii, the town buried by the Vesuvius eruption in 79 CE, huge frescos, mosaics and statues were found that explicitly depict the sex act, particularly at Lupanare, the building that used to be a brothel. There is a mosaic of a satyr mounting a nymph, and a mural showing the god Mercury with a penis half a meter long.

Sexuality is larger than life in the brothel, and we can guess why: here it is orgasm, not merely lust that is serviced. But in other times and in different contexts, scenes of copulation are not only linked to prostitution.

In the heart of India, in Madhya Pradesh, is the temple of Khajuraho. Built between 950 and 1050 CE, during the Chandela empire, the complex contained 85 structures. Only 22 still remain.

According to the chronicles, the founder of Khajuraho had a heavenly father. One night, Hemavati, the beautiful daughter of a Brahman, was bathing in the Rati River. The moon god came and seduced her. They made love and a child was born, Chandravarman. The community rejected the unwed mother, so she fled to the forest and raised her son there.

This boy later founded a kingdom. One day Chandravarman had a dream: his mother asked him to build a temple that could express the passion of human desire.

We don't know to what extent this story was just a pretext to own something visually marvelous. There are many sexually suggestive temples in India without such stories. The Meenakshi temple in Madurai and Veerananarayan in Gadag display erotic reliefs starting at the entry gates.

Whatever the reason, the reliefs of naked bodies and sexual intercourse one sees at Khajuharo cannot be equated with those found at Pompeii: in the Indian temples, stylization is dominant, and no matter how explicit the erotic scenes, what is more dominant is passion in rhythm and composition. Orgasm is merely hinted, implied in the protuberances and hollows of relief. Lust dissolves into the desire for beauty.

And isn't this what we sense in the work of I Made Budiarta whose painting of Siva disguised as a farmer seeing Dewi Sri's robes open, shows the god with an erection? There is elegance in every line of that Balinese painting. Elegance masters space. The penis, blissfully erect, appears as though just another accent of mood. The physical is part of the ongoing flow of nature.

It seems that this is where the difference between pornography and erotica lies – between the blue movies produced by Vivid, and Bertolucci's *The Dreamer*, between the pictures of sexual intercourse in Pompeii, and the reliefs at Khahujaro; between the photos in *Hustler* magazine and Balinese paintings; between cheap novels, and novels like *Jalan Tak Ada Ujung* (Road Without End) or *Supernova*.

Yet it seems that not everyone easily senses that difference. An Indonesian writer once said 'I don't like the wayang and the Mahabharata because there's too much sex in them'. He would probably have been shocked to read the *Serat Centhini,* the long 19th century Javanese work of literature. There, orgasm and lust are barely reined in by poetry.

Indeed, some people are unfamiliar with cultural lore that accepts lust as a throbbing part of life with its own mystery, between darkness and freedom, between desire and dismay. There are people whose cultural references do not recognize the exuberance of color and form, do not celebrate visible, tangible form, and who view the human body with deep suspicion.

Puritanism, which appears from time to time among Christians and Muslims, reflects this. Under the Calvinist laws of 16th century Geneva, people were forbidden to dance, sing, paint, sculpt, and to perform or watch theatre. 'Indecent' dress was punished. Something very similar goes on in Saudi Arabia today under Wahabi rule.

But in the end, Geneva still did not become a holy city, and in Saudi Arabia, people still can pretend to be holy. Puritanism can never last. Because in its eyes, bodily passion can have only one possibility: to sin – just as in pornography there is only one possibility: orgasm.

One possibility and one alone... how can this be?

'Seks' *Tempo* 19 March 2006, CP VIII: 157-60

Bandung

There, in a clearing in the Ohio woods, the old woman leads the meeting of the ex-slaves. She calls it her 'Call'. It's not a sermon. Baby Suggs just says, 'Here, in this here place, we flesh; flesh that weeps, laughs; flesh that dances on bare feet in grass.'

If there is magic in Toni Morrison's novel, *Beloved*, it is because it reminds us of the meaning of 'flesh', flesh once chained in slavery, branded like cattle, and humiliated in apartheid. 'Negro' flesh.

Being a Negro in America means trying to smile when you want to cry. It means trying to hold on to physical life amid psychological death. It means the pain of watching your children grow up with clouds of inferiority in their mental skies. It means having your legs cut off, and then being condemned for being a cripple.'

These phrases of Martin Luther King from the 1960s were probably reverberating as Morrison was writing her novel published in 1987: the story of a house known only by its number, '124', about Beloved, a ghost from the past, about Sethe who murdered her own child, and about Baby Suggs who had hope.

At the 'Call' in the woods, it is as though Baby Suggs wants to restore the 'cut off' legs of the Negro, legs that could no longer dance and feel the joy of being free to move.

But eventually she too is broken. One day, Sethe, her daughter-in-law, comes to '124'. She is escaping her boss, her owner. She has made up her mind: it is better for her and her four children to die rather than to be slaves. When the owner comes hunting her down, she kills her baby daughter, but doesn't manage to take the lives of the rest, or her own.

What could be done? Even Baby Suggs gives up. She collapses saying: in the end, the Negro has to endure anything done by the Whites.

But not all gave up. Even as the Blacks in America were oppressed, until the mid twentieth century, on other continents millions of people of varied skin color refused to be locked into colonies of the 'Whites'. From the early twentieth century they built a force. And with weapons.

They were called 'Asia-Africa'.

Clearly, the Blacks in America saw 'Asia-Africa' as a beacon. The Asia-Africa conference held in Bandung in April 1955 quickly became part of their story. So it was that Richard Wright came to Bandung. He is the author of the famous novel *Native Son*, about Bigger Thomson who is trapped within 'White' life in America and turns murderer. In Bandung, Wright wrote a 'chronicle' of this conference of nations that refused to be oppressed, titled *The Color Curtain.*

The book was published in 1956. Unfortunately, it's not very good. But Bandung echoed on. Listen to Malcolm X in November 1963, Detroit: 'At Bandung all the nations came together...black, brown, red, or yellow...The number-one thing that was not allowed to attend the Bandung conference was the white man. He couldn't come. Once they excluded the white man, they found that they could get together'.

It turned out that 'Bandung' meant many things. The Asian leaders (Sukarno and Nehru) saw it as an attempt to overcome the military tension between the Soviet Union and the United States that was threatening the whole world. To them, the A-A Conference was more a voice of peace than the embittered yell of an oppressed race.

But if 'Bandung' to them was criticism of the divided world, to Malcolm X 'Bandung' was precisely the affirmation of a divided world. At the time, he was leading the movement of Blacks who wanted separation from White America. His voice was bitter indeed. When he was only six, his father, a Baptist minister, was murdered after receiving a death threat letter from the Ku Klux Klan, and his mother became mentally disturbed. Young Malcolm and his seven brothers and sisters were on their own. 'All Negroes are angry', he said, 'and I am the angriest of all'.

Anger has its own power. Anger can be like Beloved, the ghost from the past, the spirit of the little girl who was killed, the representative of sixteen million slaves who died in a 'holocaust' that is never given that name. Anger can make history. And if to the Blacks that history is not marked by 'Bandung' as a call to peace, that is because it is not clear how that history will end: is it possible there will later be a synthesis between the 'Black' and the 'White', like the synthesis of a classless society according to Marxist theory on the history of the workers' struggle?

To Franz Fanon, the answer was depressing. One day in a corner in Paris, a girl called out 'Look, a Negro!' At that moment he was aware that he, the Negro, was framed in meaning of his self through the 'gaze' of others, a frame that was 'already there, pre-existing, waiting', and easily employed, even by children. That meaning was already soldered on the color of his skin. He was 'Negro', full stop.

It was as though 'Negro-ness' was something eternal, unaffected by history. But Fanon himself was aware, in his travels, in the world, that 'I am endlessly creating myself'. Not to renounce identity, but because it is impossible for self-identity to become either a ruse, or the contrary, to become an idol that is worshipped and unchanging.

And even Malcolm X changed. In 1964 he went to Mecca. He read the Qur'an and realized that humans, even in their anger, are still humans that are limited, and therefore have a need to be just, even to enemies. For human is not a definition. Humans are 'flesh that weeps, laughs', concrete creatures that can be happy momentarily, but can also overcome hate, hold ideals, but also, like him, Malcolm X, be murdered.

Humans such as this felt represented in Bandung: a combination of ghosts from tyrannical pasts and confidence in the future, a movement trembling yet full of hope. Wright, in *The Color Curtain* wrote of the 'Call' of April 1955: 'The despised, the insulted, the hurt, the dispossessed—in short, the underdogs of the human race were meeting.'

'Bandung' *Tempo* 10 April 2005, CP VII: 383-6

Sharp Times

A sick child, a few young women acting strangely, and people terrified. Witchcraft, the work of the Devil, they whisper. Tension grows in the fissures of the conflict of interest that people try to conceal here in this isolated place. Accusation is rife. Arrests begin. Some innocent men and women end up hanged.

This is the mood – a terrifying mixture of paranoia, religious conviction, and power – that Arthur Miller depicts in *The Crucible*, a play that will be remembered long after the death of its author at his home in Connecticut aged 89 on 11 February 2005. While *The Death of a Salesman* is a more moving work, and *All My Sons* a better crafted one, it Miller's *The Crucible* that is still more often turned to these days.

For these are times when, using faith, people can reject others and say 'anyone who is not with us is our enemy'. President Bush can utter these words with conviction, and is enthusiastically supported by the Christian Right in his country. But we know that the American fundamentalists are not alone: the Muslims, the Jews, the Hindus, all with differing political motives and theologies, and with different phrases too, are being fiercely and depressingly vocal.

Miller himself witnessed all this anxiously. A year back, in the midst of the Bush 'war against terror' hype, he wrote a short essay. He recalled that fifty years ago he had been driven to write a sentence in the speech by the judge in *The Crucible*. 'You must understand, sir', the judge says, 'a person is either with this court or he must be counted against it. There is no road between. This is a sharp time, now, a precise time – we live no longer in the dusky afternoon when evil mixed itself with good and befuddled the world.' 'Sharp times' can indeed make a comeback and *The Crucible* is their witness. The play was written when the authorities in America (long before the George W Bush era) were hunting down anyone dangerous, meaning anyone 'communist'. Because of the McCarthy campaign, dozens of people – including those in the theater and film world like Charlie Chaplin and Elia Kazan – were suspected of being 'reds'. The House Committee on Un-American Activities (a name that smacks of both paranoia and patriotism) summoned suspects to a committee of representatives to be investigated. Charlie Chaplin refused and left America for good. The director Elia Kazan gave in; he even named some of his acquaintances as 'tainted' – an act that was a blot on his name for the rest of his life.

Miller did not escape. Speaking later of the overwhelming mood of that time, he said it 'accepted the notion that conscience is not a private matter but that of state administration.' In 1956, the team of examiners investigated his earlier participation in the Left – something he himself had admitted.

He came from the generation that reached adulthood in the 1930s, when the Left seethed with anger and was full of idealism. He was in the thick of all this, even though he never became a member of the Communist Party. But he refused to testify, let alone name other 'sympathizers'. He was considered to be in contempt of the investigating committee on Capitol Hill. His passport was revoked. Fortunately he was not sentenced, once the ferocity of the 'sharp time' began to die down in the late 1950s and 'McCarthyism' became a terrible tale of bigotry. But that event seems to bear out what Miller said after writing *A View from the Bridge;* 'Once you've accepted the idea that orthodoxy is required, you have to go through the Inquisition'.

In other words, orthodoxy moves towards oppression. In the history of religion, there have been all kinds of Inquisitions that murdered countless bodies and souls, and countless good people have been their victims. In the history of Islam, in Baghdad in the 9th century the Caliph al-Ma'mun carried out the *Mihna* to enforce his religion's doctrine. He tortured Imam Hambali. In Jewish religious history, the Patriarch of Palestine at the beginning of the first millennium insisted that a young rabbi bringing the new Word be crucified; and centuries later religious experts sentenced Spinoza. In Christian history, the Inquisition burned alive hundreds of people considered to be heretics – something Calvin in Geneva imitated when he burnt Servetus at the stake.

None of this makes forced teaching win. Over and again, orthodoxy has fused with violence, and terror reemerges. *The Crucible* was an allegory for American paranoia in the 1950s. But we know that Miller took his story from a corner of Massachusetts in the 17th century, when the Puritans ruled in the colony. At a certain moment some of the people were suspected of witchcraft. Acrimonious investigations began. Over a period of a few months in 1692, dozens of men and women were dragged off to be hanged at the top of a hill beyond the village. An eighty-year-old man was crushed slowly to death under heavy stones, because he refused to enter a plea.

The Crucible adapts that historic event with the character John Proctor who ends up hanged. Proctor has long sensed that the church and its authorities offer no refuge. He does not want to attend worship because Parris, the Reverend, speaks only of 'hell and damnation'. 'You hardly ever mention God any more, Mr. Parris', Proctor says.

But of course God is always mentioned, Mr. Proctor. But the God of bigotry, in the sense of something that will always be there. Carlos Fuentes, on the occasion of Arthur Miller's 80th birthday, said that bigotry is the sin of the 21st century. If he is right, we will ask Arthur Miller to speak once again, to remind us once more.

'Begu Ganjang' *Tempo* 20 February 2005, CP VII: 355-8

Abu Ghraib

Actually, there is nothing very odd about the events at Abu Ghraib prison in Baghdad: in the jail where the Iraqi soldiers are detained, the victorious and the powerful are celebrating their power, gleefully, brutally, on the bodies of the now-powerless.

Take a good look at the photos now in circulation the world over. The first photo: an Iraqi detainee, completely naked, crawls on the floor, his neck collared to a leash. A female American soldier from Company 372 Military Police is holding the end of the leash, as though dragging some strange animal. The second photo: some detainees, stripped of their clothing, are piled up like a stack of old tires, and photographed. The written report stated that a detainee was forced to masturbate in front of the others......

But what is to be done? There has been war in Iraq, and war is, after all, sanctioned brutality that produces winners and losers. War is a wager where, in its most extreme form, to win is to live and to lose is to die. The Iraqi detainees at Abu Ghraib are creatures to be seen as old tires or snared animals. As 'the dead', what can they do about it?

One can extend this question beyond Abu Ghraib. The entire Iraq war is a statement that millions of people in the world are facing the question: what can they do? When the country with the most sophisticated weaponry on the face of the earth intends to conquer Baghdad, its will is done, even though millions of people oppose it. America does not need to explain its reasons. It does not have to apologize when its reasons turn out to be wrong. It does not have to answer to anyone at all for its attack on Iraq and all the ensuing destruction and death, other than answer to itself.

It has no need to fear. For who is that self? A figure almost entirely fevered by patriotism. And the distinction between that fever and 'jingoism', once people appear to value their leaders' 'war records' more than their 'peace records', is often unclear. They applaud when they see President Bush appear in his battle pilot uniform.....

Patriotism, and particularly 'jingoism', is the first step in separating others. And 'exceptionalism' comes from this. It was Alexis de Tocqueville in the mid nineteenth century who coined the term 'American exceptionalism', but now it has found a different expression – for what is considered acceptable and unacceptable, as something that operates for the international community yet does not have to be observed by the United States. At Abu Ghraib, one of the soldiers who took part in the torture of prisoners admitted that he had never been taught the Geneva Convention.

But this is not the only thing ignored. Prior to Abu Ghraib, America had already refused to join the International Court of Justice. It also refused to sign the agreement banning the use of landmines, which 137 countries agreed to; and it did not want to join the international agreement on biological weapons which was ratified by 413 countries.

America wants to establish that it is an exception, and it can do this. More and more, it is proving the words of Carl Schmidt, the Nazi intellectual: 'The sovereign is he who decides on the exception.'

Exception meaning complete freedom. But freedom for oneself alone – not for others.

How strange, actually, that this is what is happening. For the United States is a country that stands with an idea that there should be no 'exceptions' – a spirit of universalism that proclaims the rights of liberty for all people, for all nations. I remember back in 1955 when Bung Karno opened the Asia-Africa Conference in Bandung. He quoted Longfellow's poem, *Paul Revere's Ride* – about a revolutionary who rode his horse in the dead of night to wake up the people so they would be ready to fight for liberty. The history of the United States seemed to be the history of us all.

How distant this is now, how strange. The universalist spirit that set out to make the United States part of a free world is now fused with the spirit wanting to make this country stand apart – even when this means the sacrificing of universal liberty. For now, in the name of patriotism, there is the intent to condone censorship and ignore the principle of independent justice.

But this, it seems, is precisely the fate of all three major revolutions in history. The French Revolution ended up producing dictatorship, and then, French supremacy. The Russian Revolution in turn produced Stalin, and with Stalin, 'internationalism' that ended up as just an empty vessel for Russian influence. The American Revolution is not so different from this tragic pattern: it aimed to reach out to the world, and has ended cooped up in itself.

Maybe because the starting point is intent. When the historian Hobsbawn said that for the French, the liberation of their country was 'merely the first installment of the universal triumph of liberty', he was actually pointing out the paradox of the three great revolutions in history. All three started with the intent of changing the world. All three had a subject with a purpose, and a purpose that was achieved. And this is where a model starts.

Over time, the subject becomes synonymous with the center and example. In American history, the perception of self as the example is smeared with what is absolute, noble, and successful; 'Christianity, democracy, Americanism, the English language and culture, the growth industry and science, American institutions, they are all confounded and confused', H Richard Niebuhr writes in *The Kingdom of God in America.* In this confusion, the United States remains steadfast in its wish to be the exception. Sometimes it amazes us, sometimes it amuses us, and sometimes it terrifies.

'Abu Ghuraib' *Tempo* 16 May 2004, CP VII: 189-92

Troy

The war that lasted ten years. A thousand ships and 100,000 soldiers mobilized, and Troy, a city thought to have been on the northwestern point of Turkey, razed to the ground. People fell in droves, the warriors died. Robert Fagle's powerful translation of the famous epic depicts the battlefield brutally:

> *Idomeneus skewered Erymas straight through the mouth,*
> *the merciless brazen spearpoint raking through,*
> *up under the brain to split his glistening skull —*
> *teeth shattered out, both eyes brimmed to the lids*
> *with a gush of blood and both nostrils spurting,*
> *mouth gaping, blowing convulsive sprays of blood*
> *and death's dark clouds closed down around his corpse.*

Such savagery, for what? In the epic attributed to Homer, the supposedly blind poet who lived 2850 years ago, the Trojan War happened because Agamemnon, King of the Achaeans, wanted to reclaim his brother's abducted wife. Swords were drawn because Agamemnon was a prince from another country. Similar to the Ramayana: fascinating, but it does not make much sense.

Particularly to historians. Herodotus, the fifth-century BCE historian, was dubious about this motive of wife-freeing. So it is understandable that in our times, in the midst of the Iraq War with its fake justifications, the film *Troy* directed by Wolfgang Petersson highlights an explanation more feasible for the 21st century. Hector, the Trojan prince and warrior, according to David Benioff's scenario says; 'This is about power, not love'.

Actually, these two things do not differ, when 'love' means 'possessing'. And at a time when 'possessing' (another word for 'controlling') was important, when women were merely accessories, then Agamemnon's reason for the endless war might have been a combination between 'woman' and 'throne'. It is true that his sister-in-law, Helen, had been abducted by Paris and carried off to Troy. But it is also true that this touched on the standing and power of a kingdom.

I think this is why Jean Giraudoux wrote his satirical play *La Guerre de Troie n'aura pas lieu*. (The Trojan War will not take place), and why, when Arifin C Noer staged it at Taman Ismail Marzuki thirty years ago, he inserted coastal Javanese Tegal accent into the dialogue; to poke fun. In Act Two, Hector, who does not want war, calls in an expert on international law, Busiris. Busiris explains the legal basis for war against the Achaeans who are at sea, at the ready. But Hector, who sees how easy it is to find pretexts for war, tries to pressure Busiris to use the same pretexts for *not* going to war. '...nous devons nous précipiter pour fermer les portes de la guerre, les verrouiller, les cadenasser' (we must race to close the gates of war, padlock them, barricade them).

It is interesting that in this play, Hector sees war as something coming from outside. But 'outside' to him is not the Aechean army. He does not even want to close the gates of the city against them. What he wants to keep out is a catastrophe for the innocent.

But we know that Hector was unable to prevent that catastrophe. In Homer's telling, Hector eventually returns to the battlefield. He goes forth proudly, even though he knows that Troy will fall and he will be killed. And when the city collapses and the Greek troops come in, the innocent are indeed the victims: Hector's son,

Astuyanax, still a baby, is thrown against the wall by the conquering forces. He dies.

What is tragic to Hector is that he was right: war did not come from within or from one thousand Greek ships. In Homer's epic, the war comes from above, from the gods.

In the ancient story, Heaven is a busy Olympus: the gods eagerly drag people into savagery that people actually do not want. King Priam of Troy knows. He looks on sadly as Helen is accused of being the source of enmity, and says gently, 'My child...I lay no blame upon you, it is the gods, not you who are to blame. It is they that have brought about this terrible war with the Achaeans'.

Perhaps it is too easy to blame the gods, but in the third part of Homer's epic, this is what happens: after years of the two sides fighting without victory or defeat, they agree to settle the dispute in a manner more economical and fair: Paris, who abducted Helen, has to duel with Menelaus, who is Helen's husband and King Agamemnon's younger brother. Whoever wins will have the right to take the beautiful Helen as wife, and the war will then be over.

But it turns out the gods and goddesses of Olympus don't want peace....

Aphrodite, who loves the handsome Paris, wants him to be spared at the very instant he is to be killed. Zeus's wife Hera, basically wants Troy completely destroyed. Zeus finally gives in: the father of the gods agrees to the annihilation of Troy because Hera will then later agree to the annihilation of her favorite cities, including Argos and Sparta. And so, provoked by the gods, the two sides go back to their killing. Cruelty rages, and Troy is destroyed.

I don't know how religion can formulate its arguments with imagination such as this. But three millennia ago, Homer's epic was perhaps the beginning of an awareness of the absurdity of life and the ambivalence of faith: people believe in gods who control, but with this, people then bemoan their fate as determined by Heaven. In such dismal conditions, what can possibly give life worth?

I think the answer lies at the end of the tale: that night, Hector's father Priam comes unattended from Troy to the enemy camp. He meets Achilles who has already killed Hector and brutally dragged the body around behind his chariot. Priam wants to collect the body of his son.

Achilles is moved to see the bereaved father, and holding back his tears, he invites his guest to sit. 'The immortals know no care, yet the lot they spin for man is full of sorrow.' His tone is friendly. A moment when life seems sensed once more as having meaning, glowing anew, for people shake hands and the heavens are silenced.

'Troya' *Tempo* 28 June 2004, CP VII: 209-12

Zhivago

Every year at the end of May I quietly commemorate a poet who tried to stand apart; at a time when politics was striving to build the world with much ado, he was trying to say something else, refusing to believe that politics and history were the be all and end all. He got knocked down, of course. And Boris Pasternak died at his home in Peredelkino, thirty kilometers from Moscow, on May 30, 1960.

He was the curse of his government. The power that Lenin and Stalin had created decided that Pasternak was a traitor. The Soviet Union wanted every citizen to move like the army in battle formation, because the revolution (usually written with capital R) that had begun in October 1917 was not over. The world still had to be changed. And since Stalin had taken over the reins, even stricter discipline had been enforced, the five-year plan had been proclaimed, everyone had to roll up their sleeves, and artists had to be given direction.

In 1934, Andrey Zhdanov, one of Stalin's men, gave a speech at the Congress of the Union of Soviet Writers. That was the beginning of the principle later dubbed *Zhdanovshchina*: writers now had to apply the doctrine of 'Socialist Realism'.

Actually, to make one recipe for works of literature is impossible – but how could the bureaucrats and Communist Party officials understand the creative process? The way they saw it, writers had social engineering duties to build the 'new man'. For, as Zhdanov said, quoting Stalin, writers were 'engineers of the human soul'.

But the human spirit is more complex than cement and steel, and *Zhdanovshchina* ended up as a mechanism to control literary expression. The satirist Mikhail Zoshchenko and the poet Anna Akhmatova, who published 'apolitical, individualistic and bourgeois' works, were fired from the Union of Soviet Writers. Fear prevailed. Particularly as everyone knew that the poet Osip Mandelstam had previously been expelled and murdered, like many people who were captured and then disappeared.

Pasternak was confused and afraid. Must he join this grand endeavor that set out to drag everything, even the soul, into the project of the 'Revolution'? Or should he keep on writing poetry as he had done, and not join this 'Revolution', because there were things more urgent and meaningful to him?

I think it was at this moment that he wrote *Hamlet,* a four-line poem. Pasternak uses the Shakespearean character as a metaphor here, for he has to choose, 'to be or not to be'. But Pasternak also links Hamlet's indecision with Christ's fear in the Garden of Gethsemane, knowing the fate awaiting him. Offstage, Hamlet whispers, 'Abba, Father, take this cup from me'.

He was alone. He was like a nervous dot in the expanse of history on the move. He was surrounded, he said, by 'pharisees'. In other words, all those around him believed themselves the most right and pure, the most observant of the faith.

I find it interesting that Pasternak chose the Biblical analogy for his life situation: it seems that he equated Stalinism with a religion that hardens faith and strengthens institutions. Of course he was unable to enter that place. The religious sense expressed in his poems shows that life is precisely not as the Pharisees construe: life itself contains something sacred, even though untouched by faith. The Bible, we find in Doctor Zhivago, is not 'ethical maxims and commandments'. Christ speaks 'parables taken from life'.

And life, to Pasternak, is something intimate but marvelous, passionate yet fragile. Life is 'my little sister', as he says in his poem *Sestra moya-zhizn,* who 'swims the bright world in a wall of spring rain'. While over there the 'people with watch-chains grumble and frown'.

It is this contrast that seems to be the basic theme of Pasternak's writing: on the one hand life that is close, fascinating, free and unpredictable: on the other hand, all that is obedient, ordered and authoritative ('with watch-chains'). And between the two, the poet has made his choice. As life cannot be subjected by doctrine, he, who chooses life, refuses to join *Zhdanovshchina.* The head of the Union of Socialist Writers decided: Pasternak had to be struck down.

But secretly, he went on writing his novel, *Doctor Zhivago,* the tragic story of a doctor in the midst of the raging Revolution, someone who believed in Christ, and believed there was a power unmatched by 'unarmed truth'.

He half hoped that the novel would not be published. In 1957, *Doctor Zhivago* was published in Italy, in Russian. In 1958, Pasternak was awarded the Nobel Prize.

Not surprisingly, Pasternak became an object of the Cold War between the Soviet and 'Western' blocks. To the 'West', he was a symbol of the lack of creative freedom under communism. To the supporters of the 'Revolution' everywhere, he was someone that should be stifled. Even in Indonesia, Pramoedya Ananta Toer, who also wanted to apply Socialist Realism and who enthusiastically quoted Zhdanov's teachings, considered *Doctor Zhivago* a great sin: a 'slander' of the October Revolution.

Pasternak could not fight back. The distribution of all of his work was stopped. He lost his source of income. And it was impossible for him to get a permit to go to Stockholm to receive the Nobel Prize. In 1960, he died of lung cancer.

But could he have chosen History and Faith over poetry? Definitely not. For poetry celebrates life, with small-scale moves of intensity. For poetry:

It's a full whistle in a trice,
It's ice cracking in a gale,
It's a night turning the green to ice,
It's a duel of two nightingales.

'Zhivago' *Tempo* 20 June 2004, CP VII: 209-12

America

Which comes first: paranoia or power? I sit in the dark. Flashing before me, a line: 'When you have a hammer, all problems start to look like nails.'

The TV screen blabs on almost incessantly. CNN and BBC bring 'The War in Iraq' – or, in other words, a hammer more than adequate for the job, smashing away at a half-rusty nail. And it is not clear why.

A superpower with an unrivaled military budget. An economy that is the richest in the world, with the most innovative weapon industry. A republic 270 million strong, a patriotic population. A military force with the most sophisticated conventional weaponry and the most ready nuclear weapons...

Why on earth is America afraid of the threat of an already defeated Iraq, a country that could not refuse the UN groups carrying out inspections, an economy with no strong industry, a nation of 24 million, already exhausted, a republic with a government not supported by the people, a force that maybe does have weapons to terrify mankind, but yet is also a power that according to America itself can be quickly defeated?

Robert Kagan wrote *Of Paradise and Power*, and felt he had an answer: because America is strong. Europe, Kagan's argument goes, has greater tolerance in facing threats because it is now a relatively weak continent. Whereas America, 'being stronger, developed a lower threshold of tolerance for Saddam and his weapons of mass destruction.'

But this goes not only for Saddam. Kagan quotes an opinion poll of summer 2002. Its results showed that more Americans (compared with Europeans) were worried about the threats of Iraq, Iran, North Korea, China, Russia, the India-Pakistan confrontation, and the conflict between Israel and Arab countries.... 'When you have a hammer, all problems start to look like nails.'

There is an objection here, of course: If one does not have a hammer, one will not want to see everything as nails - even if there is indeed a nail. But such an objection, which Kagan puts forward, does not contradict what is going on: whether or not object X is a nail will be finally determined by the subjective world of the 'I'. In the beginning is the paranoia. Then the hammer.

But then again, maybe I am wrong. The TV screen changes. Now it is TV-5, the French channel, trying to explain something about America. The camera shows a building complex, in Seattle maybe, and there is the business center for designers of Boeing aircraft. Inside, a scene of jubilation: they have just won the contract from the Department of Defense for the production of a new kind of warplane. And then a scene of irritation: someone shows, on his computer, just how large were the donations given by the military industry to both the Republican and Democrat parties, who ended up reluctant to oppose war. No, it is not paranoia that brings in the hammer, but rather gain and greed.

But maybe also God? The camera moves on elsewhere. A group of neatly dressed people, middle-aged, fat, is at prayer. *The Christian Coalition* applauds George W. Bush, someone who – after a carefree life of drink in his youth –was 'reborn'. The President found Jesus. He reads the Bible every morning (does he also read the part with Christ's Sermon on the Mount, promising 'the meek shall inherit the earth'?), and like the fundamentalist Protestants who support him, he believes that the United States is the New Jerusalem. Like Israel, a Promised Land.

The camera moves. On a stage, the Stars-and-Stripes is flown beside the flag of the Star of David. Children are dancing. To these people, the United States and Israel are forever right. And over there: the Devil. The evil one – and indeed Saddam Hussein fulfills the criteria for this title – cannot be tolerated.

There is something about America in this 21st century that creates fear and anxiety. A unique variant of paranoia, profit and Protestantism? Patriotism maybe? Maybe. Alexis de Tocqueville wrote in his first volume of *Democracy in America*, after visiting there in the eighteenth century: 'Nothing is more embarrassing in the ordinary intercourse of life, than this irritable patriotism of the Americans.'

Patriotism, or narcissism. Kagan proudly admits the view that America is like a 'cowboy'. 'The United States does act as an international sheriff', he writes, 'self-appointed perhaps but widely welcomed nevertheless, trying to enforce some peace and justice in....a lawless world.'

I recall Gary Cooper in *High Noon*. There he stood at noon, alone in the suddenly-deserted street. There was a kind of loneliness there, when he had to face the bad guys who had made a *coalition of the willing*. The fascinating thing in every Western is the lone figure of the hero in a duel. And if he does appear together with others, like in *Gunfight at the OK Corral*, the weapons they carry are equal to the weapons of the opponents. He acts not because he is the stronger.

And he will wait until the opponent reaches for his gun. In the end, a battle of skill will take place, like in *The Fastest Gun Alive*. He takes his time because he is brave. Wyatt Earp even once said that the one faster to shoot is often not the accurate one.

What's more, a sheriff never fires a barrage of shots first in a pre-emptive strike, just because he thinks someone poses a threat. In that town he is bound by law.

He is utterly different to the champ in *Of Paradise and Power.*

'Amerika' *Tempo* 6 April 2003, CP VI: 397-400

Baghdad

aghdad – a city that changed from geography to a word in a fable.

This probably all began when the ninth-century Caliph al-Masur heard that the old Babylonian city of Baghdad was a place of cool afternoons in the summer. And so in 762 the Caliph moved his residence from Hashimiya, and brought all the government offices from Kufa. It took four years for 100,000 laborers and artisans to build the city. Slowly, palaces, buildings, mosques, gardens and villas appeared along the sides of the Tigris River.

And a new center was born. Baghdad (meaning 'Gift of God') changed its name to Medinah-al-Salam (City of Peace), and it became a performance, a display, and the stuff of stories and conversation. When the city was 400 years old, the Persian poet Anwari al-Khurasani was still passionate in his praise. 'Blessed be Baghdad', he wrote, and from his poem we can imagine what urban life was like there at the time.

The gardens filled with lovely nymphs equal Kashmir
And thousands of gondolas on the water

Baghdad was probably the largest city in the world in the tenth century. Its population is estimated to have reached two million. Its wealth was unmeasured. Sultan al-Muqtadir, for instance, built the Tree Pavilion, so named because in the pool in the park there was a tree, complete with branches, leaves and birds, all carved out of gold and silver.

But all that sparkled and astonished – which brought Baghdad into children's stories of genie and Aladdin – was only one aspect of that city. The other was the face that resembled a 21st century European city. In the 10th century, there were around eleven hospitals in Baghdad. Medical training was systematic – doctors were permitted to practice only if they had a 'national' diploma. Will Durant, in the 4th volume of his *The Story of Civilization,* says that in 931 there were 860 doctors with certificates to practice in Baghdad. Ali bin Isa, a vizier who was also a health expert, arranged for medical specialists to take turns visiting the sick from place to place, including daily visits in the prisons.

The power of the Abbasid dynasty, from 750-1058, certainly did not rest on a flying carpet. Al-Mansur, tall, slim, dark-skinned, aged 40, was no romantic Eastern prince, as usually depicted. He was a serious worker; he reformed the kingdom's administration, gave the army durable organization, systematized infrastructure – in short, he built an institution that was later strengthened under Harun al-Rasyid – the renowned sultan who was only 22 when he ascended the throne.

The many stories of both beneficence and cruelty under this sultan are so colorful that it is probably from them that we imagine the tales of 1001 nights. But Harun al-Rasyid, who died in 809 aged only 45, bequeathed a neat system and sizeable wealth: when he died the sum of 48 million dinar was left in the treasury, a huge sum at the time. When Al-Makmun replaced him, we find in Baghdad a ruler who had the time to hold a seminar in his palace every Tuesday about various theological and legal problems. The Sultan himself was an active participant, and did not place himself any higher than the invited experts.

Over these centuries, under the Abbassid and Umayyah dynasties, perhaps people were implementing the Prophet's famous injunction: 'Search for knowledge as far as China'. The Sultan sent people to obtain Greek texts, particularly in mathematics and medicine. In 830, Al-Makmun established the 'Hall of Wisdom' (*Baitul Hikmah*), an academy of science, an observatory, and a public library. Foreign works were faithfully translated. Under the coordination of Hunain bin Ishaq, a Christian healer of the Nestorian sect, commentaries and texts from Syrian, Greek, Pahlavi and Sanskrit were introduced to the Arab-speaking community.

This is why, while in Europe's Dark Ages the fruits of Greek civilization were virtually unknown, in the Arab world the works of Plato and Aristotle were translated almost in their entirety. A cosmopolitan spirit that was open to all directions produced an astounding cross traffic. The *Surya Siddhanta*, for instance, an ancient Indian treatise on astronomy, was brought from Hindustan. And through this kind of exchange, Muhammad bin Musa (780-850), the foremost mathematician in the world at the time, introduced his scientific works on logarithms, algebra and quadratic equations, which continue down through to this century, via various universities in Europe that now have probably forgotten them.

In times like this, and about times like this, who would foolishly talk of a 'clash of civilizations'? Since the 18th century, since the European enlightenment, 'the West' has often stated itself as the official heir to Greek civilization. But between the 9th and 12th centuries, that 'West' was actually not Europe, but 'Islam'. Ahmad al-Biruni, a scholar renowned for his work published in 1030 about Indian history (*Tarikh al-Hind*), and someone with such fluency in Sanskrit that he translated Euclid and Ptolemy into that language, still declared that it was not 'Eastern' philosophy that was his choice. He had reasons. 'India', he wrote, 'has produced no Socrates; no logical method has there expelled fantasy from science'.

'Bagdad' *Tempo* 23 February 2003, CP VI: 371-4

Bombs

Bombs and ideals – the two are allied when hope has lost politics and politics has lost hope. This story starts on a street in St. Petersburg, Russia, on March 13, 1881.

That day, someone threw a bomb from a food stall. Czar Alexander II was riding his carriage not far from the Palace. Explosions were heard. The royal vehicle was destroyed, the horses and guards wounded. But the Czar himself escaped injury. He even calmly addressed the victims and spoke gently about the potential murderer who had been immediately captured. But suddenly someone came running at the attack, shouting, 'It's too soon to be offering thanks to God!", and the second bomb exploded right at the Czar's feet. Fire and metal sliced his two legs at the calf. His stomach was ripped open. His face was destroyed. But he remained conscious for a moment, for he still was able to say 'to the palace, to die there'. And what was left of his body was taken to the Winter Palace.

'His Majesty is dead', the doctor said, after checking the bloody wrist for a pulse. The royal family witnessed all this with horror, but at the same moment a new czar stood ready. The crown prince nodded. He gave a sign to his wife to follow. He walked out of the palace. On all sides, the Preobrazhensky Regiment stood on guard, their bayonets at the ready. The young czar stood for a moment, saluted, and then jumped inside his carriage. A cossack regiment in battle formation accompanied him, their red swords glistening in the March sunlight. Russia and its dynastic power didn't seem to have been touched at all. At his coronation, Alexander III declared that he would rule with 'conviction in the might and right of autocracy'.

So, what was the point then, in the bomb that killed Alexander II? The murderers, like the terrorists in Albert Camus' play *Les Justes,* probably bore a noble ideal; liberty from repression, the restoration of human dignity. But we know that it was only in 1917, through the communist revolution, that the czar's power based on 'the might and right of autocracy' could fall. Russia truly changed.

That is why the difference between the terrorists in 1881 and the communists in 1917 is profound. Those murderers on the St. Petersburg street had no program for a change of power once the czar died, whereas in 1902 Lenin was already writing a pamphlet titled 'What Is to be Done?', which was an analysis of Russian society and the path of revolution in such a society. In other words, the 1881 bomb merely had daring and ideals, whereas the Leninist revolution had something more. This revolution, invested with its 'theory' of revolution, had a revolutionary party's might, based on a public program, and with a leadership ready to take over power. This is why it didn't only shake the world; it changed the world.

I don't know how Al-Qaeda or Jemaah Islamiyah are going to change the world. Whoever it was who detonated the bomb in Bali on 12 October last probably bore a wad of anger and hate, plus a few ideals and some courage. But, with only this, they will end up with 19th century-like terror: action where politics and hopes don't meet. Around 200 *kafir* killed, but then what? Go and kill other unbelievers? Until when? Can't the definition of what makes a *kafir* be debated unceasingly, thus making them also countless in number? Or, after attack upon attack, murder upon murder, will the Al-Qaeda or Jemaah Islamiyah have plans to defeat the United States? Say, for instance, make Bush surrender, occupy the White House, dismiss Congress, and apply 'Islamic law' from Houston to Honolulu...?

But maybe I'm wrong. Maybe I have to remind myself that the Bali bombers weren't speaking much about life. People like that speak more often of jihad, amidst plans for murder and dying as martyrs. In other words, there is no future image of an organized polity, a communal space for interaction, a comfortable and lively arena. In these bombers, bombs and ideals exist in hope that has lost politics – hope that has lost the imagination of the need for a process of managing power in the limited world.

But in this, the bombers display self-contradiction. Prepared for martyrdom, they shouldn't care about what happens in the limited world. Yet at the same time, they are disturbed about injustice in the world. On the one hand, they equate the word *kafir* with 'enemy' and claim that this confrontation is a confrontation in the path of God. But on the other hand, they are actually following the path of secular violence that began with the French Revolution – targeting groups or classes, not individuals. They don't stick the label *kafir* on the backs of the faith-less one person at a time. And so they ignore a principle of Omniscience: before God, every person, believer or unbeliever, is present whole, non-uniform, solitary, not as the representative of a group.

But they don't care. They fire volleys of ammunition into the crowd, and multitudes are murdered. One moment the terrorists can indeed be the winners, particularly at a time when politics operates without hope. But what will then be left? Maybe Camus was right. 'Modern conquerors can kill, but do not seem to be able to create.'

'Bom' *Tempo* 8 December 2002, CP VI: 323-6

Territorium

Histroy has not ended, geography is not yet dead. Or at least, it is not easy to determine these things. Endings or death are never a single full stop, and they never appear unexpectedly.

The old map of the world is indeed no longer valid: some of the huge unions (Yugoslavia, The Soviet Union, Czechoslovakia) have split apart and almost dispersed. Seeing the way that capital is amassed and circulated every second via the hyper-busy cyber highways, no longer controlled by any customs office anywhere, people go on about the 'world without borders'. Now, since September 11, 2001, it is as though the 'world without borders' has declared itself in violent serial: all sorts of countries are banding together to confront a terrorist organization (or formless organization?) which has its base in no capital city, and is citizen of no country.

But before saying that geography is finished, and a 'global village' has replaced the old map, people should come to the Rockefeller Plaza, in downtown Manhattan, New York.

Before September 11 2001, on this block measuring about 12 x 20 meters square, there stood a row of flagpoles flying all kinds of patterns and colors from all kinds of countries. But since the World Trade Center was destroyed by two hijacked planes, Americans have suddenly felt attacked, and the Stars and Stripes is showing everywhere, from short pants to tall buildings. And in that famous block of Manhattan Island, there is now no longer any symbol other than the Stars and Stripes, Stars and Stripes...

Americans don't like to be called 'nationalist'; they are proud to be called 'patriotic'. But to me, what is happening now is the upsurge of American nationalism which, like nationalism everywhere, is full of fervor, often narrow-minded, and worrying.

Two Boeing planes owned by American airline companies crashed into two tall towers in Manhattan, and over three thousand people were killed. People usually say that this was the first time that America had been attacked on its on territory. But this is clearly not so. In 1993 there was an attempt to blow up the World Trade Center by Mahmud Abouhalima and friends, and then there was the unforgettable attack in Oklahoma City that killed one hundred and sixty eight people including children, and wounded five hundred others, when a federal government building was bombed with almost two thousand kilograms of explosives. That was in 1995.

I think the idea that the September 11 was the 'first attack against America on its own territory' comes from the memory of 1941, when Pearl Harbor in Hawai'i was bombed by planes from the Empire of Japan. It is as though the photos and films about that day are on replay. There are planes. There is the clear open sky. There is an explosion. And there are 'foreigners' – meaning those who do not hold American passports. The attempt to blow up the World Trade Center in 1993, apart from being considered a failure that killed only six people, was directed by a New York taxi driver born in Egypt. And as for the attack in Oklahoma City in 1995 – Timothy McVeigh was born in America, white, with an army-style crew cut.

In other words, what is being used here is a definition from the old boundaries of nationalism – with the old yells. And all at once we witness not a United States that feels it is an integral part of the world that – like Sri Lanka, India, Algiers, Pakistan, Israel, Palestine,

Egypt, Nicaragua, or Indonesia – constantly copes with bombs and terrorist guns. Rather, what we witness is a United States closing itself off, while at the same time asking the world outside to view it with sympathy or dread. Nationalism and narcissism are interrelated. The United States, which has long viewed the United Nations with contempt, which refuses to participate in agreements on global warming, which has no interest in the idea of an international criminal court, and whose contribution to foreign aid is only 0.1 percent of GNP (lower than Japan at 0.35 per cent, and France at 0.39 per cent, not to mention Denmark at 1.01 per cent) – yes, in other words the United States, whose overseas aid can be said to equal the money spent by people in that country on their pet dogs and cats – this is the United States that is now building a long fortified wall. The idea to try those people considered foreign terrorists (before proven 'terrorists', but already proven 'foreign') in a military court like Indonesia's New Order military trials after 1965, is the most striking example of a solid national barrier brought into operation in matters of justice. And this is not counting the surveillance of foreign students, or the tightening up of visas...

But the United States is not alone in this territorial frenzy. Israel is taking the Palestinians' land, India and Pakistan are fighting over Kashmir, Australia is refusing hapless boat people from Afghanistan, and Indonesia strives – if necessary with blood and iron – for Aceh and Papua to not 'break away'. Truly, geography has not ended.

It even still has dark magic. Also to Osama bin Laden, who used to wander, but has now disappeared. And he arose because of territorial awareness. When Iraq attacked Kuwait, and the kingdom of Saudi Arabia was worried that Saddam Hussein would cross the border, Osama was close to the royal family. When the Saudi rulers invited in the US army and let them to stay in Dhahran, Osama left the palace, denouncing it. To him, when the 'infidels' stayed in the 'holy land', this had to be opposed, as though it was not only Mecca and Medina that are sacred, but the entire Saudi peninsula.

The sacralization of territory can indeed be awe-inspiring, but more often than not, it goes too far. I remember the song of praise for a country called Indonesia which the teacher taught us when I was still in primary school: 'your earth is sacred, your firmament holy.'

'Territorium' *Tempo* 13 January 2002, CP VI: 139-42

Republics

A republic is born with fine aspirations, but we often forget that there is an old connection between it and violence. The republics of Indonesia, India, China, and Algeria – to mention just a few – spilt blood in the twentieth century just as the French republic did in the eighteenth. 'The republic', says Saint-Just, a theoretician of the French revolution, 'consists of the extermination of everything that opposes it.'

'The republic' here refers to a nation-state that forced itself into history. Under Jacobin fanaticism it became The Terror, persistent, unflinching; for to the republic, unanimity in the 'new world' was a necessity.

And so, two hundred and nine years ago, the revolutionary forces came from the Capital to destroy Lyons. The city had sinned through supporting the federalist cause, which the Jacobins considered tantamount to refusing the unified march towards the future. Marseilles was dubbed 'Town-with-No-Name', as though there was no need for it on the map for its inhabitants were considered loyal only to their own locality, as if France were nothing at all.

And then of course there was Vendée. In 1793, the area of Vendée rebelled and succeeded in defeating the revolutionaries. The farmers, with the support of the clergy, restored what the revolution considered old-fashioned and exploitative and therefore to be demolished: the power of the Church. To the farmers of Vendée, the secular revolution and the republic had ripped Catholic tradition from their lives. And so they rose up, and wrote an anti-version of the revolutionary anthem, the Marseillaise: '*Allons armies catholiques, le jour de gloire est arrivé...*'.

But in mid April 1794 that 'Catholic army' was wiped out. Their day of glory was gone. Up to a quarter of a million people were killed in Vendée and its environs; that is to say, around a third of the population. The Army of the Republic was indeed an extension of The Terror. The harvest was burned, infrastructure smashed, women raped. One cold January day, two hundred inhabitants were ordered to kneel near a huge hole they had dug. They were all shot. Any who escaped were beaten with hammers. Around thirty women and children were buried alive when the hole was filled in. Vendée became Vengé, avenged.

And there stands France, proud, grand, and prosperous. History and great wars have shaken her time and again, the revolution has been betrayed, and yet the republic has no more need of slaughter. In Vendée, a destroyed past remains extinct, gone.

They say that two hundred years later, in September 1993, Alexander Solzhenitsyn came to the village of Lucs-sur-Boulogne. This great Russian writer who had lived for years in Stalin's camps for political prisoners, went there to pay homage to the victims of the French Revolution. He accompanied Philippe de Villiers, a right-wing figure who wanted to revive 'Vendée identity', with all its tradition.

Here in this French village, Solzhenitsyn greeted the past. The past was important to him, and memory essential. Revolution merely forces forgetting. 'Revolution destroys the organic character of a society', he said. This 'organic character' is connected to 'national culture': something local, enmeshed with custom, identifiable with the roots of a place. The French revolution, like the Russian revolution in 1917, severed those roots. In the name of Reason and Enlightenment, the revolutionaries destroyed the nature of old Catholic France and original Orthodox Russia.

Solzhenitsyn saw that revolution had produced a structure that warps from the 'top' what lives naturally 'below'. It sets out to make people the same. How futile. For, as Solzhenitsyn said, 'humanity does not develop in a single mould, but often through closed cultures, each with its own laws.'

This stance can certainly be tempting these days when modern forms of power are found repressive, when nostalgia for times lost is gaining strength, and when cultural differences are welcomed as liberation. But Solzhenitsyn did not explain where the boundaries of these 'closed cultures' lie. One cannot infer from him whether everyone within those cultural boundaries must or should be assumed to be the same. What happens when someone wishes to diverge from the cultural precepts within which one was raised?

Maybe Solzhenitsyn should have read Indonesian novels of the 1920s. *Siti Nurbaya* is about a young woman oppressed by a 'closed culture'. Kartini's letters in the early twentieth century desired emancipation. Abdullah bin Abdul Kadir Munsyi's records of the Malay people in Singapore in the nineteenth century tell how something local, something enmeshed with custom, identifiable with the roots of a place – that which Solzhenitsyn calls 'organic character' – can be incredibly oppressive. On the other hand, modernity can bring violence, but it can also liberate.

When the Republic of Indonesia was established, like the republics of India, China, Algeria and others, actually it was aiming for a modernity like this. It could indeed let loose dark forces within itself, spill blood, and slaughter. But finally, like the Terror of the French Revolution, it acted in the name of Reason and Enlightenment, and therefore it will be held to account by Reason and Enlightenment. It cannot escape. For the republic, modernity with all its faults does not see itself as coming from heaven. It is not sacred, its speech ended. It is not yet closed. It cannot possibly stay closed forever.

'Republik' *Tempo* 31 March 2002, CP VI: 185-8

Darwish

M aybe he is also a chunk of Palestine: something among the debris. His voice like rubble on the earth now emptied and occupied by settlers.

In this world every ruin holds a story. Within Mahmoud Darwish, the Galilean-born poet, those ruins are words. 'Land, like language, is inherited', he writes in his poem *The Tragedy of Narcissus, The Comedy of Silver*. When that language was seized by power, Darwish's poems conveyed the imagination of something no longer in existence: a complete life story, with a back, middle, and front surveying the future. Like a house that collapsed when Darwish was six years old.

He was born on 13 March in the village of Berweh, in the district of Akka, upper Galilee. When the Israeli army came in 1948 and people were shot, the young Darwish and his parents fled to Lebanon. The State of Israel was established, and the village of his birth was destroyed along with more than four hundred and seventeen others. When Darwish later became well known as a poet, a filmmaker wanted to photograph the place of his childhood. Jewish settlers prevented her, and even threatened her. The filmmaker, who was an Israeli, called the police. She did not want conflict with anyone, she said. She merely wanted to photograph the ruins of the village. 'What ruins are you talking about?' the police asked. 'The region is full of ruins.'

Darwish tries to put words together in poems as though sorting out rubble: at times irate, at times sad. He knows that language,

like land, is inherited, and therefore this inheritance might possibly
not be passed on.

I have seen all I want to see of war
A spring of water
Our forefathers squeezed
From a green stone
Our fathers inherited the water
But they did not give it to us

In 1949, Darwish and his family returned to a changed Palestine.
Israel was another country, modern, enthusiastic, democratic. But
not for Darwish, not for people like him. His status in this country
was 'present-absent alien'. Until 1966, he still had to obtain
authorization to go to another village.

It is not surprising that his poetic life (and his Palestinian-ness)
began very early: in 1950. The school headmaster invited him
to take part in Israel's birthday celebrations. And so Darwish, a
scrawny-looking pupil, stood before the microphone. In the direct
language of an eight-year-old boy, he wrote a poem about an Arab
child crying out to a Jewish one: 'You have a house, while I have
none. You have celebration, while I have none. Why can't we play
together?'

The next day Darwish was summoned by the Israeli military
governor. The short biographical sketch in the foreword to the
English translation of his collected poems, *The Adam of Two Edens*
(Syracuse University Press, 2000), tells how the governor scolded
him and mocked his Arabic. The boy went home, shaken. 'I wept
bitterly... unable to understand why a poem could so upset the
military governor.' From then on, he was often imprisoned for the
same reasons: reading poetry or travelling without a permit. Some

years later he wrote his *Ruba'iyat:* 'I have seen all I want to see of prison.'

He has certainly seen a lot: jail, death, exile. He keeps on moving: to Moscow, Cairo, Beirut, Paris, never knowing if he can return home. It is not surprising that he compared his own village, Berweh, with a native American village called Naconchtanke, feeling like someone whose birthplace has been wrenched away. The transformation of Palestine into Israel demanded mass forced displacement. As Moshe Dayan, the champion of that Israeli war said to *Ha'Aretz* newspaper on April 4, 1969: 'We came to this country which was already populated by Arabs...Jewish villages were built in the place of Arab villages...There is not one place built in this country that did not have a former Arab population.'

Dayan said this (and he was honest) because his was talking to a generation of Israelis who do not know the past. And yet war rages unceasingly in this country because the future is the past. Zionism is nationalism rooted in memory. While people in America, France, India and Indonesia built a nation through forgetting primordial ties, in Israel it is precisely those primordial ties that define: Jewishness. Palestinian nationalism is also nationalism that remembers; not ancestral religion or ethnicity, but a birthplace that is no more. This is why Darwish entreats:

> *Be memory for me*
> *So I can see what I've lost*

This poem is part of the collection *Eleven Planets in the last Andalusian Sky*, which conveys memories of Arab glory on the Iberian Peninsula in the eighth century. But what links Darwish with Andalusia is not Arab-ness or Muslim-ness, but rather the poems of Frederico Garcia Lorca:

I am Adam of two Edens lost to me twice:
Expel me slowly. Kill me slowly
With Garcia Lorca
Under my olive tree

How simple: scattered ruins in Andalusia, the rubble of Paradise perhaps, with which Darwish does not build a fortress, compact, rigid and frightening. He builds something like Lorca's poetry: nostalgic, intimate, and melancholy, like *Romancero Gitano*, gypsy song that can touch someone before death.

Maybe this is why now Palestine does not mourn alone.

'Darwish' *Tempo* 5 May 2002, CP VI: 201-4

Baku

Samuel Huntington didn't say anything new, even though it was mistaken. When he warned there would be a 'clash of civilizations', behind his assumption lay an older prejudice. And perhaps too, a more ancient obsession.

I'll quote a dialogue from a novel written by a mysterious writer named Kurban Said, a work published in 1937 in Vienna and enthusiastically received. It tells of a young Muslim man of noble birth from Baku who came to Georgia, the country where the family of Nino, the young woman he loved, lived. The host – the 'European' – invited him to camp in the forest. Ali went with him, but that night he said, 'The world of trees perplexes me, your Highness... No, I do not love trees.'

The shadows of the woods oppressed him, and it made him sad to hear the rustling of the branches. 'I love simple things: wind, sand and stones', Ali says. 'The desert is simple like the thrust of a sword. The wood is complicated like the Gordian knot. I lose my way in the woods, your Highness'.

And here a dichotomy is presented: 'the woods' and 'the desert'. In this part of the conversation, Ali Khan does not contradict when his host, a Georgian, says that this is probably the difference between East and West: in the West, man finds the woods 'full of questions'; in the East, 'The desert man has but one face, and knows but one truth, and that truth fulfils him.' From the desert comes the fanatic. From the woods, the creator.

This contrast is the start of the 'clash' of Huntington's nightmare. Reading *Ali und Nino*, one could wrongly surmise that the 'clash'

will be averted in this love story. The main character, the 'I' or Ali
Khan, falls in love with a young classmate, a Christian girl from
Georgia. Ali comes from a Persian aristocratic family that lives in
a huge house full of servants and carpets. He is clever at school,
but also a boy who in his own way makes fun of the Russian
teachers who instruct him in the town of Baku. He succeeds in
graduating from school, maintains his love for Nino, the daughter
of a Georgian prince, and intends to marry her.

If *Ali und Nino* is not a Romeo and Juliet, this is because it
is set in the period just before World War I, in a place perfect
for such a story: in Baku on the coast of the Caspian Sea, where
Georgia, Armenia and Azerbaizjan meet, in a territory under the
Russian Empire, brushing borders with Persia. And thus Ali wins
the hand of Nino. Certainly there are religious and racial obstacles
obstructing them. In the beginning, Prince Kipiani refuses Ali's
request. But all is overcome without blood and iron. An old friend
of Ali's, an Armenian named Melik Nacharayan, comes to help.
Through negotiation, Nacharayan succeeds in convincing the
Kipiani family to give their blessing to the marriage.

Nevertheless, *Ali und Nino* is not a story that welcomes the birth
of hybridization. Rather, the novel is fascinated with difference,
about the 'Asiatic' world that is thickly demarcated from 'Europe'.
And even difference becomes contrast. 'The desert' is not merely
different from 'the woods', but in opposition to it.

Everything becomes fixed. This is why, even though it was
written in the first person, the 'I' seems like a beautiful doll
displayed in an antique shop, among the carpets, the old city,
the Tehran harem, the traditional songs, and the Syi'ah rituals in
the month of Muharram. Reading this 275-page thick novel, I
encountered a neat prose structure, beautiful, yet I did not find
within it something usually present in moving love stories: an
interior.

The novel was published in German, at a time when in Austria the arts were flourishing in the climate just before the war, and evidently it was well received. Then war broke out, and the once popular work was forgotten until finally, among the ruins in Berlin, a translator found it in a second hand book shop. In 1971 the English version was published. In 2000 it appeared again, published by Anchor Books, with an epilogue by the novelist Paul Theroux.

Just like thirty years earlier, Theroux, who once wrote a review of *Ali and Nino*, praised it, which seems rather odd to me. He called it 'a bravura display of passionate ethnography', and he is right. But he doesn't consider that the novel is thus fine, but boring.

At the end of the story, Ali Khan dies while defending Baku from the occupation by the Russian Red Army. But actually, he is already long dead. He is there merely to represent 'Asia' for us; he is an 'I' without any pulsating soul. From the outset he has clumped himself into a category: at school, Ali tells his teacher that he 'rather likes Asia' and that he does not want to cross to 'Europe'. He falls in love with Nino, but doesn't seem depressed facing the world of this Christian girl from Georgia. He refuses to try to enjoy the woods. We know from the start what is driving him. And even when he kills Nacharayan, the person who helped him, merely because he heard that Nacharayan was going abduct Nino, Ali is presented as a someone without a smidgen of confusion, regret, or sadness. To this 'Easterner', to kill is like a cultural imperative. And when he bites the Armenian's neck, he does not forget to drive his identity home: 'Yes, Nacharayan, that's how we fight in Asia.... with the grip of the grey wolf.'

And that is how Ali Khan dies: frozen on the border of culture. Everything else is a historical event roaring outside of him – which actually we already know from history books. But I understand why *Ali and Nino* gripped Europeans in the 1930s, when the

Nazis were starting to show their colors. They were readers used to imagining the 'Asiatic' as a separate category of humanity; wild, savage, interesting and thus sexual in nature: inhabitants of an exotic space. This novel serves up the 'other' as something attractive, but also amusing, frightening, 'not-for-us'.

And who, in fact, was the author Kurban Said, and why did he offer the 'Asiatic' not as an interior, but rather as a panorama? Theroux once thought that 'Kurban Said' was a Tartar who died in Italy in 1942. But then it transpired that it is the pen-name of two people: Elfriede Ehrenfels, an Austrian aristocrat, and Lev Nussimbaum, a Jew born in Baku and later raised in Berlin, who converted to Islam in his youth and took the name Essad Bey. The former came from the Old Europe. The latter was a wanderer. Both of them wanted Ali Khan 'to be understood', and therefore he was not allowed to emerge untamed from his stall.

But maybe this was not their fault. From Aristotle to zookeepers, (and Samuel Huntington), humanity seems to have an obsession with two things in mutual opposition: difference and categories. Categories neatly sweep up difference: difference should free us from categories. Yet, in the name of difference, categories are often imposed, like fortresses in war, and we deny what cannot be identified. Then we live with strange words like 'reptile' and 'Asiatic'.

Every 'civilization' ends up as something rigid once people succeed in wiping out whatever is odd outside the castle. And so the clash of civilizations is not a dispute between civilizations, but rather violence within a territory wanting to be marked off as 'a civilization'. Like prison.

'Baku' *Tempo*, 3 February 2002, CP VI: 151-5

Icarus, One Day

One day, Icarus, imprisoned on the isle of Crete, wanted to escape by air, flying. His father Daedalus, an inventor, made him some wings. Eagle feathers were gathered and placed carefully, until at last there was a huge pair of wings attached to the boy's body with wax. He flew. But he flew too high, near the sun. The heat of the sun melted the wax, the wings came off, and Icarus fell to the earth, to the Aegean Sea. He drowned.

Greek mythology doesn't mention what happened when he splashed into the waves. But in 1555, Brueghel the Elder painted this scene. In his *Landscape with the Fall of Icarus*, this famous 16ᵗʰ century Flemish artist did not portray a tragic accident or a dramatic event. Precisely the opposite.

On his canvas we see a pastoral scene, light and full of color. It is a spring morning. At the front, a farmer is plowing the fields. A shepherd, leaning on his stick, is gazing up at the clear sky. His dog sits patiently, guarding a few dozen sheep that are happily grazing. A little to the right, we see the back of someone sitting facing the bay, perhaps looking at the ship sailing on the calm, green Aegean sea. Near that ship, on the practically smooth surface, a pair of legs can be seen thrashing in the water – a pair of thighs and calves showing white for an instant before drowning. This is the body of the unfortunate Icarus.

In his *Landscape with the Fall of Icarus,* normal life seems unperturbed by the fate of someone in the midst of being stricken down, dragged by Death. And what message did that canvas intend, actually? That what occurred was not a tragedy, but rather something funny, like a clown slipping on a banana skin? Doesn't that boy's life have worth, no matter what his error? The question nags. Two poets viewed Brueghel's work hanging in an art museum in Brussels and were inspired to write poems. From William Carlos we have a few telegram-like short lines, like a factual picture presented without emotion. The whole poem signals a mood of indifference – and we sense an implicit accusation of a tragedy left to occur meaninglessly.

W.H. Auden's poem, *Musée des Beaux Arts,* uses longer sentences, and more explicit protest:

> *...the plowman may*
> *Have heard the splash, the forsaken cry,*
> *But for him it was not an important failure; ...*

> *...the expensive delicate ship that must have seen*
> *Something amazing, a boy falling out of the sky,*
> *Had somewhere to get to and sailed calmly on.*

Brueghel's painting is, in the end, an example of what Auden propounds about suffering. Suffering, his poem says, '... takes place/While someone else is eating or opening a window or just walking dully/along'. The children are 'skating on a pond' while 'the dreadful martyrdom must run its course'.

But does Brueghel, as Auden surmises, really condemn this indifference? Or does he rather celebrate it? If one examines his painting, it portrays a landscape that appears to be seen from above, from the sky. Maybe to someone living in the 16th century, there was nothing untoward about this panorama. People then lived with religion as an integral part of discourse, and murder took place because of this discourse: after 1550, war in the name of faith broke out all over Europe between Catholics and Protestants. In times like these, people would say that 'the heavens' viewed Icarus's fate as no extraordinary incident. When one talks only of heaven and eternity, when all forms and events in the world are seen only as from the eternal throne on high, what is the meaning of human suffering? Of what importance, disasters and death?

Perhaps to Brueghel, Icarus's misfortune – the story of a boy who flies and doesn't make it – is part of daily life: there are farmers working and ships trading, but there are also people doing their best, yet making a mess of things. Or perhaps Icarus is an example of the vanity of humans who are proud and forget caution. So when he falls headfirst and dies, so what? Probably, to someone in the 16th century, life was better lived by accepting existing pleasures, like the shepherd grateful for the clear spring weather. Or better if pursued with honest labor, by plowing the fields and crossing the seas. Why didn't Icarus follow the hardworking plowman, the patient shepherd, or the prosperous merchant on the ship? Why did he have to go against human nature as determined, namely, that man is not a bird?

We in the 21st century can surely say that human nature cannot be formulated as simply as that. Once we feel we have succeeded in formulating 'human nature', we perhaps obliterate possibilities for people to differ – so we can call all those who differ from it, 'pigs' or 'idiots', and wipe them out.

Or we will be deceived: in formulating 'nature' or 'essence', we do not foresee a time that people will break through that formulation. Icarus did fail, but suppose there had never been anyone who dared to attempt to fly, to free himself, to be 'odd', then the world would still be like the 16th century. There would have been no Wright Brothers – the two Americans who in 1903 managed with their machine to fly for ten minutes in a North Carolina field – who thus opened the way for humans to travel like birds, or more than birds, until even space was no longer daunting.

The question has crossed my mind about what would have happened had Icarus, that mythological figure, succeeded. Probably the panorama on Brueghel's canvas would be different: everyone on the sea and in the fields would look worried. For a human who could conquer nature had arrived; who began by opposing the limits of his own body. Whoever succeeded in doing this would have power over other things. He would see himself as sovereign, full of power – humanism's image of man.

Humanism's image is indeed enticing: humans become free subjects who can determine themselves as centers of measurement of all things. But then people realize: once humans place themselves as autonomous subjects, at the same time they place what is outside of themselves as non-autonomous subjects. The 'here' conquers the 'there'. The 'there' is not just sky, fields and sea. The tillers and sailors in turn get in its clutches; or anyone considered unfit to be 'human'.

This is what happened even before the discovery of airplanes and the success of Daedalus-imitator inventors. The image of the powerful and autonomous human being, which in Europe was embodied by members of the middle class, developed not only alongside the birth of awe-inspiring civilization, but also alongside the expansion of territory and colonialism. Humans as conquerors of the ends of the earth, eventually view the creatures they conquer there as 'sub-human'. This means they have to be exterminated, or oppressed, or, in the words of Franz Fanon, a theoretician on anti-colonialism in Algeria, 'invited to become human'. Meaning the 'there' has to accommodate to the basic type of the 'here', namely the 'Western bourgeois' type.

And then colonialism collapsed. Criticism of humanism emerged from all corners. Sometimes exaggerated. For people can still demonstrate that the idea of humans as free and autonomous subjects is also what led people to oppose colonialism. To oppose, because people in Asia, Africa and Latin America no longer believed that they were a part of the 'sub-human' 'there', creatures whose 'natures' were 'powerless'. They would choose successful Icarus as a symbol. They too wanted to fly free from prison, to break out of 'character', to storm destiny.

There are, indeed, those worried about arrogance. There are religious people who now attack humanism, just as people in former times attacked Icarus as a symbol of overreaching pride, which the ancient Greeks called *hubris*. The Christian Right even equates 'humanism' with 'Titanism', a view that stamps humans with God-like omnipotence. Like fundamentalists of other religions, they want it to be God who determines the order of life on earth.

But isn't this, too, a form of anthropocentric arrogance: furnished with words and rules, God still brought among mankind as model and measure? Of course that measure is never going to fit. God is greater than words and rules, texts and laws...We recall the wings of Icarus who tried to reach the sun; he's not going to make it...

'Pada Suatu Hari, Ikarus' *Tempo* 5 January 2003, CP VI: 341-6

Baucau

In a corner of the empty Baucau coast, there stands a Portuguese-era building, filthy and extravagant. A few years ago, this thick-walled Mediterranean-style construction was turned into a rice-mill. Not far away, rather high up between coconut palms and tamarind trees, stands a tin building painted red, which used to be a government food-warehouse. All around are shacks. 'There used to be a fishermen's co-operative here', a middle-aged woman said, speaking Indonesian, her back to the stunning blue sea, 'but now it's closed, because of the war.'

Portuguese remains, Indonesian remains, total closure and futility. War, to the people of Timor Loro-Sa'e, seems to be the word to describe whatever destroyed their lives. This includes the scorched earth and murder by the militia mobilized – or at least protected – by the Indonesian army two years ago: something not war precisely, but rather one-sided brutality. The little town of Baucau was generally unharmed. The warehouse is one example of that. But as soon as one leaves Baucau in the direction of Dili, in Manatutu, all along the road there are only ruins of roofless buildings with blackened walls.

All this destruction, what was it for, exactly? I, as an Indonesian visiting in August 2001, could only look with sadness, shame, and some surprise: finally, one must conclude that the walls of those burnt out houses over in East Timor are a row of astonishing monuments left behind by Indonesia – a monument to something brutal in Indonesia's history.

Whoever that general was who ordered Operation 'Take-Back', probably wanted to demonstrate that it was the Indonesian government that had built this territory, and therefore, if East Timor wanted to free itself from Indonesia, the results of this development had to be taken back. The East Timorese must not be allowed to own them. Or there was another reason: with this rampant destruction, those generals probably wanted to leave behind a completely barren ground zero for the independent East Timorese government.

How utterly stupid: how dumb and uncivilized. No one, it seems, remembered that Great Britain let India go (the English Queen's 'jewel in the crown'), but did not want to cut ties with its ex-colony. The United States let the Philippines go while maintaining close ties. Decolonization took place, but relationships were strong. Goods, ideas, labor, services – their traffic was smooth. Indeed, this is what seems to happen in history: political power comes and goes, but trade and the traffic of culture endure. And so if East Timor had not been devastated, Indonesia would have gained a lot: not only its good name, but also a territory for export, a neighboring country with which it could maintain cultural exchange, a relationship undistorted by trauma. The buildings on the empty Baucau coast would be alive, so too the fishermen's co-operative and the coastal village, and Indonesian goods would find ready buyers.

But none of this happened. Whoever that Indonesian army general was who gave the scorched earth order was a person of shortsightedness; as short, rigid and blunt as the barrel of his pistol. He probably thought he was carrying out a patriotic duty; but we know now that the result was the condemnation of Indonesia in no uncertain measure. Eventually we have to realize that this pistol-thinking is wrong because it always considers itself superior – all because such thinking is never challenged by free debate. If there were free debate, there would not be another monument to stupidity: violence as a commodity.

The Indonesian occupation of East Timor is a story of violence as commodity. Once violence is decided upon as a money-earning enterprise, then even war and military operations become 'projects', a bureaucratic term meaning there will be big budgets and opportunities for graft. The commodification of violence eventually propagates cynicism, which spreads to the soldiers. Once the generals at the top get rich through 'projects', then the army at the bottom tries to get rich through selling explosives, even weapons, to the enemy. In Dili I heard another story: a priest was offered photos of torture carried out by Indonesian forces on East Timorese. It appears that the Indonesian forces made the photos themselves, for trade...

In Baucau and all over Timor Loro Sa'e, these days people are celebrating liberty. In Indonesia these days, people are also trying to keep liberty moving forward. Liberty: a precondition for questioning, so that the brutality cannot return.

'Baucau' *Tempo* 9 September 2001, CP VI: 75-7

Osama

Osama bin Laden – born in Riyadh around 1975, university graduate with computer expertise, business millionaire many-times-over, a Saudi who could have lived close to the royal family – ended up choosing, when he was around forty, to live in the cold caves of Afghanistan. He leads a terrorist movement that is widespread and secret. Now he is Enemy Number One in the 'first war of the twenty-first century'. Clearly, he is someone with something extraordinary about him. Faith? Islam? Anger?

I am not the one to answer this. But maybe all three are there in Osama's history. Faith is something that can be only partially explained, but we read of how people who led an extravagant youth find their place in Islam.

But that faith and Islam did not grow in isolation. Something big has been going on since the end of the last century: when religion became a sign of group identity, a kind of uniform, with religion a symbol giving communal meaning.

At that time, small and large-scale migrations became more numerous, more widespread, and almost everywhere people were meeting others who were not family, not of the same town. Suddenly difference was experienced directly. What was different became 'odd', 'unusual'. The twentieth century is the century of unease and surprise.

To Muslims, who for the most part live in poor countries and leave to seek lives in America, Europe, Australia and Japan – this narrative of unease and surprise is also a narrative about open opportunities and painful defeats. Taking off at the airport, buying jam or a jumbo jet, enjoying the piano or a porno film, we of the Third World know: those 'non-Muslim' countries have not only been wealthier for centuries, they also (to use Marx's words about the bourgeoisie) create a world after their own image. Sometimes through natural attraction, sometimes with 'blood and iron', and sometimes through buying-and-selling. And as for us, the others? We keep on asking ourselves: how can this be? How can this be opposed, contested, ended?

And then we make all kinds of grand narratives in answer. Nationalism. Capitalism. Socialism.... And we try all kinds of forms as therapy: parliamentary democracies, authoritarian bureaucratic regimes, traditional monarchies, untraditional monarchies, proletarian dictatorships, whatever dictatorships. None can assuage the sense of 'defeat' that has gone on for years.

In the Arab world, more than in other Muslim lands, this failure is almost total bitterness. Israel arose, with 'Western' assistance (especially from the United States), and the Palestinians were largely pushed out. And so 'Jews' come face to face with 'Arabs'. In this fragile situation, 'Arab' identity became a grand canopy for millions of people there, although we quickly understood that 'Arab nationalism' was an ideal heated by a distant flame. Both Baath and Nasser-type nationalism shone for a few decades, inspiring Qadhafi and who knows whom else, but the end result was authoritarian power. The further from the flame, the greater the frustration. People are still in the grip of poverty, social instability and subjugation. Palestine remains dark.

Anger rises. When the war against Israel ended only in defeat; when the wealth brought by the 'oil-economy' turned out to be insufficient to heal wounds, then that anger became even stronger, and terror became more frequently the pattern of acts of liberation. Islam as such was not itself the actor in this violence. Those carrying the banner of Islam like Hamas and Al-Qaedah did not start the path of terror Palestinians chose, but rather George Habbas, a Christian, and Arafat, a Muslim, who did not choose to translate that conflict with the language of religion. It was only in the early 1970s that Islam came with violence – when anger could find no outlet, and when people longed for a different grand narrative.

With wide-reaching cultural roots, with a history that offers a sense of pride, it is understandable that 'Islam' waves at the place where the Ka'bah stands. Islam is considered to be capable of solving all life's problems, personal or social: an 'ideology', but also a call that can unite people from Kundhus to Kudus, from Amman to Ambon.

Osama bin Laden is a Middle Eastern phenomenon that repeats, yet also changes: the Islamization of regional conflict. In this transformation, the limited becomes expansive, the profane becomes sacred, the 'worldly' becomes 'holy'. This is the case with the war against America, which has only over the past thirty years, since the Iranian revolution, been termed the "*Great Satan*". In this process, 'the West' becomes synonymous with 'Christian' (forgetting that 'Western' civilization has been influenced by Islam) and 'Israel' becomes 'Jewish' (forgetting that there are Jewish religious groups that oppose the establishment of the state of Israel).

This sacralization carries its own assumptions and consequences. Various examples of extraordinary sacrifice occur: asceticism in caves; death in America; dying in Afghanistan; imprisonment in Egypt. But sacralization can also bring action that is absolute: without any sense of responsibility to the law within human collectivity which develops to become civilization. God and purpose justify all means.

The problem then, is exactly how we see life in this world: an angry path to heaven? Or a blessing, although forever blemished?

'Usamah' *Tempo* 9 December 2001, CP VI: 119-22

Menopause

I f revolution is no dinner party, then democracy is no rice-wine
stall.

This aphorism might not be particularly novel, but
sometimes we need to be reminded that democracy – no matter
how attractive its ideals may be – is one pile of responsibilities.
This system (or process?) is not a place where people can debate
passionately, chat, drink, play chess, be sore losers or happy winners
just as long as they pay. When a number of people are together in
one place and want to strive for life without oppression, they will
soon discover that in a democracy politics is an abstruse path. It
can even sometimes be rather shameful, annoying, and boring.

'Democracy', Jean Baudrillard said, 'is the menopause of
Western society, the Grand Climacteric of the body social'. He
wrote this in a 1987 publication, only two years before the entire
Eastern Europe chose such 'menopause' as their preference, after
the communist parties were paralyzed. I don't know whether
Baudrillard merely wanted to sound controversial, or whether
his utterance displays the general ennui of European intellectuals
towards a system that has made their politics less enthralling than
a cricket match. But if democracy is menopause, what about other
systems? 'Fascism', Baudrillard said, 'is [Western society's] middle-
aged lust.'

Analogies like this can be misleading, particularly when we
imagine that middle-aged lust can also be the lust of one with
experience; something more controlled and sustained. In other
words: fascism can be more infatuating, especially when democracy

is no longer something stirring. And in our imagination Mussolini appears on a balcony in Rome: bald and brawny, like a *lingga-yoni*, and bellowing. In the streets his followers are lined up, thousands of militant people, uniformed wild paramilitary yelling enmity to anyone not 'one of us'. As though life is passion at the full, muscled masculinity, and courage to live dangerously, *vivere pericoloso*. As though war is definitely a virtue. 'It matters little who wins', Il Duce said (as found in his son-in-law's diary), 'To make a people great it is necessary to send them to battle even if you have to kick them in the pants.' A month later, in 1940, he brought Italy into combat with the Allies.

And we know what fascist politics brought about: a series of incessant ravaging. Politics such as this is indeed seductive – whether we are fascists or not. For many things become clear, straight, non-negotiable. Like battle: when two foes face each other with drawn bayonets, the settling is not through debate and considerations of truth, but rather through purity of will and deed. And often the straight, clear and pure is heard as strong, and strangely, also 'moral'.

But politics in a democracy can often precisely not be straight, clear or pure. Its workings seem never to climax: talk, talk, talk, between 'this side here' and 'that side there'. And if democracy is a pile of responsibilities, then the heaviest is the inevitability of compromise. Even with those who most disgust us. There is indeed something embarrassing, something shameful, and something not quite 'moral'.

In Indonesia, this kind of process has come to be seen as something negative – and maybe this is why democracy has to experience a 'sick' phase. For years people lived with politics hungry for repeated climaxes. Between 1958 and 1965, under Sukarno, politics united with the cry 'revolution', devouring and crushing enemies. 'Confrontation' with Malaysia was a good thing.

Between 1965 and 1998, under Soeharto, politics united with violence (murder, too) and corruption. Decisions were made after 'that side there', the contestant, had been threatened, or destroyed. Or bribed. Not only was integrity destroyed, but also the moral remnants in life were damaged. Values proffered to be acceptable to 'that side there' with dignity intact – something universal – did not apply. Basically: politics of subjugation.

Can a country go on living with politics like this? When compromise is considered to be giving in, and giving in is considered to be not only a loss of self-esteem, but also the extinction of living space, then fascism will become a communal style, consciously or not. In fascism, 'here' is essentially opposed to 'there'.

Democracy and negotiation, on the contrary, rely on a process where such essentialism does not operate. When two (or more) sides discuss and compete, they not only need to put forth interests represented by 'here', they also put forth a more universal discourse, and therefore this can be accepted by 'there'. And with this, the 'here' side makes its own experience something universal. This process, as Ernesto Laclau said, represents 'a vehicle for universalization'.

And we know that universalization is also a path towards liberation – for there are no more politics of subjugation, there will be no more Master oppressing Slave, no-one shackled as a slave, no one enslaving. Here democracy does not appear as a menopause. Nor as a passionate carnal process. It is an alternative, bland perhaps, but inevitable – when we cannot completely and endlessly love 'that there', but also cannot completely and endlessly continue fighting. When we achieve awareness of limits, right before us.

'Menopause' *Tempo* 28 January 2001, CP V: 615-8

Athena

In the beginning, politics is a common space. Our understanding about that common space is what determines whether politics is eventually merely a continuation of attempts to uphold and affirm rights and truth, or actually a process of forgiveness.

A boy kills his mother. He is avenging the death of his father, because it was his mother who did that evil deed. The boy then goes to a city, and he is hunted. In the Greek tragedy written by Aeschylus in 458 BCE, in the last part of the *Oresteia* trilogy the fate of this boy must be decided. What arises is a dilemma. The three Furies come and threaten to wreak revenge because what is true and just must be upheld. Otherwise evil will recur, and the world will collapse. But, if this is carried out and the boy, Orestes, is killed, when will the cycle of revenge cease? And won't the city, that communal space, also collapse?

This is the question Athena faces, the goddess-protector of the city who comes because the troubled Orestes summons her. But it is not easy to be the judge. There are twelve citizens whose opinions are solicited, but the three Furies have their own role.

We stand avengers at his side,
Decreeing. Thou hast wronged the dead:
We are doom's witnesses to thee.
The price of blood, his hands have shed,
We wring from him; in life, in death,
Hard at his side are we!

When the just insist forcefully that communal life must be guaranteed free of tyranny, they shout in the name of the damned. The words of the Furies in this drama are spoken repetitively 'over the victim's head'. The role of victim is one that in the past used to have meaning for the future. But what is the meaning of a future when the city, a communal space, is built from bitterness and revenge?

In Aeschylus's drama, Athena decides to save the city rather than follow justice – in this case because justice means revenge. The Furies lament: Athena has deposed Justice, while the supporters of Justice should know that they can not be swayed by the temptation of the world's wellbeing. Life will no longer be secure once compromise is made as easily as that.

But Athena considers that the Furies are serving only the 'form' of justice, and not its 'act'. Donald W. Shriver Jr, the editor of *An Ethic for Enemies*, supports Athena's argument by showing that revenge must submit to legislation and institutions. Revenge is constrained; and the stand of regarding this pure principle as something sacred moves to the stand of considering the commonality of life as sacred.

Revenge and anger even turn into civilization, when the one demanding justice is placed beneath Aeropagus: in other words, beneath the order of law. What is not faced here though, is what happens when Athena is not acknowledged as the protector of the city, and the myth about something nobler no longer operates in the community.

Here, perhaps, we need to look at forgiveness as an alternative. Eventually, once politics is a movement and an act to run a communal space, politics will be encouraged to introduce this element of forgiveness. Forgiveness is a way to stop the killing, when killing and violence destroy existing structures. But we all know how far from easy this attitude is.

The history of Indonesia is a wounded history. In a traumatic history, the problem about which should be prioritized – truth or peace – cannot be answered quickly.

Every answer will contain a sense of bitterness – and memories – for every one of us. Where will the story of violence and killing start? From the Darul Islam guerrillas from the late 1940s to the 1960s? From the war that defeated the PRRI-Permesta rebellion in 1958? From the slaughter of the people accused as communist in 1965-1966? Or when the army shot a group of protesters dead in Tanjungpriok in the 1980s? Or in East Timor? Aceh? Papua?

Like it or not, pasts are always attributed limits. Like it or not, every limit to these pasts will be determined by what we are going to use all of this for. If, eventually, reconciliation or a state of mutual kindness is more important, then those limits perhaps cannot be left stuck in one time and place. The terror of tyranny in Indonesia's history is varied, with actors from various quarters, and its sufferers are also various. The only thing that unites them is the face of the victim in pain and suffering – and the idea that every victim is created equal.

To me, the middle path Athena takes is the more pragmatic one to save an existing city – a conservative stance. To me, what is important is not a city that is safe and secure. What is important is a communal space that is safe and secure where the weakest – those who will thus never become Furies – are not muzzled.

'Athena' *Tempo* 27 February 2000, CP V: 437-9

Mirror

Alaa Hamid wrote a poem:

They ordered my thoughts to be captured,
Stuffed them in a sack,
And threw them on the back of a donkey.
They opened it in court
And it was empty
They asked why.
Because the donkey got hungry and ate them.

What were Alaa Hamid's thoughts?

Clearly, he was punished for them. According to the *Economist* of 25 January 1992, this rather obscure Egyptian writer was sentenced in Cairo to eight years' imprisonment. 'My only fault', this 53-year-old tax inspector said, 'was to allow myself to think.'

In his small room, in his spare time, he had written a novel. But the novel, *A Distance in a Man's Mind*, was ill fated. It told the story of an imaginary journey of a man some time in the future. He meets the prophets from the past and challenges them, in a teasing and sometimes 'cheeky' way. At the end of the story, a court sentences the accused, who attempted to challenge religious law with philosophical argument, to death.

'My mistake was that I did not understand the extent of liberty in Egypt', Hamid said. 'It is like this', he added, drawing a tiny circle with his finger.

Yet this was not his only mistake. He was most probably not aware of the tendency more and more prevalent in Islamic countries these days, namely the tendency towards what Mohammed Arkoun has called ' logocentrism' in the thinking of the *ulama* and jurists: that is, regarding spiritually revealed truth as something that can be grasped and controlled with grammatical analysis and through the meaning of words in texts. However, Arkoun says, even language exists within a historical context. Logocentrism regards evaluation as something fixed, without alternatives. A structuralist or post-structuralist approach does not.

At the same time, Arkoun also sees that the imaginative side of Muslim life is almost extinct. It is something evident in 'folk' traditions, in culture that springs from its place of origin; a social imagination that has always been spontaneous and which allows for authentic artistic expression in Muslim societies. All this is threatened. 'The modernist movement', the increased formalization of worship, together with the process of urbanization, have all wiped out that rich aspect of Muslim life.

And we are faced with the push towards uniformity in the way we relate to God.

It turns out that this it is not only Alaa Hamid who had to face this. The chief judge who sentenced Hamid was Said Ashmawy. He is regarded as an expert on Islamic law, and has written a number of books. However, last January the *ulama* from Alazhar confiscated five of his books at the International Book Fair in Cairo. Ironic indeed.

But Ashmawy was lucky: his ideas may not be in keeping with the ideas of the *ulama*, but his criticism of ideas about an 'Islamic state' pleases the Egyptian government. In the end, President Mubarak ordered that Ashmawy's books be returned to circulation.

So who, then, decides what is error and what is not? The *ulama*, the president, the judges, the armed forces, the ones who owns the prisons? And from where and whom do they get this right? And it is possible that this right can be legally challenged?

Such questions are, of course, expressions of 'liberal' thought –
a stigma cursed in the Third World. Some say that 'liberal' thought
is not just ideas. It is also a statement of the pragmatic need of a
group of religious minorities. 'Liberal' thought, which underlines
press freedom, freedom of artistic expression, rule of law, the
dignity of the individual and so forth, is basically not a reflection
of the needs of the majority of the lower class.

In other words, the basis is weak. Particularly in the Middle
East, as Leonard Binder points out in *Islamic Liberalism* (1988),
where the existing culture is heavily influenced by the ongoing
need to communicate with the illiterate and the poor, who don't
care who does or does not have the right to forbid people to read
books.

But the problem is perhaps not only one of the importance
of writing and reading books. Religion, truth, matters to do with
God and man, and matters that do not have to be always related
to forms and needs. 'Truth is like a God-given mirror that is now
broken', said Mohsen Makhmalbaf, the well-known Iranian film
director, as quoted in the *Kompas* newspaper. Man picks up the
pieces, and each person then sees his reflection in one of the pieces
and thinks that he has seen truth. The real difficulty is later, if he
uses that piece of glass to stab someone who holds a different piece.

'Kaca' *Tempo* 1 February 1992, CP IV: 259-61

Khomeini

When an elephant dies it leaves behind its ivory. Khomeini died leaving behind him nothing as bright as ivory: just a block of land, an unfurnished house, a poem.

What is the definition of a great person? Great people are those who are able to keep the space of their souls clear when threatened on all sides by the pressure of material things, and they achieve this because they seek a more meaningful freedom. Great people are those who work for the cause of eternity as though each day will be their last, and work for the world as though they will live forever – but who lack any personal greed.

No matter how differently Khomeini saw things from Gandhi or Mao, the three all had one thing in common: to them the ideal of changing the world was something of the utmost importance, completely engrossing, so that possessions and wealth were seen only as obstructions. 'Revolution is not a dinner party.'

Ordinary people, those who do not measure with the great, are not able to practice such strict asceticism. They are not able to take on the full burden of a specific idea. They may wish to change the world – but how far, and for how long? For most people, the effort of changing the world has to be let go at some stage. For people like Khomeini, Mao or Gandhi, the effort is never-ending: one merely sometimes slackens in one's resolve.

Therefore most people are impressed, moved, awestruck and bowled over when they enter the shadow of a great person. They themselves lack the mental stamina, they wonder where such incredible power comes from, and then they recognize that they need an imposing figure like this to follow. Often they submit totally and make the leap of faith. Often, too, they find real peace in this shelter.

Then one day the idea will come to them: 'We must follow his example.' And the teachings of the great person will be collected together and disseminated.

At a time of deep crisis, it is common for a leader to emerge whom people expect to be complete: not only a political leader or social manager, but also a type of moral guiding light.

There are countries in this world that are rocked by revolution – or by the speed of their own sudden birth. The past is shaved off from the present and the future, but the break is a fragile one. In countries like these, no fixed points of measure remain. Everything is in flux. People are confused, following this and that, trying to find a model for attitude and behavior. It is not surprising that in such a situation, the idea of 'complete leadership' finds quick acceptance. The move to 'follow the leader' soon becomes a movement for the teaching of good behavior, the mobilization of sermonizing and upgrading courses in political ideology, like the P-4 *Pancasila* courses in Indonesia.

Consciously or not, in this way we form the basis of our legitimation: we only accept the leaders – those at the top level of power – once they have demonstrated some expression of moral purity. In the 1950s Bung Hatta expressed his hope for 'honest and honorable leaders'. How good this would be. But in just a few decades we in these unstable countries have aged with disappointment and a little more wisdom. We know now that legitimation that relies on morality is an inconclusive legitimation. It is unsatisfactory, and can even bring with it its own confusion.

The morality of a leader can indeed be powerful – as an example. But perhaps this is all. For not everyone in Iran can be like Khomeini, just as not every Chinese is a Mao or every Indian a Gandhi. The majority of people, wherever they may be, are not great – honest, honorable and of moral strength.

So when a great person dies and leaves behind a country that is bereft, then we are aware of the extent of our laziness: we have not prepared a system that as far as is possible is able to handle those things termed 'honest', 'honorable' or 'moral'. In short, we have not developed the basis of legitimation from *morality* to become *law*. 'Law', in this sense, whether we like it or not, means law that all voluntarily agree to.

Without this, any existing legitimation is just a sham. Without this, any certainty is entirely dependent on the moral certainty determined from a single viewpoint. And as we are busy talking about the morality of the leader, we may forget that power is not something that, as the Javanese say, is *sepi ing pamrih* – without personal ambition. Power holds within itself its own concerns.

Democracy with its fixed laws is needed because of this. Life with great men like Khomeini is not enough.

'Khomeini' *Tempo* 24 June 1989, CP III: 549-51

The West

The West always makes us disturbed. Almost everyone in the Third World senses, or knows, that 'the West' is an undefined territory, peopled by those who once colonized us, with a power that formerly placed us at their feet, that humiliated us, and that now remains something in which we can see our own reflection. We scrutinize ourselves before this mirror: are we smaller than them? Larger than them?

Larger, said Sanusi Pane half a century ago. Arjuna is a more complete hero than Faust. We are made up of both body and soul. They – those Westerners, epitomized in the human creatures of Goethe's creation – are Faust. They will join forces with the devil, if necessary, for the sake of science. For us, the soul and God are not dead. But for them....

Sanusi Pane was one in a stream of such voices. In India there was Tagore, in Pakistan Muhammad Iqbal, in Egypt Qutub, in Iran Ali Ayaru'ati and so forth. Japan has Kita Ikki and his Yusonsha club – and Africa has Franz Fanon.

Even in the West these ideas have become a cliché. Forty years before the Beatles left on their pilgrimage to the spiritual teachers of India, the character 'A.D.' in a novel by André Malraux departed for 'the East', just like the writer himself. In the last letter in the novel he utters a kind of farewell to Europe, that 'great cemetery where only dead conquerors sleep ... you leave me with only a naked horizon and the mirror of solitude's old master, despair.'

Malraux titled his novel, written in the form of letters, *La Tentation de l'Occident*. The word *'tentation'* means in English both 'temptation' and 'test' or 'trial'. In the East, people are indeed tempted by the West. In the West they are tested. 'This great troubled drama which is beginning, dear friend, is one of the temptations of the West,' writes A.D. to his friend Ling in Malraux's novel.

This is an unfinished process, and will perhaps never come to an end. Every now and then we may carry out a 'week of hate' as in Orwell's novel *1984*. 'The West' is then a sort of ghoul that we can mock. Or we can remain indifferent. We order Swanson ice cream and supersonic F-16As, we order Gucci designer wear and high-tech equipment. But whether we hate or remain indifferent – two very different reactions – in fact we are never sure where we should begin and end in speaking about that thing, 'the West'.

Are we able to distinguish between the west that has produced computers but also novels, striptease but also Mother Teresa, nuclear bombs but also humor? In other words, can we talk about the West as 'one' when the Middle Ages have long given way to a post industrial age, and the concerned 1960s have given way to the cautious 1980s?

It is not only Europe that changes. The West may indeed reflect us, in an unexpected way as a sudden surprise. The way we regard it depends partly on the reflection itself and partly on our own situation.

In his famous fourteenth-century work *Muqaddimah*, Ibnu Khaldun wrote about a 'country of the Franks' in the realm of 'Rome' that was situated to the north of the Mediterranean, ruled over by the kind 'Sanluwis bin Luwis'. He praised this country, especially for its scientific knowledge, particularly philosophy. Ibnu Khaldun does not appear to have known much about the West. To him, the West was not important. But it is exactly in this that Ibnu Khaldun differs from us today. He did not feel inferior, but neither was he overawed. He could praise in passing.

In those times, the test of the West had not yet begun. When the drama began, not a single person could avoid it. In the Third World, we, like Ling in Malraux's novel, can write as he did to his Westerner friend. '*Cher Monsieur*, how can I find myself except in an examination of your race?'

'Barat' *Tempo* 12 May 1984, CP II: 487-9

Imagination, not just Blood and Iron

How is a nation born? Otto von Bismarck, with his terrifying face, huge body and heavy clothes would answer, 'through blood and iron'. The echo resounds near and far.

Germany may have been born *'durch Blut und Eisen'* after the advance of the Prussians who trampled over the land in their jackboots, shooting and killing. War may be the father of all if one believes only the fine words of Heraclitus. True, it has been proven that war can indeed create new boundaries, ignite a new collective pride, confer power or destroy it. War made a loser of Hitler, produced a bombed Hiroshima and an independent Asia.

But if we believe only this, we then believe that history is the product of pistols and sergeants – and that the only things born outside of warfare are bastards. However, although a nation can be born through the trials of blood and iron, it is also essential to hold on to myths and even dreams – no matter if the dreams are a little stupid, or are something called 'imagination'.

Garibaldi might be an example: he would not have succeeded in unifying Italy as a nation had he not had 'imagination'. Yes he fought, of course, but it is as though all the large steps of his life were determined by the whims of a novelist in fantasyland. Even his appearance seemed to be deliberately fashioned to fulfill an ideal: his flowing hair and long moustache were like the marks of a prophet. It is not surprising that when he visited London wearing a red shirt and a Latin American poncho, half a million people, captivated, came to greet him.

This truly bizarre romantic hero did not start his life story in warfare. He began with a message from Giuseppe Mazzini, an Italian nationalist prophet who made the somewhat grandiose prophecy of a nation that would be 'a single people with the same language, who would come together with the same civil and political rights and with the same aims,'

In practice, a nation-state is not as beautiful as this: people who speak the same language can indeed come together, but then one group may exploit another, or civil and political rights can be altered and 'common aims' can become unclear. But Giuseppe Mazzini succeeded in charging Giuseppe Garibaldi with 'imagination'. Italy was at that time fragmented, and the area unified through the language of Dante was divided into parts ruled by Austria, the Bourbons and the Hapsburgs. On 5 May 1860 Garibaldi summoned his resolve, and together with a few volunteers who called themselves 'The Thousand', he left in the dead of night for Sicily.

Once in Sicily, these budding nation-builders were rather shaken to learn that the people on this island did not care much about Italian nationalism, the unification of Italy or other such big talk. They were worried about the salt tax, which they thought was too high, and the price of bread. The economic situation was bad and they thought the Bourbon government was corrupt. But the romantic dream of creating a new nation...?

But the dream did survive. 'The Thousand' and their handsome, dedicated leader were able to attract the people. The farmers came to join them with all kinds of tools and equipment, and the women and children helped build the barricades.

The first fighting broke out in the village of Calarafimi. 'The Thousand', impressive in their red shirts but inexperienced in war, attacked a few times and were forced into retreat.

The romantic spirit remained, however. The dream (even though rather confused) was kept alive, and imagination won in the end.

Once, the story goes, Garibaldi was hit by a stone during a battle. He shouted out that the enemy must have run out of ammunition. The redshirts, hearing this, doubled their resolve and attacked again, with hand-to-hand combat. The enemy was defeated.

Sicily fell. A few months later Italy was unified. As Garibaldi delivered the nation to King Victor Emmanuel near the city of Teano, he cried out *'Saluto il primo Re d'Italia!'* The cry resounded throughout all Europe.

The echo of this cry was heard even in Indonesia: Sukarno read Mazzini and the biography of Garibaldi. After many 17 August Independence Day celebrations, we know that there was blood and iron in the forming and holding together of this republic. We have been tested with civil wars, with unrest, and with killings. The fact that today, thank God, the Republic has not fragmented, shows that the myth of unity, this imagination, this very difficult dream, still holds value. No, not *'durch Blut und Eisen'*.

'Imajinasi, bukan hanya darah dan besi' *Tempo* 20 August 1983,
CP II: 341-3

In Granada

How hard it is for the bright midday sun
To say farewell to Granada!

Federico Garcia Lorca

Not only the midday sun, but also the past finds it difficult to say farewell to Granada. History seems to wrap itself around the cypress trees – or hide underwater, or stick to the red stone of the Alhambra. And behind, standing as an age-old backdrop, are the Sierra Nevada Hills, the 'snow-capped back of the mountain range'.

In the eleventh century it was here that the remnants of the Berbers set down roots, after Islam was expelled from Spain. Things were not then as magnificent as they had been in the ninth century when the Umayyad kingdom was a famous center of culture in Cordoba. Cautiously, however, what remained of this kingdom in Granada regained some of its strength, and there arose a civilization that made Andalusia, to quote one historian, 'an honor to the human race'.

In 1248, Muhammad Ibnu al-Ahmar ordered the construction of the Alhambra, a palace that looks out over two clear rivers flowing below. It is beautiful. However, it is not only the beauty of the castle that thrills us.

Like its life history, the red Alhambra palace (the word comes from *al-qala-hamra* meaning the red fortress) shows great contrasts. From the outside, it gives the impression of an invincible fortress.

Within, however, there are tall columns, fine carving and feminine decoration – giving an impression of almost exaggerated softness.

The Alhambra began as a fort. It was constructed in the ninth century, and the original building, Alcazar (from the Arab *al-qasba* for citadel), was like a Middle Eastern defense post. But this fort changed two hundred years later to become a residence. Fighting subsided and life was easy. Little by little, richly decorated rooms were added within the rough outer walls – rooms that completely indulged the senses. And then came defeat.

'Only God is victorious', spells the beautiful calligraphy carved there. But it was in one of the most exquisite rooms, the Salon de Embajadores, that the last Berber ruler four hundred years ago decided to submit to King Ferdinand and Queen Isabella. Islamic power came to an end. Some years later King Carlos V was looking out from the palace at the view below of the Darro and Genil rivers. As he gazed at the lush garden he said: 'What a terrible fate for the people that lost all of this!'

Was it fate, or carelessness? The usual interpretation is that the historical destruction of the Spanish Islamic kingdom is an example of that well-known pattern: a group starts out strong, invincible and eager to progress, but then, trapped by indulgence in the fruits of progress, it falls.

Before the Alhambra fell, wasn't the power of Islam also under pressure because the rulers in Cordoba and Seville had become indulgent and corrupt? And didn't Andalusia rise again because of the arrival in the twelfth century of Abu Aqua Yusuf, descendant of the follower of Innu Tumor, who called for a more severe, restrained and simple lifestyle?

A hard, simple life of strong faith: such an attitude is attractive in a time of decadence and injustice. It is not surprising that in the history of Islamic thought this attitude recurs from one era to the next. It is based on the lifestyle of early Islam and the followers of the Prophet, and therefore has a moral force and strength of spirit: purity, cleanliness and strength.

But there is also the tendency to judge other lives that do not follow this kind of simplicity and severity, as symptomatic of ruin or straying from the path.

Certainly there is truth in this. But it could also be that history is like the Alhambra palace. There is no single group that can exist continuously with a fortress-culture of constant alert. There are the temptations of the flowers and the trees, of enjoyment and play, there are some things to be found through art and creativity – and there are not always people around as holy as the Prophet.

Alhambra. Cordoba. Seville. Is beauty itself a cursed attribute?

'Di Granada' *Tempo* 13 November 1982, CP II: 195-7

Graham Greene, White Man in Indochina

Two white men were speaking about the people of a country in Indochina. One was worried that the country would fall to a communist government. The other didn't appear to be worried – although he knew that it was going to happen.

'They don't want communism.'

'They want rice, I said, 'they don't want to be shot at. They want one day to be much the same as another. They don't want our white skins around telling them what they want.'

'If Indo-China goes –'

'I know that record. Siam goes. Malaya goes. Indonesia goes. What does 'go' mean? ...'

'They'll be forced to believe what they're told; they won't be allowed to think for themselves.'

'Thoughts are luxury. Do you think the peasant sits and thinks of God and democracy when he gets inside his mud hut at night?'

'You talk as if the whole country were peasant. What about the educated? Are they going to be happy?'

'Oh no', I said, 'we've brought them up in our ideas. We've taught them dangerous games, and that's why we are waiting here, hoping we don't get our throats cut. We deserve to have them cut...'

The Quiet American, 1956

Almost a quarter of a century after Graham Greene wrote this dialogue, much came to pass in Indochina.

Take Samlaut in 1966. Samlaut is a small town east of Battambang, Cambodia. It is located in an isolated forest area, home to the Pors people who were forgotten in the modernization program in Cambodia under Prince Sihanouk.

One day the authorities in Battambang decided to build a sugar factory at Kampong Kol near Samlaut. They brought land from the farmers, but the farmers did not receive adequate compensation. There was dissatisfaction and they revolted.

Of course there was some element of 'subversion' in this revolt. There were Vietnamese communist cadres among the population who had been there since the beginning of the fighting in Indochina. After the Geneva Agreement in 1954, the Party probably told them to remain there. There were about two hundred guns hidden in the forest. The *jacquerie* at Samlaut broke out at the urging of the Vietnamese cadres.

The central government at Phnom Penh acted quickly – but over-reacted. The army was sent in. Police too. These armed forces, without much consideration, shot the troublemakers, killed many people and burned their houses. The people fled to the forest, but they did not forget this injustice and cruelty, and the communists got more supporters.

It is not common for farmers to discuss communism or God, as Graham Greene writes. But is it true that they only want rice? Is it true that 'thought is a luxury' for them? Graham Greene, the white man, like so many other white intellectuals, often feels himself to be the 'defender' of the farmers in Asia – but from an unconsciously patronizing position: the white man thinks that the farmer in his hut will not think about democracy.

Of course not. But the anger of the farmers at Samlaut, without grand discussions of democracy, is anger at the lack of recognition of rights. When the farmers in China come to their capital city and demand human rights, or when the farmers in Cambodia and Vietnam escape as refugees, is it true that all they want is rice?

'They are not buffalo, nor are they cattle', said Sihanouk of his oppressed people. A bit late – but he is nearer the truth than the white man Graham Greene a quarter of a century ago.

'Orang putih Graham Greene di Indocina' *Tempo* 20 January
1979, CP I: 445-7

III
Mythic and Sacred

Mecca

How Mecca has changed. Sitting in a corner of the Haram Mosque as the heat of the day begins to ease, you can feel the shadows of a building that soars to the sky in the south.

And indeed, across from the King Abdul Aziz Gate stands a mega building (officially opened last August), called *Abraj al Bait.* It is a giant over 600 meters high: the tallest clock tower in the world. The four clock faces at its peak are all copies of London's Big Ben, which they dwarf in size: they are each 46 meters in diameter and the hands span 22 meters. And unlike Big Ben, the pinnacle is lit by two million LED bulbs spelling الله أكبر 'Allahu Akbar'. God is great.

The *Abraj al Bait* houses twenty floors of shops and an eight hundred room hotel. Plus apartments. Its garage has parking for one thousand cars. But guests and residents can also arrive by helicopter (there is a helipad large enough for two), because this is a place for those wealthy enough to hire, or own, helicopters. The price for a room for the night at the Mecca Clock Royal Tower is around $700.

There, in an air-conditioned room, the well-heeled can see below – yes, far below – the thousands of pilgrims circling the Ka'bah, like ants circling a piece of chocolate.

I cannot imagine how anyone in that position could write as the Indonesian writer Hamka did in 1938. What is the meaning today of being 'beneath the protection of the Ka'bah?' Nowadays it is as though the simple Ka'bah with its aura beneath the protection of the towering buildings, particularly the luxurious, glittering *Abraj al Bait* with its lights beaming out thirty kilometers, probably even eliminating the moon in the sky.

How Mecca has changed. 'It is the end of Mecca', Irfan al-Alawi the executive director of the Islamic Heritage Research Foundation in London said to *The Guardian*. He spoke disconsolately, as did Sami Angawi, the architect who almost forty years ago established the Hajj Research Center in Jeddah. Mecca is under the control of real estate businessmen and developers. 'They are turning the holy sanctuary into a machine, a city which has no identity, no heritage, no culture and no natural environment. They've even taken away the mountains', *The Guardian* quotes him saying.

Perhaps the 64-year-old Angawi is too romantic. He probably does not want to know about the laws of supply and demand: the number of people making the hajj continues to increase; calculation for the future is urgent. Mecca must be prepared. But Angawi sees that this is the problem. He sees the 'historical layers' of Mecca being bulldozed and turned into parking lots.

He himself, born in Mecca, ended up moving to Jeddah, and lives in a house designed in traditional Hijazi style. When the *Abraj al Bait* was constructed like some super-sized Big Ben, he felt completely defeated. 'We are aping like monkeys', he said. He now prefers living in Cairo.

But can the brakes be put on Mecca's transformation? Capitalism turns a city into a pile of molten metal to be poured into molds any which way. With this proviso: in the case of Mecca, this city has lost its uniqueness not only because of 'the commercialization of the House of God'. Angawi mentions an additional factor unique to Saudi Arabia: Wahabi-ism.

Wahabi-ism, Angawi says, is the force behind the destruction of the remains of the past. He has noted that over the past fifty years, around three hundred historic buildings have been destroyed. The prevailing Wahabi-ism in Saudi Arabia wants to guard against the 'idolatry' of people making pilgrimages to sites associated with the Prophet, regarding His every trace as holy – and therefore to be worshipped.

Saudi Arabia's history records the routine destruction of historic sites. In April 1925, in Medina, the dome of the Al-Baqi' tomb was destroyed. Parts of the famous verse by al-Busiri (1211-1294), which were engraved on the Prophet's tomb as a hymn of praise, were painted over to make them illegible. In Mecca, the tomb of Khadijjah, the Prophet's wife, was demolished. The place where her house stood was turned into public toilets.

There are many other examples, and also protests against the actions of the Wahabi rulers. In early 1926, a 'Hijaz Committee' was established in Indonesia at the residence of K.H. Abdul Wahab Khasbullah in Surabaya, as an expression of the ulamas' concern.

Such world reaction managed to stop the destruction. But now, in the 21st century, Wahabi-ism and capitalism have joined forces, and Mecca is changing.

It is shocking, actually. Writing in 1940, Bung Karno quoted the book by Julius Abdulkarim Germanus, *Allah Akbar, Im Banne des Islams*. He depicted the Wahabis as people who were violently and terrifyingly suspicious of 'modernity'; they even dismantled radio antennae and rejected electricity poles. But these days, as seen in the luxury of *Abraj al Bait*, it is not only electric lights that are acceptable, but the whole transformation of Mecca into something like London & Las Vegas. What is going on?

Maybe Wahabi-ism has not changed, Wiping out traces (abolishing the past), and rejecting 'modernity' (abolishing the future) are both anti-Time. The huge *Abraj al Bait* clock finally merely turns Time into iron hands. Dead things. And to those who consider Time something dead, there is only the formula of religious observance, with no historical process.

But what is the meaning of religious pilgrimage, without treading on traces of history and without viewing what is bitter and amazing of the past?

Probably an instant excursion to glamor.

'Mekkah' *Tempo* 11 November 2012, CP X: 395-8

Leda

– In memory of Putri, aged 16, who committed suicide
after the syariah police in Langsa, Aceh accused her of being
a prostitute

A sudden blow: the great wings beating still
Above the staggering girl, her thighs caressed
By the dark webs, her nape caught in his bill,
He holds her helpless breast upon his breast.

The story of Leda raped by the mysterious swan has been
circulating ever since Europe discovered it in ancient Greek
mythology. From one era to the next, the erotic, the brutal
and the shocking in this tale have never failed to attract painters
and poets. With it they build various imaginings, in expression
sometimes refined and sometimes crude, sometimes profound and
often just shallow.

But it was only in the 20th century, that century of rebellion,
that this story of rape became so gripping. Particularly when W.B.
Yeats, the nationalist Irish poet, wrote it in a sonnet from which I
have quoted a few lines above: the full poem is fourteen lines long
and opens with a throbbing rhythm.

Yeats finds no need to explain that the swan is Zeus in disguise.
He considers that his readers are familiar with the Greek story, and
also know that the king of the heavens is a merciless force: he is
impassioned, he is powerful, he exists. Whatever his name, as long
as he is manifest only in brute force, we cannot hope for justice.

Nor does Yeats mention Leda's name. Perhaps he wants to stress that what he is portraying is not just the fate of the wife of Tyndareos, the King of Sparta. Yeats's poem is merely depicting a person suddenly plummeted into a situation incomparable and unique; and in that situation touches the hearts of people anywhere, at any time: universal.

Nonetheless, Yeats wrote this poem in the years of the Irish struggle for independence from English colonization. It is not surprising that the woman ravished by Zeus is interpreted as a symbol of the oppressed, hitherto silenced. Yeats's story is a political history: from a brutal and repressive situation, new violence is born. In particular, the violence of one nation upon another, and the tragedy that happens during and after that.

And Greek mythology tells just this, because from Zeus's act, Leda gives birth to Helen, the woman who caused the ten year long Trojan War. The last six lines of Yeats's sonnet mention 'The broken wall, the burning roof and tower/ And Agamemnon dead.' In the *Iliad*, the victorious king of the Trojan War was indeed eventually murdered in his own house, and thus spread the series of acts of revenge that ended in the extermination of the descendants of the family of Atreus.

When the early twentieth century was left behind, a new interpretation came along. The Leda of Yeats's poem changed: she symbolized the figure of woman raped by patriarchal force. Zeus, like depictions of God in other religions, is 'male'. The experience is one of the crushing of women, squeezed between laws, between institutions.

And all this is carried out as though without any tyranny whatsoever. One story has Zeus, at the beginning, turning himself into a swan in order to ask for protection. In Leonardo da Vinci's 15th century painting, we do not see the brutality. On the neat canvas, the swan merely snuggles close to the naked Leda in a garden.

The fact that Zeus disguises himself as a swan before indulging his passion shows how effective the power of deception is in power relations between the genders. The upholders of patriarchy say that they are exalting women when in fact they are hemming them in. The Muslim clerics in Saudi Arabia and the syariah police in Aceh state that women have to be protected and to protect themselves for their own good, but this is not what happens. In the end, women become citizens under constant suspicion.

But, they say, don't the women themselves agree to it?

Indeed, it is not easy to determine what is going on: powerlessness or acquiescence. Yeats himself questioned this:

> *How can those terrified vague fingers push*
> *The feathered glory from her loosening thighs?*
> *And how can body, laid in that white rush,*
> *But feel the strange heart beating where it lies?*

Yeats uses the word 'glory' to depict Zeus's might as the swan, rather than another word that would show something vile and evil. He also mentions the 'strange heart beating' in the body of that pressing creature, not the savage, panting breath that Leda senses.

Maybe in each of Zeus's claws there is something enthralling; maybe in every one of the victim's cries of pain there is another intense, unforgettable feeling. Maybe because Zeus, and the other gods, are forever ambiguous: in them there is brutality and jealousy, but also nobility and intimacy. This is why the story of Leda and the swan can be told as it is in Leonardo da Vinci's painting: an atmosphere intimate and sensual, not barbaric.

But despite all, according to the ancient Greek tale Leda ends up committing suicide. She has been raped. And she has been made to feel that she has sinned. And this is what Yeats does not say: injustice has occurred.

'Leda' *Tempo* 23 September 2012, CP X: 367-70

Sirius

Just after dawn, from a hill at Munduk in north Bali under a naked sky, I saw Sirius. The star was far distant, like the last actor on stage in the firmament before the night's curtain is taken down. Brilliant, as one expects at this hour in the month of June, when the dark sky begins to tinge blue.

'Do you know that it takes eight years for the light from Sirius to reach the retina of our eyes, here on this cold hill?'

'A whole eight years travelling?'

'Yes, because the distance between the Dog Star and Earth, according to astronomers' calculations, is 8,611 light years.'

I was lost in thought. What do I really experience of that world beyond? It seems there are two interchanging moments. In one, astronomy gives information about a great distance. In the other, my direct experience has no connection to that figure of light years. In this moment, I am meeting there and then a clear star on the edge of dawn.

I cannot say that Sirius and its distance are just a construction by experts using their language and mathematical symbols. Stars and space really exist outside of telescopes. But nor can I say that the entirety of Sirius's presence at this moment is completely determined by thousands of telescopes as part of the curiosity of astronomy. In my visual space, there in the sky above Munduk, Sirius is part of my enchantment.

Anyone enchanted by stars knows that experience is an ongoing renewal. I cannot add anything to that figure of 8,611 light years. But every time I look at Sirius, from this hill at this moment or from another hill on another night, I experience it as though for the first time: something new.

It doesn't feel important to fuss about what and who makes it new. What is clear is that my awareness is really merely passive; it is not directing my experience at that moment. All I do is gaze at space. But my position, my body, my memory and my whole self are actually not the same as they were before. And so it is with Sirius, that far distant star that man has known since ancient Egypt. In its eight-year-long journey of light, it changes: it could be just its position above this hill, in its relation to shapes and the position of the moon in the sky. Or it could be because of differently falling mists.

Experience is a creative process. It 'creates' what was not there before, not from nothing of course. Life is a flow, at any particular time an event, and every event is a 'production of novelty' as Alfred North Whitehead says. Within, parts are components of the past, but other parts are components of the future – possibilities not entirely known.

Take, for instance, when we stand before Raden Saleh's canvases: we see a work from the mid 19th century, but at that instant we also seem to see something unfinished. This unfinished-ness is sensed not only in the portrait he painted of a Javanese bridal couple, holding hands as they gaze directly at us. Indeed, on this canvas, the background and the brush strokes on the face seem to have been made fleetingly, unlike the background and other figures that seem full.

But this unfinished-ness is also sensed in the most complete canvases – because every work is an event that continuously stimulates us, fascinates us, pleases us.

On such and such a day, we vividly encounter the eyes in the portrait of Sultan Alkadri, or the ferocious expression of the stabbed lion, or the details of the medals on the chest of some colonial official, or the pattern on the batik cloth of an old woman on another canvas. Or the green of the ferns in the road climbing to Megamendung.

On another day we return, and the same painting unpredictably appears before us as something in yet another process of 'becoming'. We still recall our previous experience, but we are open to an experience we do not anticipate.

So when it is said that these works are eternal, this is not because they are more than a century old. The canvases can deteriorate – some of them are neglected and beginning to deteriorate – and colors can change. But there is something 'lasting'. Keats's famous lines say something about the quality of beauty:

A thing of beauty is a joy for ever:/Its loveliness increases; it will never/Pass into nothingness; ...

What the poem perhaps incorrectly conveys is that beauty is outside of time, 'a joy forever'. 'It will never pass into nothingness'. But we never view beauty as something free from its temporal form, a wooden statue that will mildew, say.

This is why what is eternal in the beauty of Raden Saleh's paintings – what is not 'cracked by heat nor mildewed by rain' as the Malay saying goes – and in my moment of wonder as I meet the light of Sirius, is not something that exists outside of time. It exists within time. Objects and moments will not last, memory will fade, but wonder in events of beauty – as in moments of loving – return, like reincarnations that do not recognize their original forms

Maybe this is one reason for us to be thankful: there is something 'eternal' in the temporal, and Sirius above the hill is not just the repetition of a thing that arrives eight years later. Life is not a line of machines with ready-made patterns. Life is a profound creativity. Anyone who feels that she or he can predict its direction will be disillusioned, or bored.

'Sirius' *Tempo* 24 June 2012, CP X: 315-8

Myth

"Jackie Chan is a myth."

Jackie Chan

B ut Jackie Chan breathes. He eats, sleeps, smiles, shits, runs, acts, does acrobatic leaps, and enjoys sex. But like most people with particular fame, he has shadows. At almost every moment these shadows, in the form of Jackie Chan but sometimes a bit larger in size, are close behind him. Or in front of him.

What makes these shadows appear is of course the ways and actions of Jackie Chan himself; don't forget: this is an essential part of the world of film. But more important, those shadows are there because of others, fans or critics, who have produced them – as a way of 'capturing' Jackie Chan who always escapes definition.

What is extraordinary about this character (or his shadow, or his image) is his agile movement, his flexibility in getting himself out of traps, his slightly simple and slightly playful attitude, yet his ability to get knocked about and show remarkable endurance.

Of course that's not why he calls himself a 'myth'. But nonetheless, one aspect of myth is 'movement': a myth, like Jackie Chan in film, is never stagnant. This is why, as I said, he constantly escapes definition. A myth never becomes an unchangeable source of truth, fixed outside of time. The 'truth' of a myth is not in its neat fit between 'fable' and 'fact'; the weight of its narrative floats between one human experience and the next.

But this is precisely why myth is inseparable from daily life. When Marlene Dietrich, in contrast to Jackie Chan, said that she was *not* a myth, she was both right and wrong. Like many people, she thought that the opposite of myth is real life. But she forgot that the 'real' is always seen in eclipse, with penumbra – the opaque light that reveals partially, like Marlene herself in *Blue Angel*.

When I was young, I once crossed the Dieng Plateau, in Central Java. The plateau, the floor of an ancient caldera 2000 meters above sea level, has for three millennia, it seems, emitted a strange aura. The name 'Dieng' comes from '*di Hyang*', the place where the gods ('*hyang*') reside. Anyone who has visited that high place will see a row of eight small Hindu temples. But back then I believed – as did those with me – that there were only five. It was said that the five constructions were the place where the five Pandawa warriors in the *Mahabharata* came to meditate on certain nights, reflecting upon their sins in war and in power.

When I became adult, I laughed at that story. Archeologists point out that the eight small temples that were constructed around 750 CE are the remains of an original total of 400 built to worship Shiva. There is the carving of a mask with an evil face and sea monsters on that architecture, which probably led to the beauty of the Prambanan temple almost 200 years later. There are no signs of the *Mahabharata*.

But the *Mahabharata*, in that place of my childhood, was not just an epic. Even though the majority of the population was Muslim, the names of the Hindu gods, the good, bold warriors and the evil characters in that epic were alive in daily life and language. Performances of *wayang kulit* that showed the last scenes of the final war of the Bharata family, where the heroes died in glory or disgrace, were rare. To the villagers that I knew, performances of these dreadful battles demanded solemn rituals. People were afraid of something that might befall them in the future, which just might be induced by the violence, misery and futility of the Bharatayudha.

Around the late 1960s there was a *wayang kulit* performance that went on for a whole month and depicted the life stories of the Pandawa and Kurawa from their youth until their death in or after battle. When the performance was over, a ceremony followed: the body of Sengkuni (nothing more than a shape carved from buffalo hide) was taken to the Indian Ocean to be cast into the sea. Sengkuni was the most despicable character in the performance. He had been killed. He had to be thrown into the sea and not permitted to return to life.

It seems that myth is not merely fantasy, but also part of life that answers the human need to transcend limitations and darkness. Myth, Karen Armstrong says, looks into 'the heart of a great silence'. Silence about the appearance and disappearance of happiness and sadness, silence about *sangkan paraning dumadi* as the Javanese phrase goes, the origins and direction of everything that was, is and will be.

Looking into that silence, people feel they get something: an experience that cannot be put into words. Neanderthal man has been found buried in caves with the body placed like a fetus in the womb. It is said that this was an expression of their experience of the riddle of life and the wonder of birth. Whatever the meaning is of the pictures of animals on the Lascaux caves from about 17,300 years ago; they seem to be attempting to recapture what is fascinating in life from one season to the next. Man is the creature that is fascinated and expresses his fascination. And this is also where myth is born.

And all these tens of thousands of millennia later – in the time of Jackie Chan – it turns out that this fascination has not ceased. Nor the sense of marvel and dread at the grand silence. Some think that science and technology have wiped this fascination, just as they will in time defeat religion. But, like Jackie Chan in film, myth continues, giving meaning to life that is not completely clear.

'Mithos' *Tempo* 13 January 2013

Abraham

Slaughtering an innocent child; slaughtering your own innocent child – could you do it? Abraham had heard the voice. He believed it was the command of God, and this was what he must do. He was being tested to see how close he was to God who must be obeyed in all things. He departed.

If I were ordered to do that, I would almost definitely refuse. Respectfully and fearfully. I would say, let me go to Hell. Let me be cursed, but save the child. Pity for that innocent boy would sway me more than the will of the Almighty.

But I am not Abraham. I am not a Biblical character. The Danish philosopher Kierkegaard, in his book *Frygt og Bæven* (Fear and Trembling) published in 1843, described Abraham's faith as something that surmounted the universal 'good' that applies to anyone, anywhere, at any time. Abraham was not anyone. He was unique, singular, alone. No values or laws can condone his act on Mount Moriah. Abraham could carry out the act only because he placed his belief in 'the power of something absurd'. Kierkegaard considered Abraham no tragic hero. He was not like the Emperor Brutus who, broken-hearted, had to kill his son in order to uphold the Roman law that applied to everyone, anywhere and at any time. Kierkegaard saw Abraham, in contrast, as a 'knight of faith'.

But it is still not easy to imagine a 'knight of faith' having to cut his own son's throat. How could he possibly bear being right?

This seems to be why the Qur'an depicts Abraham placing his son face down. The history of Al-Tabari mentions that the boy (the Qur'an does not name him either Ishmael or Isaac) says to his father: 'Father, when you lay me out for the sacrifice, then set my face downwards, not to the side: for I fear that if you see my face, you will be overtaken by a sense of pity, and fail to carry out God's command.'

There is a painting by the famous Dutch painter Rembrandt, dated 1635, titled 'The Sacrifice of Isaac'. I saw it once at the Hermitage Museum in St Petersburg. I remember it well: the painting shows Abraham covering his son's face while he draws his knife. He cannot bear to look his tortured son in the eye.

But interestingly, Rembrandt does not depict Abraham in fear and trembling, as Kierkegaard explains it. In quoting the Bible story, Kierkegaard chooses to focus more on the initial command of God: Abraham, or Ibrahim, must kill his own son. Kierkegaard does not continue his reading to the second of God's commands. Rembrandt, though, captures precisely this moment. As is written in Genesis:

> And Abraham stretched forth his hand, and took the knife to slay his son.
> And the angel of the Lord called unto him out of heaven, and said, Abraham, Abraham: and he said, Here am I.
> And he said, Lay not thine hand upon the lad, neither do thou any thing unto him: for now I know that thou fearest God, seeing thou hast not withheld thy son, thine only son from me.

The painting shows the angel's hand restraining Abraham's right arm. The knife has fallen. Abraham's left hand is still covering his son's face. His eyes turn to the gentle angel: the pupils of his dark eyes seem part of a smile yet to break.

Evidently, Rembrandt painted this scene when, aged 29, he had just experienced the death of his own infant son. This seems to have made his painting more sympathetic to the bitterness of senseless loss of an innocent child. His Abraham is not executing the initial command of God.

Rembrandt would probably prefer the interpretation of Emmanuel Lévinas, the French philosopher and Talmudic commentator. Lévinas criticized Kierkegaard's explanation of Abraham. In his essay *"A propos Kierkegaard Vivant"*, Lévinas writes; 'that Abraham obeyed the first voice is astonishing: that he had sufficient distance with respect to that obedience to hear the second voice—that is essential.'

For it is at this moment that Abraham looks again at the face of the near-sacrifice. The face of a child. The face of humanity. The infinite face. That cannot become an object. The face that causes God's command to have meaning: 'Do not kill.

And to Lévinas, as to us, every face calls to us. We respond, take responsibility, do not easily abuse. We recall Abraham at that moment. He becomes meaningful because of this.

'Ibrahim' *Tempo* 28 November 2010, CP IX: 727-9

Casting Stones

There is an old story, a well-known Biblical story that begins early one morning in the grounds of the temple, as Jesus sat teaching. The story, as told in the King James Bible, begins:

> *And the scribes and Pharisees brought unto him a woman taken in adultery; and when they had set her in the midst, they said unto him, Master, this woman was taken in adultery, in the very act.*
>
> *Now Moses in the law commanded us, that such should be stoned: but what sayest thou?*

To John, recording this incident, the scribes and Pharisees wanted to 'trap' Jesus. They wanted this figure they called 'Master' (mockingly, perhaps?) to say something wrong.

I am a Muslim, and no Bible expert. I can only imagine the background to this incident: the scribes and Pharisees were suspicious that Jesus was teaching heresy. They thought that he ignored the teachings of the Law; after all, had he not infringed the prohibition against working on the Sabbath? Probably they had already heard Jesus' view that faith cannot be regulated by legal experts. To have faith is to experience the life that God is continuously creating and tending with love.

But to these Jewish leaders, this dismissal of the Law could not be tolerated, particularly in the eyes of the Pharisees who, among the various Jewish groups, were the most persistent in their desire to purify daily life by ensuring consistency of belief.

So that morning they wanted to 'trap' Jesus. Jesus did not reply. As John tells it:

> *But Jesus stooped down, and with his finger wrote on the ground, as though he heard them not. So when they continued asking him, he lifted up himself, and said unto them, He that is without sin among you, let him first cast a stone at her. And again he stooped down, and wrote on the ground.*
>
> *All was suddenly still. No one made a move. No one was prepared to cast that first stone.*
>
> *And they which heard it, being convicted by their own conscience, went out one by one, beginning at the eldest, even unto the last: and Jesus was left alone, and the woman standing in the midst.*
>
> *When Jesus had lifted up himself, and saw none but the woman, he said unto her, Woman, where are those thine accusers? Hath no man condemned thee?*
>
> *She said, No man, Lord. And Jesus said unto her, Neither do I condemn thee: go, and sin no more.*

There was no stoning. There was no punishment. The event of that morning became an example: endless punishment of sinners will not change anything at all. On the other hand, empathy, compassion and forgiveness are transformative actions.

But to me, the more interesting moment is when Jesus bends over and writes something in the ground with his fingers. What did he write?

No one knows. I can only imagine: He was making a sign. When Jesus wrote letters in the sand, he wanted to show how every literal construction inevitably has elements that are not fixed. Words – even in the Law of the Torah – are never free from the earth, even though they are not shaped by the earth. Words are shaped by the body ('fingers'), although they are not extensions of the body. The sand will be trampled by passers by: on the face of the earth, meaning is always there for the passing, but something inevitably changes or is lost from that meaning.

In the temple grounds, Jesus did not seem to reject the Law. He did not deny the sentence of stoning. But in a radical way, he changed that law into an aspect of experience, making it part of the lives of every single person at a certain moment in a certain place. The law was no longer written for anyone, anywhere, at any time. When Jesus said, 'let he who is without sin cast the first stone', then the law suddenly touched the 'who' rather than the 'what' – with the souls, desires, and memories of every person present in the temple grounds that morning.

The stone-throwers-to-be were no longer machines defending the faith. Suddenly, each one looked into himself. I myself am not entirely at one with God's law. I am a complex situation shaped by a web of multiplication. What did I do yesterday? And what will I do?

And at that same moment, the accused was no longer an example of 'women like that'. She was a person, a face, and a story that was singular, incomparable – and thus incapable of formulation. She was a story that did not exist yesterday, that tomorrow will not be repeated, and is today something I cannot fully understand. Do I even know her name, and how she came to be accused?

The woman, and all those in the temple grounds, were destiny that comes from and goes to who-knows-where. Chairil Anwar was right: 'Destiny is every person's private silence'.

In his essay about these events in the temple grounds, René Girard, who considers mimesis to be vitally important in human life – points out an interesting scene: after being struck by Jesus' words, the people 'went out one by one, beginning at the eldest, even unto the last.' At that moment, the impetus for mimesis – the human urge to copy what others do – ceased to be the factor governing behavior. From the gathering of the crowd, there emerged individuals, persons. 'The Gospel text can be read almost allegorically,' Girard writes, 'as the emergence of genuine person-hood out of the primordial mob.'

But who does religion speak to, really: to every person in their private silence? Or to 'the mob'? I do not know. In that yard, Jesus bent over, silent, and scribbled with his fingers. When he stood up, he spoke to the crowd. But that scribbling did not shout.

'Perajam' *Tempo* 4 October 2009, CP IX: 481-4

Atheists

Religion will remain part of human life, but should one defend it?

The British writer Christopher Hitchens has recently attracted attention with the publication of his book *God is Not Great: How religion poisons everything*. His is not a sole voice at the beginning of the 21st century. In 2004, Sam Harris's book *The End of Faith* came out, and last year he hardened his position by attacking Christianity in *Letter to a Christian Nation*. Richard Dawkins, the biologist, quotes another writer in his book *The God Delusion*: 'When one person suffers from a delusion, it is called insanity. When many people suffer from a delusion, it is called Religion.'

I have not read all these books thoroughly, but I feel something between perturbed, offended, stimulated, intellectually challenged, and glad. Let me tell you why I am glad: because now there are a few atheists fluent in argument as sharp as a surgeon's knife. And they use their analysis to attack all religions, without exception, at a time with faith is paraded with fear, and fear soon turns into hate. The world is not a more peaceful place because of religion. So who knows, the world might have been waiting for Hitchens, Harris and Dawkins. Who knows, it might be these atheists who make religious communities change tack and stop fighting one another.

And indeed there is truth in Christopher Hitchens's words about faith and a sense of safety. Just one week before that historic day of September 11, he was asked in a radio interview whether he would feel more or less safe if he were in a foreign city at dusk and was approached by a crowd of people, and he knew that this crowd had just come from a prayer session.

Hitchens, who has lived in Belfast, Beirut, Bombay, Beograd, Bethlehem and Baghdad, answered: 'Less safe.'

He is not speaking from imagination. He has witnessed enmity between Catholics and Protestants in Ulster; Muslims and Christians in Beirut and Bethlehem; Croatian Catholics and the Serbian Orthodox Church against Muslims in former Yugoslavia; between Sunnis and Shiites in Baghdad – thousands of people killed, maimed and abandoned.

So to Hitchens, religion 'has been an enormous multiplier of tribal suspicion and hatred.' And yet interestingly enough, Hitchens does not say that religion is the source of this negativity.

In this he differs from Sam Harris. To Harris, the bloody conflict between Catholics and Protestants in Ireland which began in the 17th century, has its source in Biblical text, and has no relation to the politics of land affairs at that time. Harris does not see the sediment of history in every interpretation of belief – in this he is like a Christian or Muslim fundamentalist. His history-denying view is able to say that it was Qur'anic doctrine that made a group of people destroy the Twin Towers in New York and kill around 3000 people on 11 September 2001. Harris does not see that on that day 'Islam' was synonymous with anger from the bitterness of colonialism in the Middle East, Africa and Asia, and the defeat of the Arab world in Palestine.

Indeed there is truth in the famous apology: it is not religions that are wrong, it is their people.

But the problem doesn't rest there. Atheists like Hitchens would ask: if it is the human factor that corrupts in any religious community, then this means that there is no role for religion in bettering that community. And if this is so, if belief is determined by history and not the other way around, then what use is religion in fixing the world?

Maybe none at all. When these days one sees so many murders committed in the name of religion, it is an easy slide to Hitchens' atheism and his conclusion: religion poisons everything.

But we could also come to a different conclusion: religion might indeed have no role in fixing the world. The role of religion might be something else entirely – particularly when seen from the perspective of the birth of religions.

Karen Armstrong, in her talk to the Islamic Religious Council of Singapore last June, said something unusual: religion is born from recoil from violence. Even Islam, which nowadays is constantly associated with bombs, suicide, and the bloody conflicts in Iraq, Afghanistan and Pakistan, appeared first as a peace-builder in and around Mecca, among the most wild of Arab peoples.

But Karen Armstrong could probably take this further: if religion is indeed born from recoil from violence, then that recoil is linked to an awareness of weakness. Because of this, religion does not feel it has the power to fix the world; rather, it lives with the excluded, it befriends the weak – and this is very evident when people are tortured.

But these days, as it tries to compete with the vigor of modernity, religion tends to forget its own 'originary empathy'. Muslims celebrate Hijrah, the flight of the Prophet from Mecca to Medina, not with a sense of loyalty and empathy towards those terrorized, even though Hijrah began with the fate of a pursued minority. People celebrate Hijrah more as a victory. Probably in this way they can forget their own experience of powerlessness; just two weeks ago, in the name of 'Islam', some people threatened a group of Carmelite nuns who were gathering to pray at the valley of Cikanyere in Cianjur.

When it forgets the powerless, religion can be a terrifying force. But it can also become a force that knows no limits. And at times like this, don't we need the atheists to come and speak out?

'Atheis' *Tempo* 5 August 2007, CP IX: 13-6

Dialogue 7

The text, made up of twenty-six dialogues, is now forgotten. The dialogues took place towards the end of 1391. At the time, Byzantium was not yet part of Turkey, nonetheless its ruler Manuel II had to keep a low profile. Although he still had the title of 'king' or 'Autokrator', in fact he was merely a vassal of the sultan ruling in Anatolia.

Byzantium had been fragile and dependent since 1379. When he was 29, because of a dispute with his brother over the throne, Manuel sought protection from Sultan Murad I. This was the beginning of the demand for Byzantium to pay tribute and join a military alliance with its neighbor on the Bosphorus. And Manuel was always ready to obey.

In 1391, he was ordered to take part in the battle on the coast of the Black Sea. But it seems that while in Ankara he found time for something else. From October until December, he conversed with a local religious court judge. And from this – even though in fact this exchange of views was probably not completely factual – was born the text *Twenty Six Dialogues with a Persian*. This document was rarely consulted – until Pope Benedict XVI quoted it in a lecture he gave at the Regensburg University in Germany two weeks' ago.

I myself have never read Manuel II's text, but it does not surprise me that in it one finds strong anti-Islamic sentiment. The Autokrator was heir to conflict and defeat by the Turkish power, which at the time was synonymous with 'Islam'. His father had ruled in perilous times after the Ottoman Empire had defeated Macedonia and Serbia in the 1380s; he also had to face internal threats to his throne. In order to keep his father as king of Byzantium, Manuel steeled himself to become a vassal in the Sultan's palace. He was prepared to accept all kinds of insult. When Sultan Bayazid I forbade the strengthening of the walls of Constantinople, the prohibition came with a threat: if the construction did not cease, Manuel would be blinded.

Manuel kept quiet, but he came to his own conclusion. 'Only evil and inhuman', he said of the teachings of Muhammad, God's Prophet in Mecca.

Manuel's source was close at hand: the tome titled 'Defense of Christianity' (against Islam) had been compiled by his grandfather, Johannes Cantacuzenus, drawing on the polemic *Confutatio Alchorani* written by Bruder Ricoldo from Montecroce, which refuted the Qur'an.

But all polemics contain the politics of quotation. When Manuel quoted the Qur'anic sura saying 'there is no compulsion in religion', he said that this sentence came from the time when the Muslims were powerless. In other words, he gave historical context to the text. But he did not employ the same historicity in *Dialogue 7* when referring to another text, namely the call attributed to the Prophet to 'spread faith by the sword'. In other words, Manuel did not attempt to find any historical context when the Prophet advocated not kind greetings but the sword.

Islam is only 'evil and inhuman' Manuel says. This is typically an essentialist voice, which considers all identities determined in unchanging 'essence', and which does not acknowledge that every 'essence' is actually produced by the shaping of discourse.

Pope Benedict, like Manuel, is an essentialist. He quotes Theodore Khoury (the editor of the republished *Twenty-six Dialogues with a Persian*) who quotes R.Arnaldez, a 'French Islamist', who in turn quotes Ibn Hazn who stated that God is not bound even by His own word. In this view, what appears is 'the image of a capricious God, who is not even bound to truth and goodness'.

It must be pointed out that the Pope does *not* consider this to be the image spread by Islam: he says only that it is the view of Ibn Hazn. More significantly, he also states that in the history of Christian thought there was Duns Scotus from the 13th century, who had similar ideas; that we can know only God's *voluntas ordinata*: beyond that, it is entirely freedom 'in virtue of which He could have done the opposite of everything He has actually done.'

Actually, there are not only Ibn Hazn and Duns Scotus. The Pope did not mention the occasionalist philosophers of Islam and Christianity, like Al Ghazali from Iran in the 11th century and Malebranche from France in the 17th century. To them, every change in objects and thought occurs because of the will of God: 'cotton is consumed by fire not because it is ignited by a match, but because God has willed it to be so.' There is no relation of cause and effect such as scientists discover and formulate using reason. God is beyond reason.

But to Pope Benedict, reason is *logos*, the Greek word that also means 'word' as found in Genesis. So reason fuses with faith. Manuel, the Pope says, was able to say that not to act with reason is contrary to God's nature.

And here, according to the Pope, is the intrinsic encounter between the Bible and Greek inquiry. The product of this encounter changed the world – and formed the foundation of what is called 'Europe'.

Europe? But when 'Europe' with its Hellenic elements is synonymous with 'Christian', then how can the 'non-Europe' believe in the love of Jesus? Isn't that 'foundation' merely the construction of discourse, which was formed to distinguish itself from – and to marginalize – what must be expelled, silenced; in the past, the Jews, and nowadays, the Muslim immigrants?

The thesis at Regensburg campus, it seems, is merely a polemic: the political process of quotation and memory, when information A is noted and B is hidden.

Meaning that a similar polemic could be put forward by Muslims, by stressing that it is Islam that has a rational basis to faith, for the Hadith says 'religion is reason'. It is also Islam, in the figure of Ibn Rushd, which introduced the world of Greek thought to Europe.

Meaning that other religions are sheer stupidity....

And as for religion and violence: isn't this clearly etched into the history of Islam – as too it is etched in Europe's past – something forgotten that day of the speech?

'Percakapan 7' *Tempo* 2 October 2006, CP VIII: 261-4

Laozi

aybe Laozi never existed. Maybe a better name for him is 'the gentleman who left no trace' or 'Yinjunzi', as the historian Sima Quian dubbed him. Perhaps he was merely the fictional character created by Zhuangzi, a thinker who lived in the 4th century BCE and continues to fascinate us today.

But there are those who say that Laozi was born in the town of Ku in the state of Chu. Regarded as the founder of Daoism, he lived during the Zhou dynasty as keeper of court archives. Even Confucius visited him, they say. But exactly who he was – known also as 'Lao Tan' – not even Confucius could tell.

'Master, you've seen Lao Tan – what estimation would you make of him?'

The Teacher said, 'At last I may say that I have seen a dragon – a dragon that coils to show his body at its best…riding on the breath of the clouds, feeding on the yin and yang. My mouth fell open and I couldn't close it; my tongue flew up and I couldn't even stammer. How could I possibly make any estimation of Lao Tan!'

No one is able to fully appraise another – probably this is what we can take from the Master's reply. Other people always have strange sides to them, inexplicable, mysterious. And when facing that enigma, tongues fly up and we cannot even stammer.

Or, here's another wise thought implied in that answer: there is no need to know precisely the beginnings of good teaching. Good teaching has a history when it is performed, now, and not when it was revered in some past. Every beginning is merely a point determined in the past, but that point, like all points in geometry, cannot stand alone. It is always linked to other points in a trajectory. All beginnings are relative.

So too when we tell the story of philosophies such as Daoism or Confucianism, or even religions of revelation. Religions may state that they originate from the word of God whispered to a prophet, but don't those prophets exist within a history, within a language, and these are not free from beginnings whose starting points cannot be precise?

And what is 'the beginning' of our religions, beliefs or knowledge other than attempts to seek the origin of all origins – for which there is no easy final answer? Daoism talks about this in the same way it talks about its own roots, by acknowledging existing mysteries: the beginning is something nameless, between being and non being, 'the mystery of mysteries, gateway of untold secrets'. The *Daodejing* says: 'Who knows whose child it is, this ancestor of the gods? …Something great and wonderful flows into all things, and they spring up. But the beginning does not claim ownership or lordship over them'.

In other words, there is no *archĕ* as in Aristotelian thought: a 'principle' that begins all things and controls all things. 'Dao' or 'The Way' is indeed a process, meaning movement. But Daoism does not view movement in a cause-and-effect relationship. To Aristotle, all things move but they are always set in motion by another thing. Only at the very end does there have to be 'the unmovable first cause', *to proton kinoun akineton.*

Aristotle's view, which came from physics, found resonance in monotheistic theology, entering from the 12ᵗʰ century via the commentary of Ibnu Rushd the Muslim, Maimonides the Jew, and Thomas Aquinas the Christian.

Not all monotheist thinkers agreed on the explanation of God as merely a beginning point in a chain of cause and effect. And Aristotle's theory about the universe seemed monolithic and authoritarian. The word *archĕ,* (according to those skilled in Greek etymology) apart from meaning 'beginning' and 'principle', also means 'ruler' and 'political office'. In his work on metaphysics, Aristotle compares this first principle to 'a general in the army'.

The *Daoidejing* is different in this: it gives no assurance of any 'first cause' present, having presence. The universe is not seen as an army, but rather as a manifestation of 'the Way'. An army appears with a clear purpose. But 'the Way', in the imagination of people in the 4th century BCE, was otherwise: 'the Way' exists because people open it and together travel it, without a common direction or purpose and probably without any predetermined direction. On the 'way', and not in the army, there is no single authority that directs the march and brings all the different feet into step.

There is something non-authoritarian and non-imperialistic in Daoism. Perhaps this is because it grew when China was being torn apart by war over two centuries or more from 405 BCE. In Daoism, there is no illusion of any single and everlasting power. There is no belief that mankind was created as special with the status of God's Representative, charged with ruling over the earth. Daoism offers no 'onto-theology': Anticipating the questioning of humanist thinking by 1500 years, Zhuangzi saw that man was not the center of all things. 'Of all the myriad created things…Is not he, as compared with all creation, but as the tip of a hair upon a horse's skin?' he questioned.

So when Confucianism aimed to mend the world and the political life of the time, which was in such dire straits, Daoism took a quiet, wise approach. Daoism is not convinced that man is capable of acting, even to make life happier, without destroying.

To a Daoist, a wise person braves action without acting – this is *wu wei.* She moves without being dictated by targets and purpose. He knows the meaning of 'empty'. Take the gate and the water vessel: It is the part that is 'empty' that makes them meaningful to others. It is precisely man feeling herself full of truth, sanctity and power that can be destructive.

And so along 'the Way', where all kinds of people meet and pass, the selfless person makes herself a gateway to give space, and makes himself a water vessel for the quenching of thirst.

'Laozi' *Tempo* 12 February 2006, CP VIII: 137-40

Prayer

All prayer holds tension. Prayer is always moving between copious expression and quiet, between the impulse to comprehend and a sense of wonder that is also reverent. Before the Divine, the Ineffable, the tongue cannot put on airs.

If religious institutions are antagonistic towards poetry, it is because they forget that it is also a kind of prayer. 'I am knocking at Your door/and cannot turn away' Chairil Anwar wrote in his most religious period. Poetry, particularly at its most bleak, is disappointment but also unacknowledged gratitude.

This is why God never abandons metaphor. Every metaphor shows just how poor and how ingenious human language is. A scholar of Arab literature said that metaphor is synonymous with isti'ara, which literally is said to mean 'borrow'. Humans, metaphor-creating creatures, formulators of parable and analogy, are creatures who borrow and lend. When 'God' is depicted as 'door', and 'Fate' is said to 'strike' people, we see how words beg for help from other distant words to convey meaning – and often obtain it unpredictably. The metaphor is a leap 'to borrow', it is flight back and forth between the abstract and the concrete, when one feels the need for the abstract to be realized in a metaphor or picture perceptible by the senses.

People have debated whether the phrases of sacred books should be interpreted literally; in other words, to what extent language can guarantee fidelity of meaning. But people forget that language, including that considered to be chosen by God, is shaped by deficiency and desire, by memory and forgetting, by the need to tend and to be invasive, by the sense of community and solitude. Metaphor is the product of these conflicting proclivities, because history, where language is wrought, is unfinished contradiction. Every language on the face of the earth is rooted like a teak tree and soars like a shooting star. Verbal pictures about God, and quotes of His Word, inevitably take their leave from the world of finite language, even though they move to greet the infinite.

Symbols alone are eventually inadequate. Symbols are gradually replaced by 'signs', Julia Kristeva wrote in 1966. The Middle Ages ended in Europe, and Christianity encountered society no longer able to accept symbols. Symbols are realizations made to refer to an object with a fixed meaning, but this stability is only possible because it is assisted by a kind of 'law'. Red lights, signs of the cross, letters of the alphabet: interpretations of all these were fixed and single. But then came the era when symbols had to compete with 'signs'. 'Red lights' were no longer only signals to stop; they were also signs of prostitution zones. 'The cross' became increasingly separated from the story of Jesus' suffering; it also appeared on national flags. Letters were no longer phonetic signs: 'f' can mean gulden, just as 'T' is linked with 'T-shirt'.

Symbols began to lose their monopoly once people no longer accepted the Church's claim to be the single interpreter of all things. 'Thus, up until 1350, it is the Word, in the guise of Jesus Christ, which creates the world,' Kristeva writes. After the Word was pushed aside, the 'sign' emerged – represented by the picture of 'an old man who measures the earth with a compass and throws the sun and stars into the heavens'. The Word lost its power when humans – who experience time and mortality – became the center of discourse, and the bestowers of meanings that are changeable and diverse. Once the authority of the Word was dislodged by signs that are permeable at every corner, then meaning was no longer shaped by relationships in a vertical way. A sign is no longer determined with total authority by the content of 'meaning' it signifies. Once the Middle Ages ended in Europe, meaning came to be shaped in horizontal chains: we grasp the meaning of 'the cross' after we see it on a church spire and not on an ambulance.

Thus symbols were replaced by signs, and in Europe the novel was born, says Kristeva. The novel (rather than the sermon) was indeed an arena where various voices and signs collided and passed fleetingly. Kristeva is right, but actually there is an older example that she does not observe: there had been incessant centrifugal tension between The Word and poetry

Tension between the Word (as center) and poetry (that liberates self from center) was particularly acute in the history of Arab literature. This probably all began because the Qur'an, with its poetic expression, developed as a text in an environment where poetry was celebrated in oral form. The Syrian poet Adonis, in his *Introduction to Arab Poetics* (the translation of his 1984 lecture at the Collège de France) quotes al-Jurjānī, a 10th century literary theoretician: who said that writing poetry is 'a kind of sedition', '…an alchemy which gives a doubtful argument the authority of proof, and turns proof into doubtful argument.'

Indeed, poetry does not promise any center and stability at all. Creative interpretation of a text is always 'dynamic, explosive, unfettered', Adonis says. The creative text never ceases to move us because it builds images and not symbols, because it inspires and is inspired by a sense of wonder, because, to use Ibnu Sina's words about poetry, it is a meeting of *takhyil* and *ta'jib*.

Does it do wrong? It has been said that poetry is a cursed form. It seems that there are moments when the hastily uttered curse of faith means taking the attitude of 'I-already-know', with sour-faced conviction. The sour expression refuses to welcome life as something extraordinary.

And it can win. But only those who accept life as something extraordinary, as something to marvel, will write poetry and/or pray.

'Doa' *Tempo* 4 September 2005, CP VIII: 41-4

Seven

Numbers can be imaginative. When I was a child, I was fascinated listening to the old people speaking about *Lail tul qadr*: 'the Night of Power better than a thousand months', the night of the revelation of the Qur'an, the 21st, 23rd, 25th, 27th and 29th nights of the month of Ramadan, when the outpouring of light would take place...

Once I grew up, I realized that the Qur'an does not state specifically which night in the holy month the revelation took place. Nor does it say that on the 27th there will be an outpouring of light from heaven.

But need this disappoint us? After all, with a measure of reflection and conviction, can't we already call the event of the revelation a miracle?

Miracles are always felt at times that we are 'touched' by God. Without a sense of awe and trepidation, faith will be sensed as only a thesis. Without any holy books to help them, people can always be astounded by His greatness. At such moments, even numbers tremble and grow in imaginative being.

This is found in various traditions. Outside of Islam, there are those who merge the Kabbalah spirit of mystic Judaism with secrets of numbers, as found in numerology. In Christianity, the number seven seems to have a special attraction. In a terrifying depiction of doomsday, the Bible speaks of the 'seven seals' on the biblical scrolls in God's hand, the 'seven angels with seven trumpets' and the 'seven bowls of God's wrath' of that day.

The number 'seven' here probably holds symbols from hidden lore; nonetheless it certainly conveys an impression of mystery. I don't know whether this was also the case when the Prophet said that the Qur'an is revealed in 'seven readings'.

What is meant by 'the seven different readings', the *sab'at-i-ahruf*? Is the number seven used to designate a specific sum, rather than a metaphor? And what does 'readings' or 'ways of reading' mean?

I once heard an ulema quote a hadith (saying of the Prophet) passed on by Ubayy bin Ka'b. The Prophet said that one day the Angel Gabriel came to say that Allah had ordered that the Qur'an be recited in only one dialect. The Prophet was reluctant. He replied that his ummah would not be capable of this. The Angel Gabriel insisted, but the Prophet continued to argue his point. Finally, after much to-and-fro, the Angel Gabriel stated Allah's decision: man was permitted to read the Qur'an in seven ways, and all of them were true.

I don't speak Arabic, nor am I an expert on the Qur'an or hadith. My own impression is simple: 'seven' here means what the number means: a certain sum. But why 'seven' and not 'eight'? It seems, true to God's mystery, that there is mystery in this. And just as important, it appears that what this says is that diversity is sanctioned. A single certainty was not chosen. Muhammad, Peace be upon Him, was very wise: he knew more about the plurality of his ummah that an angel who had never lived with a body limited in space and time.

If diversity of 'ways of reading' is not outlawed, then the problem is this: what does the hadith mean by 'ways of reading'? Is it ways of reciting, or ways of interpreting?

I never got around to asking. I know only of what occurred so often in history: imagination is not always secure. It is often disturbing, and is therefore reined in by the desire for certainty.

Especially when numbers are concerned, intrinsic as they are to exact science. Numbers are so easily skimmed off from the imaginative; they easily become abstract.

Nevertheless, obliterating metaphor from language is inconceivable, and it is impossible to do away with analogy and allegory, even in numbers. 'One thousand and one nights' does not represent a sum, nor does 'one thousand months' or 'one thousand years'. These numbers are not concepts, nor are they sums of calculation; they are products of the imagination.

This is where metaphor is born. Al-Jurjani, the 11th century literary theorist, once said that one of the qualities and beauties of *isti'ara* or metaphor was that it can make the non-living alive and communicative, and bland forms become expressive. *Isti'ara* allows for concepts 'buried in the intellect' to change into physical forms that appear to be seen by the eyes.

But herein lies the risk: physical forms give the impression of fleetingness and inconstancy. And people are often anxious – how can the inconstant record God's command? The history of religions shows that there are always efforts to canonize the meaning of holy words, because there is always tension: if plurality in reading is unavoidable, as the Prophet himself acknowledged, then how can that plurality not cause conflict?

This is what seems to have been behind the compilation, recording and codification of the Qur'an from the time of Caliph Abu Bakar, and particularly since the Caliph Usman. It was Caliph Usman who is supposed to have said, around nineteen years after the Prophet's death: 'My view is that we should unite the people in a single text (*mushaf waahid*), then there will be no further division or disagreement'. And so after this single text was completed, it was ordered that all other Qur'anic material, whether full texts or written fragments, be burnt.

History notes that the effort to impose a single *mushaf* was achieved, although it was limited. Varied ways of reading or dialects continued, so that only three centuries after Usman's death, a great ulema named Ibn Majahid succeeded in restricting them to seven in number. But did dispute cease? The Caliph Usman was murdered, followed in turn by Ali, there was the split between Sunni and Shiah, and heated debate – often profound and rigorous – has continued to the present day. Perhaps it is not only the numbers 'seven' or 'one thousand' that need to be interpreted imaginatively, but also the number 'one'.

'Tujuh' *Tempo* 6 November 2005, CP VIII: 77-80

Tso Wang

God and TV, faith and the Internet, sermons incessantly crossing diverse places; maybe this is what makes religion extend to all corners these days, overcoming space and time. Maybe too, this is what makes religion not find ground. Place has become something virtual.

One feels something is lost in all this. Place interacts with body. 'Body' meaning the body that is born and gives birth, the physical that has language and makes love, the body that matures and dies. In this story of the body, the rites of life-passage are institutionalized and celebrated, and thus tradition is created. And history takes on its special characteristics. But the special can be ignored, once TV and the Internet make the communicative urge so important for crossing boundaries, reaching into all corners. Place is then easily ignored, and the body is given no role to play.

That is the moment fundamentalism is spread.

Some think that fundamentalism is the desire to rediscover fundaments, so that tradition and history are not forgotten. Derrida, for instance, regards fundamentalist violence as the reaction against a kind of globalization he calls '*mondialatinisation*' – the Latinization of the world. In this process, the other, the non-Latin without links to 'Latin' history, is crowded out. 'Latin' here can mean something with connections to the Christian world in Europe. But 'Latin' can also shape the form of understanding of the world that equates 'knowing' with 'mastering'.

And so reaction arises. The 'non-Latin' does not wish to be swallowed up by 'Latinization'; the 'here' does not want to be gripped within the power of 'there'. When there is bloodshed, when there is massacre and hacking, bodies carved and destroyed (as is said to be happening in the Algerian violence between the 'Islamists' and their enemies), then according to Derrida all this is 'revenge' against the tendency of science and technology to turn others into mere things placed on a glass screen, dry and flat, body- less, like virtual creatures in computer games. Fundamentalism, often claimed to be anti-modernity, rejects this.

But in this I think Derrida was wrong. I think fundamentalism is actually on a par with digital technology: just as everything passes to and fro in the virtual world, religiosity does not speak to other people as figures-in-space-and-bodies. Fundamentalism regards itself as the most perfect, and this means not touching the soil, having no relation with geography or history of any kind, and unshaped by the earth and the physical which differ from place to place and time to time. Fundamentalism even views language, used by sacred texts, as something *not* formed by specific bodies and certain social relations. It sees itself as the bearer of the eternal and universal word, and with this conviction, it pushes on.

To practice this kind of religion – particularly when it too is part of the ongoing traffic going on in pervasive, communication technology-without-borders – is to practice religion that eventually has no more desire or opportunity to be still.

'To be still' means to find place, but it also means no noise or restlessness. In finding place, in that noiselessness and restfulness, to be religious is to rediscover a sense of thanksgiving. For in stillness, thinking is meditation, and meditation is to offer thanks. *Das Denken dankt,* Heidegger said.

In that still thanksgiving, in a state that a 10th century Javanese mystical poem described as '*sepi, sepah, samun*' (silent, vacant, secret), passivity is actually a state of openness to intimacy with the other, with the wonder and mystery of the other – especially The All Other.

This is probably why the theme of being is still a theme found everywhere, as long as faith has not yet lost meditation, nor is yet busying itself with the outside; when piety has not become self exhibition, when religion is not yet lashed by communicative longing, and certainly before digital technology has become pervasive. In the 14th century, Meister Eckhart, the mystic who died in Cologne in 1327, said that the passive state is 'more perfect' than the active. The passive state is when we have neither ambition nor aggression to attain, tug at, and take over the All Other. The passive state is when 'knowing' in its most profound sense is un-knowing.

Long before Eckhart, in the 4th century BCE, Zhuangzi, the Chinese philosopher of the famous Daoist School, also spoke of being still and 'knowing'. The highest stage of knowledge, he said, is stillness without movement within what cannot be known absolutely with reason. And in that stillness, it is intuition that is at work, in the state of *tso wang*.

Tso wang means, approximately, 'sitting-in-oblivion'. Someone 'sits-in-oblivion' when limbs and body are shed, when activity of the ears and eyes is annihilated, when one liberates oneself from the ego that hardens in identity, and one unites with The All Present. 'Look into the closed room', the Teacher says to Yen Hui 'and see, that the empty interior generates a bright whiteness.'

'All the blessings of he world', the Teacher goes on, 'come to reside in the stillness.'

But our times seem to give no more place to tranquility. These days, religion tends to move, pushing forward, often noisy and expansive. Sermons on television, text messaging, the Internet and pamphlets, have shaped a new language: not the language that utters the bitterness of loss before mystery, but rather language that promises things of utter clarity to all. And along with this new language comes a new conviction – the conviction that does not care whether 'knowing' is really 'un-knowing'.

'Tso Wang' *Tempo* 21 December 2003, CP VII: 99-102

Horror

When Akbar still went by his childhood name, Muhammad, he had already earned the title *Ghazi*, 'butcher of infidels'. Aged only fourteen, as prince he had been invited to demonstrate his courage and skill, and had passed the test: he cut the throat of a Hindu prisoner in a single stroke.

Descendant of Genghis Khan, descendant of Tamburlaine, herder of wild horses, artful wielder of arms in combat, one who played polo at night if need be (and for that purpose invented a ball that would shine when the light was too dim), Akbar could walk sixty kilometers without tiring. All this discipline and energy he mustered when, in 1560 and aged only eighteen, as adult he assumed full rule and became the third maharaja of his dynasty.

At that time, the Moghul Empire was only one eighth of India's size today. But with the fire of his ancestors, he extended that territory to almost all of Hindustan.

But with this breadth came complexity. Akbar knew why: he, a Muslim and new arrival of foreign descent, ruled over a majority of a different creed, in a continent that since ancient times had produced all kinds of sacred texts and holy men. Even Christianity was arriving, with Catholic priests already in Delhi. Hindustan was entering a tense time of transition.

Akbar knew, but more than that, he thought, he reflected: there was something worrying when people mingled with their different faiths. He made great efforts: he married Rajput princesses who were Hindu, he agreed to the Jainists' demand to stop hunting, he gave the Jesuits free rein to proselytize, and he wore his holy Zoroaster shirt with respect.

But he was dissatisfied. 'My mind cannot rest amidst this diversity of sects and creeds... Besides this outward pomp and circumstance, what will make me satisfied.... can I undertake the sway of empire? I am waiting for some discreet man of principle who will resolve the problems in my conscience....'

So he invited the wise and esteemed from various sects to his halls. Long days were spent discussing fundamentals of science, secrets of revelation, strange events in history, or oddities in nature. Representatives of the various religions also attended. Akbar was in their midst, but also stood apart from them. He was a rationalist, and he viewed religion in that way. 'The superiority of man', he said, 'rests in the jewel of reason.'

Not all his guests were happy to hear this. Particularly when Akbar took the next step. One day, he invited the scholars and his military commanders from cities near Agra to the capital city. He addressed that esteemed gathering as follows: 'one bad thing for an empire ruled by a single head is to have its members divided among themselves and opposing each other.... Therefore, we ought to bring them all into one, but in such a way that they should be both "one" and "all"; this will give benefits to everyone. Any one faith will not lose what is good in it, while it will gain whatever is better in another.'

It seems that the longing for peace and tolerance, together with faith in rationalism, and of course the politics of security and integration, made Akbar take this extraordinary decision: on that day he established a new religion. He named it Din Illahi, which is roughly 'the religion of God'. He himself would govern this new religion. It is said that the forms of worship its followers had to observe were an amalgam of various laws, more or less all mixed together.

But we know that Din Illahi did not succeed in replacing Islam, Hinduism, Buddhism, Zoroastrianism, Christianity, or anything else. It had only a few thousand followers, and it lasted no longer than Akbar. All that remains today of this religion that sprang from and existed for a dream of peace is a temple at Fathpur-Sikri.

Of course, peace does not automatically mean fusion. But more than that, I think there was a basic reason why Din Illahi did not survive: Akbar did not see that faith is belief in the light while also believing in the dark. When faith touches the sacred, then this touch is not a greeting of hands, for horror also lies there – as the Bhagavad-Gita depicts when Arjuna witnesses Vishnu appearing near him before the great Bharatayuda war. 'Place me in your fangs', Arjuna says trembling, bowing before the god who has made himself manifest.

The Sufi poet, Amir Hamzah, seems to echo this: 'I am prey in your clutches'. Or Chairil Anwar, 'I am formless, fractured', or like the words of Jeremiah to God, 'Lord you rape me, I am overcome…': God does not enter our hearts with any guarantee that there will be only tranquility, as an absolute protection, with all things made comprehensible.

But Akbar lived in a secure palace that answered every need, and he had proved to himself that he could govern anything – Hindustan, his own disciplined body, political affairs, and diverse philosophies. He felt fortunate to possess that jewel: reason. If he had been closer to misery, been more bitter in facing destiny, more despairing in witnessing despotism and torture, or if he had lived in the twentieth century, like Simone Weil, then perhaps he would not have offered a faith like an architect offering a tidy construction design.

'The beauty of the world is the entrance of the labyrinth', said Weil, the philosopher who died emaciated. 'The imprudent person who, having entered, takes a few steps, is after some time unable to find his way back... If he doesn't have courage, if he continues to walk, it is absolutely certain that he will arrive at the center of the labyrinth. And there, God is waiting for him, to eat him. Later he will leave again, but changed, become other, having been eaten and digested by God.'

'Horor' *Tempo* 8 February 2004, CP VII: 133-6

Trees

Anyone who has planted a tree knows that what grows is not merely an object in space, but also a mark in time. How many centuries are gathered in the virgin forest around Lake Tamblingan? Thousands of trees, ancient, young, crowd together, interweaving with the bushes, tendrils and vines; the dense foliage thickened by ferns that have hidden the path since time immemorial.

I was walking there that evening, along the lake in the hills of north Bali, forging through the undergrowth and losing a sense of distance in a solitude disturbed only by the sound of my tread. Far to the east, on the edge of the lake, was a small temple, entirely protected. At that moment, in that green half-light, the everlasting appeared. Eternity moved. Each second seemed to slip and fuse into the chlorophyll of the trees. Centuries seemed to tremble in the forks of the tree trunks.

Maybe this is why, when forests are felled, time changes. Like a plot of barren earth, where roads will be laid and markets built, time too is strewn, flat, ready for measure. That sight – forest felled, time trimmed – has no more magic. It has only a price. It has only a use. Every bit has been discarded, yielding to the tug of human calculation. Awe-inspiring time, and 'that vigorous and pacific tribe', as Proust called trees, are extinct, never to be reborn.

The Forest, I think, is the end zone where Mystery is not yet lost, where Mystery is not yet mapped. This is why, in times past, old and infirm kings went away to the forest as ascetics to await death, like Destarastra, accompanied by Gandari and Kunthi, in the last section of the *Mahabharata*. Rulers who transformed themselves into ascetics had no further desire to conquer the world. They came to the jungle to rediscover trees (wearing clothes of bark and woven leaves) hoping to be one once more with the Mystery they had previously forgotten.

How long has that Mystery been forgotten, for the magic of nature to vanish? The 'disenchantment of the world' began with the arrival of 'modernity', Max Weber's famous work stated. But perhaps the forgetting and vanishing is much older than 17th century Europe. To me, forgetting can come any time at all, when people view the world as merely a group of objects ready in their grasp, to be summed up in 'knowledge', or to be tinkered with as tools. At that moment, people forget that they were once enchanted by what in Javanese philosophy is called *sangkan paraning dumadi*, 'the source and what will be of becoming'. At this moment, those who forget are no longer moved by what Islamic mystics call *wujūd*.

At that moment, people are busy with what can be seen and heard, with all that can be felt and smelt, with what is there right before them – and they ignore 'being' (*wujūd*) as something miraculous, in fact: Why does being 'be'? Why not 'not being'?

A disturbing question, but not out to disturb. It is actually a wake-up tremor. In the meditation cave protected by trees – that 'vigorous and pacific tribe' – the long-forgotten wake-up tremor seeks redemption. Calmly, silently, willingly, letting go of desire. With 'wise passiveness', as Wordsworth says,

There, static space melts with time past. The ascetic allows, invites, anything outside his ego to celebrate *wujūd*. He does not defeat time. He does not cut it down, level it, all measured, like the developers who plunder the forest. The ascetic, the king-turned-recluse, has no more wish to determine. He is determined. 'Now, Time, it is not my turn...,' says one of Amir Hamzah's meditative poems. The ascetic attempts to absorb all the centuries forming trunks, the years connecting branches, and, near his feet, the dew forming soft lace between the grasses and moss. He or she even senses dampness as a moment in the continual movement of water, from who knows where, to who knows where. Eternity, perhaps.

A Sufi, it is said, will say that this is the moment he discovers *tajalli,* the self-manifestation of The Ineffable. The Sufi will recall one of the Prophet's sayings, that God hides himself 'behind seventy thousand veils of light and darkness'. The Sufi immediately senses how true and beautiful that phrase is: both elements in that veil are present, and the dark will not expel the light, nor the light the dark.

For the Sufi is one who used to be like a king, or an imperial subject, wanting to drive the world outside of himself, and therefore not allowing dark things to appear. Now, as a passive but wise ascetic, he offers thanks, that darkness too is part of the blessing. For, as the *Hadith* says, if God were to strip off all the veils, the light that would stream from His Countenance would 'blind all creatures that dared to gaze upon it'.

Perhaps *tajalli* is *Lichtung* – Heidegger's word for when Being *(Sein)* declares itself, when The Ineffable is manifest. George Steiner, Heidegger's commentator, describes *Lichtung* as 'Like the light which plays around objects in the dark of the wood even though we cannot place its source'.

Dark forest, primeval jungle, but sometimes revealing enchanting light of no clear source – maybe this is a good metaphor for today: humankind's longing for each trembling of the Eternity of the All-mysterious, and the All-beautiful, where life is dense trees giving thanks to the sun. Yet we fell them, we destroy them, and terrifying nihilism begins.

'Pohon-pohon' *Tempo* 16 November 2003, CP VII: 79-82

Allah

People often worship a miniaturized God. Centuries ago, in towns bordering the desert, where the sky is expansive and the nights inhabited by stories and secrets, prophets came to warn people. They denounced idols. They denounced prayers that imagined God – if we use a contemporary metaphor – like a bonsai tree. Idols or bonsai: things attractive precisely because they are placed in a fixed box, as though alive, although in fact it is just God miniaturized by humans, a worshipping very far from the essence of Him, the Almighty.

Muslims have a story from the Qur'an.

Standing before the Pharoah, so the story goes, Moses gave an unexpected reply when the King of Egypt asked, 'And what is the Lord of the worlds?' That question, *'Ma rabbu al-alamina?'* was coaxing a definition. But Moses' answer was different, and sharp. 'God', he said, is 'the Lord of the East and the West and what is between them.'

Moses did not give a definition, for God-defined is the same as God-confined, tightly, within language. Moses' reply was actually a description, or, more correctly, a depiction that did not stop at one conclusion. We can interpret it as an attempt to show, using metaphor, that God is greatness manifest on the horizon in the east, where the rays of light beam, and also in the west, where the dark departs. In other words: God is *Rabb-i–* 'possessor', 'lord' and 'carer' – of all things, visible and invisible, all bright in clarity and all finding obscurity.

This is why He is 'One'. In Indonesian, we use the word '*esa*' for this absolute singularity, and not the word '*satu*', which is the word for the number 'one'. For the divine cannot be counted. He is not like the sun and moon.

Nor is He the God of *Thus Spake Zarathustra*: The God depicted by Nietzsche as an 'old grim-beard of a God', a jealous God saying: 'I am the Lord Thy God! Thou shalt not put strange Gods before me!' In *Zarathustra,* after this statement, all the other gods die – not because they are exterminated, but from laughter.

To me, Nietzsche's caricature fails to capture the attitude of the virtuous, who believe that the divine is one. The monotheists did not come to reduce number. Their intention was not to condense matters. Precisely the opposite. The Almighty is one because He is so great and inscrutable. He is the foundation and the source of a power that makes one tremble – a force that makes all things appear within clarity, 'being'.

Whoever is moved by that force and tries to call the source behind it by name, with a word, will feel this as inadequate. Chairil Anwar bemoaned this in one of his poems he titled 'Prayer': 'How truly difficult it is/ to recall the all of You.'

A 'You' that is 'the all of You' cannot be a miniaturized God. Ibn 'Arabi, a Sufist and great Spanish intellectual of the 12th century, used the word *haqq* for 'the Absolute'. In the sense of 'the most indeterminate of all indeterminates', or *ankar al-nakirat,* the most mysterious of all mystery, 'the most unknown of all the unknown'.

He is unknowable because He transcends all qualification operating in the world of mankind.

But people often worship a minaturized God. Sometimes they treat God as a ruler of a territory, a king with rigid boundaries. These days, there are many who think that when the Qur'an was revealed and said the name 'Allah', Islam aimed to introduce yet another figure of god within an already-cluttered pantheon.

As though 'Allah' was not a name used by the Arabs in pre-Islamic times, by both the ignorant and virtuous, by both the polytheists and Christians. As though 'Allah' is solely God-of-the-Muslims, ruling in a kingdom with its own specific customs. 'Their God is different to our God', say the Christian fundamentalists who view the Islamic world suspiciously. As though the Christian-God, the Jewish-God and a whole line up of other gods, are in competition – precisely like the jealous God of *Zarathustra*.

Maybe this is why there is no need for prophets to come again. But could they? I went back to Ibn 'Arabi's *Fusus al-Hikam* (the Bezels of Wisdom), written in 1229, as discussed in *Sufism and Taoism*, a careful and lucid commentary by the Japanese writer, Toshihiko Izutsu, the foremost scholar of Ibn 'Arabi. I am beginning to see why God is The Absolute. And yet we live in a world, it seems, ruled by ahl *'aql wa-taqyid wa-hasr"*, those who approach Mystery while 'restricting, binding, limiting, restricting'. God is miniaturized. He ends up as just the divine, deserted.

A God like that can be seen everywhere, like some variant of the statues of traffic-police we have in Indonesia; just an idol beside the road, to alert, instil fear, and control. God is no longer a source of '*rahmah al-imtinan*', 'mercy of gracious gift', as Ibn Arabi portrayed; a mercy that reaches anyone and anything without any expectation of any kind – mercy that is not a reward for those who do good.

With a God lacking this kind of mercy, we are living in times marked by *Fehl Gottes*, 'the default of God', as Heidegger said. Despite His name being cited ceaselessly, 'the world becomes without healing, unholy'. A line of Charil Anwar's perhaps conveys this: 'Your pure burning light/now no more than an evening's flickering candle'.

Are we talking about 'secularism' here? I don't think so. Perhaps we are rather talking of a climate where 'the pure' has turned banal, when 'the sacred' has been placed as routine in daily life, organizing its trifles. At that moment, God is indeed busily marketed and exhibited. But He is put in a box, like a bonsai tree.

'Allah' *Tempo* 30 November 2003, CP VII: 87-90

Soroush

A person of faith and afraid of doubt is a person of faith with the door closed, legs quaking. This is why I admire someone like Abdulkarim Soroush. He strides through his doubt with courage, but he does not celebrate atheism. In 1995, an American journalist, Robin Wright from the *Los Angeles Times*, called him 'The Luther of Islam'.

Not quite right: Soroush did not produce an independent force of politics and faith as Martin Luther did. In Germany's sixteenth century, Luther set Protestantism in motion. Its reception spread fast, with the shock felt not only in the body of the Church, but over all Europe.

In Iran, the land of his birth, Soroush is certainly a voice that rebels against doctrinal fetters and institutional religion. Charles Kurzman, in his book *Liberal Islam: A Source Book,* which contains a range of ideas of Muslim thinkers whom he calls 'liberal' – among them Nurcholish Madjid from Indonesia – states how Soroush takes risks. He has had death threats. He has even been physically attacked twice. His voice was considered too sharp in its accusation of contemporary post-revolutionary thought in Iran. However he is not one to shout and get angry. He is a reflective, soft-spoken person. But because of his more reflective tendencies, also probably because he is close in spirit to the poetry of Sa'di and Rumi, Souroush's influence is not explosive.

Soroush is not Luther also because Islam does not recognise a spiritual institution like the Vatican. Islam recognises only ecclesiastical shadows: something unclear in structure, and yet influential and inspiring fear and trembling in the deeds and thoughts of Muslim scholars and intellectuals; something that emerges from the idea of a single community of faithful that crosses space and time because of the teaching that constituted it. In Iran, these shadows are often represented by the *velayat-e-faqih*, the guardians of religious law. But the ayatollahs never created a monolith, and the possibility for disagreement is still negotiable.

Soroush is an example of this process of negotiation. He joined Ayatollah Khomeni's forces in the Iranian revolution. He even joined the advisory board for 'cleansing' universities of 'non-Islamic' elements before these educational institutions were permitted to reopen. Later he did, indeed, retire from that, but he is not an intellectual considered an 'outsider'. Mahmoud Sadri and Ahmad Sadri collected Soroush's writings and translated them in *Reason, Freedom, and Democracy in Islam*, and described the singularity of this thinker as a rare combination: he has an understanding of traditional Islamic law, but he also has a basis in exact sciences, literature and humanities. His book about the Sufi poetry of Rumi is considered to be one of the most influential in the field.

But from Rumi, too, he entered dangerous territory. He, who once admired Al Ghazali, ultimately concluded that there was mysticism based on fear, but, as Al Ghazali portrayed, there was also mysticism based on love, as Rumi extolled. 'I ultimately realized that there is such a thing as an individual religion based on personal experiences, whose teacher is Rumi, just as there is such a thing as a collective religion which is what *shari'ah* and *fiq'h* teach and which is Al-Ghazzali's domain', Soroush said in conversation with Mahmoud Sadri and Ahmad Sadri.

It is precisely this collective religion that has become increasingly visible since the Iranian revolution – and then developed in other places too, as, in Soroush's words, 'Islam of identity' which differs from 'Islam of truth'. In such an atmosphere, there surges an attempt to ideologize Islam. And here, Ali Shari'ati, a renowned thinker from the periods both prior to and following the revolution, and whose writings are revered by the younger Muslim generation, including in Indonesia, has also played an important role.

Soroush feels uncomfortable with this. To him, there is another alternative, which he calls the 'expansion and contraction of interpretation'. He voices the manifestation of plurality. To him, all kinds of truth are 'compatible'. There is no one truth that clashes with another. 'They are all inhabitants of the same mansion and stars of the same constellation.' One cannot possess all truth, and one needs other places and other people to help open up different aspects of that truth: 'religious knowledge as a whole would appear as a mixture of right, wrong, old, and new, that flows on like a vast river', Soroush says.

Thus to Soroush, just as Ahmad Wahib reflected in Indonesia almost a quarter of a century before him, Islam is not, and does not have to become, an ideology – something assumed to be capable of explaining all things, of guiding all affairs. 'Shari'ati wanted to make religion plumper, but I want to make it leaner', Soroush says.

This reminds me of a letter. Ahmad Sahal (a young intellectual from an Islamic school in central Java who studied Adorno's philosophy in Jakarta) explained to me what he meant by 'liberal Islam'. Just as the concept of liberal in politics demands that the State be present only as much as necessary in the organization of daily life, so too, he said, does the concept of liberal in religion demand that religion not control all nooks and crannies of life from A to Z. In a 'lean situation', religion can be more attractive and more inspiring, not more burdensome. 'The greatest pathology of religion that I have noticed after the revolution is that it has become plump, even swollen', Soroush says.

'Soroush' *Tempo* 23 December 2001, CP VI: 127-30

Jerusalem

Jerusalem: here the name of God is uttered every minute and hate is shouted every day. Perhaps every alley in this ancient city is a street of suffering, a *via dolorosa*, and every passer-by is an enthusiastic witness of absolute power. Between the yellowing walls and olive trees, it is as though all these things appear: faith, absolutism, sacrifice, hatred, reawakening, and bitterness. And the desire for immortality.

Just a few metres from the beautiful *Al Aqsa* Mosque still stands the Wailing Wall, weathered for over two millennia. A few hundred meters from this place of Jewish worship stands the Church of the Holy Sepulchre, blackened by centuries of passing dust. I once asked why God had created all this – a cluster of differences that are not accepted as differences – and a world that has become a large Jerusalem: a place witnessing never-ending bloodshed. A friend replied, 'You really think it was God that made all this?'

God created hate, or the other way around, hate created God.... Is that the question? I am afraid to draw any conclusion, afraid lest there is a two-in-one relationship between the sacred and the profane, and there is something terrifying, even disgusting, in every truth. An etching by William Blake, *Jerusalem*, is inscribed with a series of perturbing questions:

> ...*What is a Church & What is a Theatre? are they Two & not One? Can they Exist Separate? Are not Religion & Politics the Same Thing? Brotherhood is Religion, O Demonstrations of Reason Dividing Families in Cruelty and Pride!*

Blake wrote this in the eighteenth century, but here in the twenty-first century we are still asking how precise, actually, that line of division is: what exactly is a church, the place where God is worshipped, and what is a stage, a place of spectacle performing illusion? Are they not just the same thing? Is not religion also politics? And does not religion – which creates a sense of brotherhood between people – 'divide families in cruelty and pride'?

There is a tone of bitterness in Blake's questions. Perhaps his hope for one hundred per cent pure religious behaviour was exaggerated. How could that be? 'Church' is riveted to 'stage', and 'religion' to 'politics' because man never interprets his God standing by himself. No one today is 'like Moses on Mt Sinai', to take a line from Amir Hamzah's poetry. On that mount there was just one human confronting God, but now we do not live on mountain peaks or in deserts, but in crowds, in particular places, at particular times. God speaks and becomes history.

When God becomes history, His word travels from place to place and from time to time. It crosses the diverse, and it discovers the unpredicted. It becomes a narrative, a retelling of aspiration and deed. And we know that deeds are always carried out by a body, brave, but governed by limits. There is no longer anything that can be absolute, nothing that can become final meaning. In this way, the Word is never alone, it lives amongst others; and debates, answers back, grows, branches out.

But there are times when God becomes history, and other times when history becomes God. All that is made and done by humans– with their diverse bodies, fates and times – develops to become The One. Deeds become experience, and experience is codified as teaching. Once teaching is divorced from its metaphor, it quickly or slowly becomes doctrine, something worshipped.

Tragedy occurs when God stops being history and history appears as God. In other words, when belief, which arose in the past, is no longer entwined with the frailty of human affairs today. It is then that the eternal takes over from the mortal.

In Sophocles' play, the gods take up Oedipus's fate. He is destined to murder his father and marry his own mother. He tries to escape this fate, but fails. And yet he is punished for this deed – in the name of justice. In Shakespeare's play, the indecisive Hamlet eventually does something that causes tragedy when his father's ghost, appearing from the realm of the dead, succeeds in pushing him to take revenge. In the *Bhagavad Gita*, Arjuna, who is reluctant to wipe out his own kin, finally joins the battle when Krishna, with his authority and knowledge as Vishnu, succeeds in persuading this reluctant son of Pandu. And the fratricidal war between the Bharata families becomes more savage, eventually ending in futile victory.

There is something noble and moving in these actions, particularly when we ignore the raging cruelty and hate, and the bodies piled up, dead. Perhaps this is what is celebrated in Jerusalem, with its repeated tragedies: man has been killing and being killed since the Crusades, both for martyrdom and through fear.

Until when, we don't know. Once history becomes God, then that historical hate can even be perpetuated to become something eternal. Maybe John Lennon was right: 'God is a concept by which we measure our pain.'

'Jerusalem' *Tempo* 29 October 2000, CP V: 565-7

The Body

From the early mist of the morning, thousands of deer gather, look about, or meander untended in the pine forest of the city of Nara. No one disturbs them in this vast park. It is as though their lord is still enchanted by them, so too the tourists who become more numerous in the heat of the day: since 752, at the Todai-ji temple, a statue of Buddha has stood, sixteen meters high. People say that this figure dominating the *Daibutsuden* space represents a depiction of the essential noble nature of Buddha.

Status and stature – it is as though the two are linked. Strange, actually. How can it be that grandeur is upheld in honoring someone who came into the world precisely to deny grandeur? Didn't Siddharta Gautama leave the palace and return to the people to teach, in the Deer Park, about a life of suffering as long as man remains tempted by desire?

This question of grandeur could be applied just about anywhere. In the coastal town of Amalfi in southern Italy is the Santo Andrea Basilica, a structure that combines elegant Romanesque style with Byzantine goldwork. In one of the far corners is a statue of the Virgin Mary. She stands beside the body of Jesus, lying with blood flowing. The Blessed Lady wears the dress of nobility, dark in colour and embedded with jewels, and on her head is placed a queen's crown.

Why does purity end up dressed in worldly garb? Why is grandeur eventually realized in a stone construction of thousands of cubic meters? I am reminded of Amir Hamzah's poem, when he expresses his longing for God. 'I am human, longing for feeling, longing for form.' Faith is the mother of all kinds of architecture. In our souls it forms peaks and crannies, and builds fences to safeguard what-is-within from the pollution coming from what-is-without. In the space of the world, it builds holy temples and sacred mosques in a longing for feeling and form. Whether a large room or small, a stark building or a decorated one, a statue or calligraphy – all is exuberance of the senses to praise God. The body craves its satisfaction, even in matters concerning the depiction of spiritual desire.

The body, in religion, is indeed a paradox. There are so many rules imposed by sacral command to regulate the body, as though this part of man forever gives rise to anxiety, and therefore needs to be safeguarded against. And yet, at the same time, it is as though there is also the admission that the body is of such importance that worship – and sacrifice – are always an expression of the physical. Perhaps this is why there are some who think that the elimination of apostasy and the removal of difference in faith can only be carried out through the annihilation of the body, not through persuasion. We read about how Al Hallaj was burned, just like those burned at the stake in the Spanish Inquisition.

The body is indeed a point of contradiction: is it the center of defilement, and thus to be denied, or at least controlled? Yet is it not also a presence in deed, so that only through the body can good be enacted?

There is a debate in Confucian thought, particularly in old Japanese manuscripts, which illustrates to me a controversy about the body – a controversy that also continues in the history of Buddhist, Hindu, Christian or Islamic thought, or in anything that aims to translate good deed in the world. At least, this is what I concluded from the Naoki Sarai's explanation in his book *Voices of the Past*, which is most impressive for both its research and philosophical content.

The main character is Ito Jinsai. He is an expert on exegesis of Confucian thought of seventeenth century Japan, who explains his philosophical position through commenting on earlier interpretations found in classical Chinese works. Ito positions himself as one who denies "Song rationalism", particularly the experts from the Zhu Xi school.

Good, according to the Zhu Xi school, is within the thought of man as part of his nature, which is everywhere and forever the same. The self ('I') is in harmony with the universality of the heavens. Almighty awareness pervades and shapes my consciousness, and makes my goodness universal. With this guidance, my behavior is valid. Here, the control of body by thought occurs, and in this way the path towards good can be followed.

Ito Jinsai, on the other hand, emphasises the significance of the body. To Ito, it is not the universality within the soul that unifies mankind, but rather togetherness: the soul or self as Zhu Xi depicts it, is basically assumed to be self sufficient, and needs nothing outside itself, nothing else. In Zhu Xi's philosophy, the world and steps leaving traces in the dust of its path, have no influence on the soul. Even though it is precisely within the world, in the brushing up against others, that good occurs.

The body is not as the Song rationalists imagine: the material cannot be fully planned. There is always the unpredictable. Because of this, the enactment of goodness is not an easy thing. It is not only humility that is important here, but also a feeling of togetherness: each self alone will be insufficient, will be unfinished. As Ito says, 'The Way is like the road; it is that by means of which people come, go and encounter. It is named the Way by virtue of the fact that it enables people to encounter one another.'

A simple path, certainly, not a grandiose space and form, closed, and saying, "Take witness, this is perfection".

'Tubuh' *Tempo* 6 February 2000, CP V: 425-7

Visnu

V isnu sleeps, and humanity feeds dreams to his slumber. Visnu sleeps on the Endless Ocean and lets the dreams run, for he wishes to always recall what is of beauty and the non-vile of the world.

This is what mankind must do, according to one Hindu belief: we must carry out our *dharma,* so that the beautiful is never extinct, and becomes a reminiscence of human life. This reminiscence will be an important part of Visnu's dream. And with good dreams, in the time to come after the universe is destroyed, Visnu the creator can make another universe that brings no disillusionment...

There is anxiety in this Hindu story, but also hope. Our problem these days is that we are further and further away from such conviction; the conviction that there will be apocalyptic change, a total destruction that will be followed by a better world. Perhaps the world is becoming older and more tired. There are piles of scribbles describing revolutions intending to destroy and rebuild, but which turn into trite epics: what is demolished is not completely destroyed, and what is rebuilt is disappointing. Now perhaps we can still imagine the sleeping Visnu, but we doubt that there is an Endless Ocean. What is becoming increasingly clear is that it is the dream that is limited.

It is not that there are no longer angry people demanding change. Actually, there are more of them. Marxists used to assume that because capitalism controlled the entire world and had a tight grip over all sectors of life, transformation would occur and be carried out by a single petitioner and reformer, namely the proletariat. This was not because this class had become a mythical creature as some kind of holy vanguard, but rather because, with capitalism's tentacles spreading everywhere, practically everyone had been sapped of energy. And in this way the anger and demands of the workers could become the anger and demands of anyone and everyone: something universal.

But now times have moved to a different stage, and Marx is long gone: capital has indeed penetrated everywhere, but it is as though people have lost the universal. The workers' protest is only one of many protests heard. There are also the screams of the women's fight, the yells of the black, the brown and the yellow, the petitions of various religious groups and the claims for rights of denied cultural expression. A cacophony. Politics has become a competition between disconnected desires. What people want to destroy and rebuild are no longer one. The universal has been replaced with the particular.

It is not surprising that in all this din, people are not only more doubtful about whether 'universal humanism' exists, but also whether it is true that a system will collapse and change will come about. Just look around us: Indonesia appears to be undergoing transformation, but then again, no – perhaps because Indonesia (as V.S. Naipaul said of India) has become 'a million mutinies', and 'a million mutinies' will eventually not show any great reformation. In fact, in those parts of the world where capitalism has become a system that can no longer be prized open, Revolution (with a capital R) is no longer mentioned. Disconnected rebellions are handled one at a time. Monday, confronting the demands of the workers – which are maybe met, maybe not. Tuesday, hearing the women's protests – accepted or ignored. Wednesday, the system listens to the claims of X, Thursday, Y.... and at the end of each year the system still has not collapsed.

I don't know if this is what is called 'post-modern political struggle' – or in other words, particularism, with limited dreams. I don't know whether I, living in Indonesia, can complain with Slavoj Zizek, a Slovenian intellectual who frequently addresses Western Europe, that there is no longer any opposition to the 'totality of Capital'. I myself am dubious whether one is only able to change the world within the confines of the horizon that currently binds one, for this horizon ultimately is formed through our own steps in guessing the size of space. In other words: the limitation of our dreams is ultimately our own construction.

Indeed, there is something disturbing in the limitation, and the din, of 'a million mutinies'. I feel disturbed not because they are diverse, loud and many. I am troubled because when we never cease celebrating the particular, we deny the ties that give politics worth: the ties between victims. A historian complained that what unifies mankind these days is actually the awareness that mankind is no longer one – and I think there is nothing sadder than this. When a murdered Palestinian child no longer has any tie with an old Israeli who is killed, and a Muslim who is slaughtered does not have the same fate as a Christian who is beheaded, then it is not only the universal that is lost, but life itself is negated.

Each of us is indeed not Visnu – a god who creates from his dreams on the Endless Ocean. We have our limits, and we know that history does not spring from the universal, but rather starts from particular destinies. But the world has never changed through an isolated strangled voice, has it?

'Visnu' *Tempo* 5 November 2000, CP V: 569-71

God

God was gagged and His name yelled in Ayodhya. The Babri Mosque had been standing since the sixteenth century, causing no trouble. But last week it was destroyed by those convinced that faith had called them: a large group of followers of Hindu 'revivalism'.

Since then, around seven hundred people have died. The Muslims attack the Hindus, the Hindus attack the Muslims, regardless of whether or not they had anything to do with the Ayodhya incident. Who is wrong and who is right has become obscure. God is proclaimed, with differing names, in this carnival of hate that they think is a parade of truth. But is He listening?

No – not if we view God as Tagore did, not if we worship God as Tagore worshipped him. 'I know thou takest pleasure in my singing. I know that only as a singer I come before thy presence', Tagore described his relationship with God. A song is love that radiates, clear, free and simple, without complicated ritual, grand ceremony, and fancy places of worship. Without pretention. Those who love and sing are not going to consider their own way the expression for people in all places, at all times. Love, like song, is not law. Love, like song, differs from one person to the next. Love, like song, does not spread anger.

But in Ayodhya there was only the yell of war. There were no individuals. Only the mass, the group. In the midst of thunderous noise, mouths foaming, Tagore was not mentioned; he might sound like a softhearted poet, a loner. The God he mentions in *Gitanjali*

– Thou hast brought the distant near and made us brother of the stranger' – has become a strange God.

It is astounding that God can be worshipped in ways different to Tagore's – or to the way a Muslim recalls God daily as The Compassionate and Merciful. God is sometimes even imagined as the One sanctioning hate and destruction. But is there really a way that is most correct to interpret Him? Who knows? How difficult, indeed, to project His complete image, uninfluenced by our habits, our behaviour, our concerns – in other words, our limitations.

Here we enter a tricky problem: interpretation. It seems to be no coincidence that intellectuals are once again tied up in knots in the intricacies of how, really, the process of 'knowledge' or 'knowing' works – in other words, the epistemological process. There are no more prophets receiving new revelation. At the same time, life detects more and more circumstances that cannot always be clarified by extant concepts, models or examples. Old paradigms quickly become as dead as corpses. Last year's theories are quickly stale. People need revised interpretations, particularly if they concern knowledge about humankind, its origin and end. People are even beginning to be uncertain as to whether there can be a consensus about all this, and whether we can claim there is a single center that can forge this consensus. And thus aware, people are now seriously analyzing whether all of this isn't grounded in the way we give meaning to the world, just as a reader gives meaning to a text. The 'post-structuralists' even pay great attention to this matter of textual interpretation. To them, it impossible for human language to offer a single, finished meaning, without always sliding into other meanings.

Chaos? Confusion making many victims? Frightening indeed, if the problem extends to the way God appears in our consciousness: as The Avenger, like in Ayodhya, or as the One we can love with simplicity and humility?

Well, I prefer to return to Tagore, who can be so beautiful: 'You hide yourself in your own glory, my King', he wrote in his long poem, *Crossing*. 'The sand-grain and the dew-drop are more proudly apparent than yourself.'

'Tuhan' *Tempo* 19 December 1992, CP IV: 371-3

Saladin

I tried to pray for Saladin's soul beside his tomb in a small crypt behind the more-than-twelve-centuries-old Umayyah Mosque in Damascus. But my concentration wasn't right.

Something must have been troubling me. This tomb – the tomb of a person so revered in history, so renowned, so admired even by his enemies – felt murky and dull. The room was grey, like half-hidden sadness.

Here was a grave with a high metal tombstone that was so worn away it looked like worm-eaten wood. The room, measuring four by six meters, was like a room that no one was interested in any more. The colors were washed out. Pale light. Thick cobwebs. Dust. No one would guess that here Sultan Saladin, the Islamic hero of the Crusades, is buried. There is just an ugly paper picture, of his face perhaps, on the wall.

Graves should not be made into exhibition halls, of course. A grave is a sign of our own transience, and of the limitations of heroes. And shouldn't humankind pause and reflect? 'Reflect on everything good', a line of Chairil Anwar's poetry reads, 'and my eternal love'. Doesn't the past have something eternal that can be represented by a sign, a symbol, an attitude of reverence?

I tried to pray before Saladin's tomb in Damascus, for his soul, but also for something good in history, yet I felt there was something wrong in this room. Stepping outside and walking back to the open inner courtyard of the mosque, I could hear the sound of the Shia pilgrims wailing near the relic of Hussein who died in

Kerbala centuries ago. On the high walls one could still make out the traces of Byzantine murals.

The past does not disappear easily, even if we don't wish to view it. On one of the walls of the Umayyah Mosque, which used to be the Cathedral of Saint John the Baptist until it was altered to become a mosque around 700 CE, a historian found the trace of an inscription that read: 'Your Kingdom, Christ, is the eternal kingdom...'.

But if the past does not disappear easily, then which part of Saladin's story will come to us here today? Which myth will we keep alive from this murky tomb?

Saladin's tale is a tale of war. We hear stories from his times of how religion could inspire courage and a spirit of sacrifice, even inspire killing if necessary.

But a large number of the tales of Saladin, tales that spread in both the West and the East about the Crusades in the twelfth century, tell of a man valiant in battle who in fact did not like to spill blood.

Saladin reclaimed Jerusalem in the summer of 1187. Just before the battle, he gave the Christian holders of the city a chance to prepare themselves so they would be able to defend themselves with dignity against his forces. And when the Christians eventually lost, Saladin did not take the people as slaves, but rather freed them without exacting revenge – even though the European crusaders, when they had taken Jerusalem in 1099, hacked to pieces 70,000 Muslims from the city, and dragged the remaining Jews off to the synagogue to be burnt.

'My child', the dying Sultan addressed his son, az-Zahir, 'do not spill blood, for split blood never rests.'

During his life of only fifty-five years, Saladin seems to have followed this ideal. Of course he was not always without fault, nor was it uncommon for him to give orders for killings. Yet we know

– even from Hollywood movies – how this Muslim leader showed kindness towards Richard the Lionheart, who had come from England to defeat him. When Richard lay ill during the battle, Saladin sent him a fresh pear packed in snow, and a doctor. The peace agreement was signed on 2 September 1192. Celebrations and all kinds of tournaments were held, and the Europeans were amazed that Islam could produce such a good man.

We too can be amazed that those times could have produced such a good man, especially now when people are trying to revive all that is aggressive and belligerent from the twelfth century while ignoring all that is peaceful and tolerant from those warlike times.

But is the past important, really? On a day in the 1970s, I left this neglected tomb of a great Kurd and returned to the center of Damascus, passing the busy bazaar in front of the Umayyah Mosque. The city was bustling – a bustling that seemed to be without history.

'Saladin' *Tempo* 19 January 1991, CP IV: 105-7

Family

A few moments before taking up arms, Arjuna doubted. We know this part of the story. We know why this Pendawa hero did not let his arrow fly at once: he was reluctant to kill his own kin.

However, we also know what happened. The battle continued fiercely. The two sides of the Bharata family went on destroying each other. Some of the elders were killed, and almost all of the youths. There was spilling of blood, gnawing bitterness and endless wailing.

The *Mahabharata* tells us that war has to happen. There are matters and injustices that must be settled. A new world has to be created. Yet it is interesting that the *Mahabharata* holds a certain ambivalence that seems to be in accordance with the widespread feeling of a society leaving behind something usually termed a kinship system.

On the one hand, there is general condoning of the dismantling of a kinship system in the attempt to construct a new world with new values. On the other hand, there is a sense of guilt and loss. Unlike a Mandarin martial arts story, the *Mahabharata* does not portray any happy ending after the great Bharatayudha war is over, What is depicted is mainly dying, and finally a procession of the Pendawas to the meeting with Death.

This is probably why we find the *Mahabharata* far more gripping than the *Ramayana*. In the *Ramayana* there is not the bitterness of the dismantling of family ties – except the well-known conflict between Rahwana and his two brothers, Wibisana and Kumbakarna. To put it simply, the *Ramayana* is the story of a battle between us (*kita*) and the outsiders (*orang asing*), but the *Mahabharata* tells of a war within one family.

And so this story, performed over and over again in Java with such deep respect, seems to give expression to an anxiety and tension in our souls of which we are not fully aware: an anxiety and tension that was felt the most intensely around the time that the *Bharata Yuda* was adapted in Java in the twelfth century.

Ever so slowly, but surely, one can sense now the weakening of our kinship system as the main hinge of our socio-political framework. No longer do people feel united with their distant relatives from the same village, or with people from the village claiming the same ancestral founder. Now a wider unit has been formed, with more people of more diversity. We call this 'a country', and as a single, complete operational unit, 'the state'.

The transformation is not without a sense of sadness. Feelings like this must emerge amongst members of society living in the midst of such a process, for in effect their anchor lines, their ties of loyalty are altered. And so a war within a family becomes not only possible, but is even given a moral cause. We see how Kreshna could assure Arjuna that he need not take family ties into account. Personal relationships – including the relationship between teacher and pupil – need not be considered. The moment had come for Arjuna to link himself to something impersonal: his duty as a *ksatriya* – or something along these lines.

So if the 'call of duty' must be given priority over the bind of loyalty to origins, where do I stand? If the ideals of building a new world and new values are greater than the virtue of doing good to and within one's family, then what do I have to lean on?

With the emergence of feelings like this, something happens in our awareness. An expert has called this the movement of 'separation' towards 'individuation'. The movement contains a certain fear, and this fear brings a demand for protection. And so people create a series of symbols.

In this giving of symbols, we call our country 'a family'. At the head is the 'father' (*bapak*), usually the king or the head of state. It is as though we are able in this way to replace something that is lost when we 'separate' and become our own selves.

However, the difficulty is that the symbol comes to be no longer seen as a symbol, even though a country is never a family, and a head of state can never be like a real father to the citizens. And how is it possible to operate an economy in a 'family-like' way, when the state itself needs something that cannot be based on kinship – namely the law, and in particular law that protects the individual's rights of ownership? Doesn't the state, after all, definitely require a mechanism that is impersonal, namely bureaucracy?

And did Arjuna, on the Kurusetra battlefield, act as a bureaucrat: as one who, for the sake of duty, does not distinguish between what is family and what is not?

Maybe not. Maybe Arjuna is the eternal humanist: he was unsure of whether to fight not because he was disgusted to kill people of the same origin as himself, but because he did not want to destroy people who had done no wrong other than to be on the wrong side. Bhisma could not be accused of being wrong merely because he was in the Kurawa branch of the family and therefore fighting with the 'others'.

The end of a system based on kinship can therefore open the door to a new dawn, where people do their duty, die, are cursed or praised because of themselves. Family and the group are only a trace.

'Keluarga' *Tempo* 3 August 1991, CP IV: 189-91

Ego

A poem hangs on an old grave in Delhi, the burial site of an Islamic saint. The poem was written by Muhammad Iqbal, a Muslim poet from the Indian continent who composed it when he was twenty-seven years old. He wrote in praise of the great Sufi saint Nizamuddin Auliya.

This was around the year 1903, and at this time Iqbal was still very close to Sufism. Two years later he left for Europe. He studied at Cambridge, London and Munich, and there, in the lively activity of Europe, he found a valuable model. 'Through their ambition for action,' he wrote, 'the Western nations have towered over the other nations of the world.' According to Iqbal, the literature and ideas of the West provide the best guide for Eastern nations wishing to appreciate the 'secret of life'.

Iqbal was not without criticism of the West, and in this he differs little from other Islamic or Eastern thinkers. However, Iqbal, who regarded modern Western thinking as the 'direct descendant' of the culture of medieval Islam in Spain and Sicily, later voiced more strident criticism of something in his own past – Sufism.

Iqbal's poem on Nizamuddin Auliya's grave remains, even though Iqbal himself changed. He was no longer a devotee of Sufism. 'Mysticism is the sign of decline in a nation' he is quoted as saying. 'All religious teaching that obstructs the flowering of the human identity' is something 'worthless'. In other words, Iqbal had become an 'activist' who saw self as one with the wave: 'If I roll, I exist. If I stop, I no longer exist.' But Sufism is passive. Sufis stress the striving for 'extinction of self' within the Almighty. There, the self vanishes like a drop of water in the ocean. There, human identity is blotted our. To Iqbal, this is not what should happen. As Rajmohan Gandhi wrote in his work *Understanding the Muslim Mind*, 'Iqbal hoped for man to become a gem, an emerald, not a drop of water.'

Iqbal did not seek union (*wisal*) with God, but *firaq* or separation. He wrote in a poem that in union there is the desire for death, but in separation there is the enjoyment of searching.

Man is not just a creature that lays his head with faint whining in God's lap. Man does not need to speak as Chairil Anwar did when he knocked on God's door: 'I am lost, destroyed.' Man is rather God's partner. His creative colleague. Man has his own independence. In a collection of Iqbal's poems, *Payam-i-Mashriq*, Iqbal relates a conversation between man and God: 'You created the night – but I turn on the light. You created the clay – but I make the pots. You created the wide expanses – but I create the gardens.'

Iqbal goes on to speak further of that important pivot of his well known philosophy, *khudi*. This word can mean 'self', 'ego', or 'identity'. To Iqbal, its meaning is close to 'declaration', 'reality' or 'self-realization'. For Iqbal sees that Adam (meaning man) was sent into the world from Paradise not in order to be punished but rather to be God's representative. Man is not burdened with sin, but rather is given freedom, and it is this that Iqbal calls 'the freedom of the human ego'.

The difficulty for man is that this freedom is often frightening. Therefore, man calls upon laws and sets limitations. But how far, for how long, and by whom? For those living souls that give birth to wisdom and poetry and those active minds that engender new ideas and discoveries cannot all merely be handed established timeworn limits *ad infinitum*. Here lies man's capacity to resist becoming 'lost and destroyed.'

So, how can man's *khudi* move freely and yet not deviate? If we read the writing of Rajmohan Gandhi, Mahatma Gandhi's grandson, who in the book mentioned above seems to be trying to understand Iqbal's teaching, then Iqbal himself was eventually unable to find a satisfactory answer to this complex problem.

On 20 April 1938 Iqbal died. We recall a line from his last poem, sad and anxious: 'another wisdom will follow – but then again, maybe not.'

'Ego' *Tempo* 15 April 1989, CP III: 517-9

The Cube

The Ka'bah is plain simplicity. Once I went inside. It was dark. There was nothing awe-inspiring, nothing special. There was nothing to say that this room held a magical secret.

But something made me uneasy: this happened when I heard a whisper from somewhere in front of me, saying that I should start to pray, and at that instant I was aware, not only as thought but also in a physical sense, that God was not here – that God was not anywhere, but remained distant, and could not be reached from where I stood. God is not within measurement.

But at the moment that one understands this, or more precisely, that one experiences it, one surrenders. Just as a poet said, 'we submit beneath the shadow of His might'. And at that moment, He is very near.

That day I was reminded again of Chairil Anwar's poem: 'I knock at Your door, Lord/ and I cannot turn my back on You.'

The Ka'bah is simplicity: it is a sign of man's surrender before Him, and that sign is the Cube, covered in black. It is large, but apart from the calligraphy on the covering cloth, it is practically without any decoration or ornament, without any ostentation. It just stands there in the square of the Haram Mosque, nothing attractive.

Muhammad Asad, the Islamic writer of European Jewish descent, is right. In his fine autobiography *The Road to Mecca*, he describes in beautiful language what I am trying to say: 'I have seen in various Muslim countries mosques in which the hands of great artists had created inspired works of art', he writes, but 'in the utter simplicity of a cube, in the complete renunciation of all beauty of line and form', a certain attitude is encapsulated. 'Whatever the beauty man may be able to create with his hands, it will be only conceit to deem it worthy of God: therefore the simplest that man can conceive is the greatest that he can do to express the glory of God.'

The Ka'bah is 'a quiet island', Asad says, 'much quieter than any other work of architecture anywhere in the world.' The Ka'bah is a quiet island because the people who first built it knew that in one's ambition for greatness and determination for success, all this pales the instant that one is aware of one's true position. The Cube is a product of this awareness. It is a statement of humility. The poet Rainer Maria Rilke sings of God and touches on this eternal theme: 'God, Your meaning is humility.'

On that day, inside the Ka'bah people were praying – facing any direction. Outside, all the faithful were praying, but all facing the same direction, the direction of the Ka'bah. Yet in fact they could also face any direction. They surrender.

'Imagine yourself as a particle of iron in a huge magnetic field', Ali Shariati urges in his famous small treatise on making the Haj. 'Or as though you are among millions of doves ascending to Heaven.'

A particle of iron amongst millions of other iron particles, one white dove amongst millions of other white doves: who am I, who are we? Clearly we are not just a mass. The paradox of the 'mass' is that on the one hand personal identity is not important, but on the other hand it can merge with others to become a potentially powerful force. Totalitarianism, like fascism and communism, speaks of 'the masses' as though this word is a mantra or lucky charm to be used in battle. The masses are given special place. In these creeds, we can hear at once both the anger and faith that declared that the 'masses' are always right and are destined to win in the end.

In other words, a kind of arrogance. Therefore, in fact we cannot equate the movement of the thousands of faithful who walk circling the Ka'bah with the 'masses' of totalitarianism. For this prescribed action is an act of homage and surrender – any socio-political significance ascribed to this act cannot stray far from this basic inherent meaning.

Ali Shariati writes: 'Mecca is a safe and peaceful city that is not marked by fear, hate or conflict, but by security and peace.' Sadly, much has changed since he wrote this.

Let us imagine we all recall that we are iron particles or birds in flight – that we face the Ka'bah, circle it, make a statement of surrender (*mituhu*) within the One Will.

'Kubus' *Tempo* 15 August 1987, CP III: 277-9

Wounds

Islam is a religion that is full of *élan,* but its community of believers has a wounded heart. A friend once called it, in a tone of melancholy, 'a wounded civilization'.

This description comes from V.S. Naipaul, of course, writing about the distant land of his forefathers in *India: A Wounded Civilization.* In history it seems there is always a civilization that soars only to be later struck down, and the 'wounded civilization' syndrome appears. In Islam, this wound is relatively new: at least its traces are still felt acutely at the end of the twentieth century. In other words, the wound is not completely healed.

Formerly, when newly arrived on the face of history, the Muslim community accepted life with hearts of joy and conviction. They didn't balk at searching for knowledge in China, copying Greek works, tapping poetry from Persia or theater from the Far East. From all of this they created many things, discovered many things. It was as though they were carrying out a mandate given by God to become caliphs on earth, and to affirm a covenant.

But then Islamic countries got cornered. In this twentieth century the majority of Muslims are living in a vast territory called 'The Third World'. They are at the very bottom according to current measures of achievement. And when people still recall Ibnu Khaldun or Avicenna it is precisely with a sense of pain in their hearts.

What happens then is a process, with consequences occasionally depressing, occasionally brilliant. The depressing is a sense of hopelessness. This lack of hope is maybe what makes people desert religion. Or perhaps they don't desert what they believe in: rather, some of them decide to exercise *takfir* (disavowal) – namely to disavow the entire contemporary world outside of themselves as the space of the *kafir* or unbelievers.

That world outside is indeed not always comprehensible and acceptable. It is full of things whose origins are 'non-Islamic', and even, and especially, 'Western'. There are machines, large-scale businesses, democracy and basic respect of individual rights; there are also porno films and the philosophy of Karl Marx. These things have a strong presence, and in one way or another seem to mock those of us who choose not to go along with them. And so it is understandable that we tend to reject them.

But to reject does not mean to conquer, and this is the problem. Maybe this is where 'takfirism' is born, a term I prefer within Islam's own history compared, say, to the term 'fundamentalism'. Not yet able to defeat that world with all its wrongs, some Muslims cut off contact with every bit of influence from outside their world of reference. And so the attempt to purify behaviour begins. The stronger one senses the world of those 'kafir' (unbelievers) over there, the more vigorous the will to purify.

'Takfirism' inevitably involves an attitude of rejection and opposition. This rejection can be very extensive: because constitutional democracy and pluralism come from 'the West', for instance, then they too can even be seen as conflicting with Islam. Here, a constant sense of suspicion prevails. Scientific experiments, artistic innovation, and cultural diversity usually local and indigenous in nature, are also, in turn, an anathema.

Needless to say, it is more difficult for the 'takfirists' to accept compromise. Purity precisely seeks life without compromise. For as seen in history, teachings, mental attitudes or values all prove to be factors that cannot in themselves create the objective world. Thus we cannot really blame Muslims' misguided thinking or deviant teachings and prohibitions, however manifest, as the source of economic backwardness, just as Hindu culture cannot completely explain poverty. However perceptive Max Weber and Sombart may be, there are many holes in their theories that argue Protestantism in northern Europe brought about the progress of capitalism.

Because of this, the 'takfirists', adhering to the purity of teachings, will be disappointed yet again when they see the modern world continuing to shunt believers aside. For purity or contamination of doctrine does not always determine history. There are so many factors of chance that put us within the level of the 'Third World', as a wounded civilization.

Fortunately, a wounded civilization sometimes produces brilliant things. Like Islamic communities everywhere, in Indonesia it too feels under pressure. And yet, at the same time as in Indonesia increasing numbers of educated are to be found among more traditional Muslim adherents, there is also in Muslim circles a rainbow and explosion of thinking that seems livelier than in other circles. These people do not all agree with one other. But neither do they all despair that the situation is beyond hope, and that outside all is black.

Maybe because of this, that rainbow and explosion is called divine mercy. For this wounded civilization is precisely a civilization that is not yet dead – and is even healing itself. It can't be written off that easily.

'Luka', *Tempo* 3 November 1984, CP II: 583-5

Solar Eclipse over Borobudur

It was as though the Buddha statues in their stupas had suddenly gone mute. These stones had been standing for centuries at Borobudur without movement. But when the eclipse happened and the strange filtered light fell even to the distant hills, the sensation of silence was sudden. Astonishing.

What really happened? Everything, perhaps – but then again maybe only a sign of time itself. The sky so distant and so primeval. An unfathomable time cycle from some never-never land: this ninth-century temple standing here amongst us witnessed the same event three and a half centuries ago – also three and a half centuries before that, and three and a half centuries before that again,

Four times this black monument on the hill has been touched by such a complete eclipse – when dark falls at noon and the temperature drops. Four is a small figure. But between each time, hundreds of years have been swallowed up, millions of people have come and gone, and dozens of disasters, wars and times of fortune have gone by.

Time cannot be reduced to merely a succession of seconds or years. It cannot be explained completely, except through witnessing that which is finite.

And what is finite? Are we? The answer to this can be at once cutting and flippant: we creatures who are invisible from endless outer space, we inhabitants beneath an ancient temple that when measured in astronomical time is still in its infancy – only four eclipses old – we are merely dust.

It is not surprising that an eclipse like this inspires people to prayer. Nor is it surprising that it can touch us in a way that inspires humility. For we surely do not know where we were at the eclipse before this one, three years before Sultan Agung departed from a place close to this very village to attack Batavia (now Jakarta). Nor do we know where we will be when the next eclipse occurs – the fifth eclipse for Borobudur.

The distance between the seventeenth century and the twentieth century is great, even when it is linked through the sequence of history. So many have vanished without trace – so much is unknown.

And the distance from the twentieth to the twenty-third century is unimaginable (despite the attempts of Herman Kahn). Change is so fast. The earth is more and more inestimable. Science fiction stories give us ever-stranger fantasies. On the one hand we could be chatting to ET, or on the other hand we could be wiped out like the inhabitants of the planet Krypton in *Superman*.

No matter what happens, in the end all of us who experienced the eclipse – those who squinted at the stars through telescopes, those who feared being dragged off by the police, the politicians who posed beside the stupas, the fishermen who were prevented from going to sea, the tourists who paid for the sensation – all of us are merely a fleeting gathering of specks. As Chairil Anwar wrote in that now-famous phrase, 'Life merely delays defeat'.

Merely delays defeat? Is human life just an accident with no meaning except as witness to the greatness of the Creator?

Here is the problem. Something that has no meaning at all is more depressing than, say, an old locomotive. That old loco can give us a ride to the Cepu forest – it can entertain us, and it is not superfluous.

So all through their lives, humans seek a synthesis between the humility needed to admit that one is merely dust, and the need to deny that one is only a product without any worth. Religion gives answers, if our existence is linked to God. Not only God the Almighty, but also God the All-Merciful.

And the eclipses could be symbols of time: life is like a shower, soothing but fleeting (or fleeting but soothing), to use the analogy of the desert. We are shaken by that power, but we are also entertained by the fact that we can witness it. Then we realize that both three hundred and fifty years ago and in three hundred and fifty years' time we are different from a stone temple: more perishable yes, but more meaningful within a sense of thanksgiving and wonder.

'Gerhana Matahari di Borobudur' *Tempo* 18 June 1983, CP II:
311-3

Mosques

We can probably remember the mosque in the village where we grew up. It had no tall minaret. On top of the roof, almost mid-center, was just a small room with wooden walls, which was the prayer-calling room. You got there by climbing up a bamboo ladder. There was no big dome. There were no loudspeakers. The architecture of the building and its location in the village were not ostentatious, nor did they compete with the houses of the poor villagers around. But inside it was cooler. The floor was cleaner, the well deeper. And the water for ceremonial washing before prayer never ran dry.

These are not mosques considered fit to be photographed for a history book. Perhaps they do not even feel they have a history. Like the faces of the old mosque-keepers, they have just always been there. If the roof leaks, it is fixed up as best as can be. When Idul Fitri celebration time comes around, the walls are whitewashed just as much as is necessary. These mosques, built for small cost and maintained with minimal expense, are free from dependence on big-shot donors. They can go on without begging for the attention of important bureaucrats.

In the large mosques, usually you find that the authority is shared between the mosque religious officials and the state officials. Sometimes this is a happy union – sometimes not. But in our village mosques there is never this union, honorable or not.

For these are not mosques like the huge Istiqlal Mosque (in Jakarta) which can draw in so much money, and save so much through donations, that corruption scandals are a constant liability. They are also not the mosques around Baghdad, with crystal chandeliers, silver or gold engraved doors and brightly colored or golden minarets and domes, all restored with government funds for which the resident religious leaders must express grateful thanks to all who visit. Our village mosques are also not places with tombs for the eminent, in secure, fragrant enclosures scattered with coins of the alms-givers. They are not flashy in the midst of people living lives of poverty and detachment.

An Egyptian architect at the Sultan Hassan Mosque in Cairo, which is often hailed as a great example of Islamic architecture, once said, 'If I stand at the Sultan Hassan Mosque, where is the place for me?' While he could acknowledge the monumental nature of the structure, he had to admit that this mosque was built as a symbol of the power and prestige of the Sultan and his government – a symbol built just at the time that Islamic thought and culture was at its lowest ebb.

At times when we feel inferior, we often puff ourselves up. The fact that our village mosques feel no need to be flashy is perhaps because they stand for no other purpose than as places of prayer. They are a reflection of the people they serve who, because they are at one with their environment, feel no need to be ostentatious.

Structures do indeed reflect the attitude of the people who construct them. Seyyed Hossein Nasr has written of this in his lengthy article, 'The Contemporary Muslim and the Architectural Transformation of the Urban Environment of the Islamic World'. Nasr points out that the outer environment created by humankind for itself is no other than a reflection of its spirit. He speaks sadly of the contemporary crisis that is taking place in the construction of cities and buildings in many Islamic countries, and the loss of the humility and self-respect that used to be found in traditional architecture.

In other words, he speaks of a spiritual crisis. But is it true that its cause is secularism? Or is it that religion has narrowed to become merely a system of laws and rules of behavior, while ignoring compassion and concern for one's own environment? Or is it that Muslims are no longer humble, but rather lacking in confidence? Or that, in fact, cities and Muslims cannot be free from the developments of these times that are so frequently bad and haphazard?

Perhaps we should think back on those mosques in the villages where we grew up: most of us never visit them any more.

'Masjid-masjid' *Tempo* 24 November 1979, CP I: 619-21

Sacred Poetry

If sacred texts were merely books of law without poetry, humans would have been living for a long time with barren spirits. The Bhagavad Gita, the Bible, the Qur'an: in the midst of our contemporary experience one thing we need is to revive the poetry found within them.

And this doesn't mean merely to translate them with verbal decoration or to read them in a beautiful style. The poetic translation of the Qur'an pioneered by Mohammad Diponegoro in Indonesia some years back, or Nyoman S. Pendit's attempts with the Bhagavad Gita, proved they did not have to ornament. For we do not need such ornament. More fundamental to the revival of the poetry of sacred texts is actually to revive our own spirituality. To me this means a renewal of attitude, so as to be able to accept sacred texts as not just a kind of code of criminal law.

For indeed, God spoke in human language, in poetry. And poetry, with its symbolism, rhythm, with all its energy, does not dictate. Poetry is speech to the soul, which involves the acknowledgement of the other as a person, with all that this implies. Accepting sacred texts as living poetry means to accept the word of God not as a decree, but rather as an invitation to dialogue; not as intimidation, but rather as the bestowal of love. In this way, we free ourselves from a biased, confining view about God and mankind; God as a kind of tyrant, and humans like His colonized subjects, already exiled, and forever distrusted.

Too often we are asked to be in fear of Him, and all too frequently we forget that we can actually be attracted to Him and love Him.

Henry Miller, in his autobiography, writes that once he suddenly noticed on a wall in Chicago writing in ten-foot high letters: *Good News! God is Love!* As though this good news had to be made into a headline – even though this 'news' was not actually any new truth. For this not-new truth had been long stifled, and mankind had, for a long time, not known of it. We know the character Hasan in Achdiat K. Mihardja's novel, *The Atheist*: he suffers because since his childhood God has been depicted to him as the Owner of Hell, speaking only of threats and never of consolation.

A God who does not cheer is a God depicted not as the All-loving and All-forgiving, but rather as the All-hating. And if so, he is a futile creator. For then our life loses its meaning, man is just one absurd product. And then we forget that life is a gift, that the world is not a cursed place of exile, that man is important, a caliph on earth, and not a hunted dog.

To accept the important meaning of man is actually our problem now. If we believe there is no coercion in religion, if we are open enough to live within the poetry of God's words and not merely to live within His threats, then we have to trust man with his freedom. For God bestows upon us what Iqbal calls the 'freedom of human ego'. The relationship between man and God, which these days is called a relationship between 'I-and-Thou' is a relationship of Subject-to-subject. It is only through the poetry of sacred texts that this kind of relationship can be experienced: my self is not submerged, but rather emerges, with a living spirit, in liberty. In short, a relationship without ambition, where humans can give thanks within a situation of devotion and intimacy, a direct contact without any other person as intermediary – for in the end, poetry cannot be determined by a go-between.

Indeed, in the end, God's conversation with man in poetic experience is not determined by a third party. We can get assistance from someone else to interpret the Word of God, but then it is up to us to determine our attitude. Through poetry, the words of God convey not merely His being, but also His mystery. For in the meeting transformed by poetry, language is enriched, approaching comprehensive depiction, and portraying realities that cannot be completely clarified by analysis. Poetic articulation does not speak of details, little by little. Its articulation contains its own ambiguity, and yet can still communicate. Through poetic language such as this God can appear in our hearts, creating an inner experience, which made the poet Chairil Anwar write:

Although it is truly difficult
to remember the all of You

He experienced the mystery of God, which opened up all kinds of possibilities of interpretation, without there ever being fullness of depiction. No one can resemble God, and no one can claim to have found the one and only Truth of Him. That is why God gives each of us the opportunity to relate to Him. In this way, to revive the poetry of sacred texts means to open the door to a free, authentic and individual communication between God and man. To revive that poetry means to avoid the tendency towards stasis in our systems of belief. Faith cannot be transplanted, religion cannot be regimented, and interpretation about God cannot be monopolized.

I think we need awareness like this in our times.

'Puisi Kitab Suci' *Harian Kami* 1968, *Kata Waktu*: 19-21

IV
New Essays

That Photo

...and the grave
Proves the child ephemeral...
                    --W.H. Auden

That photo – that shocking photo, the one we can't bear to look at, the one we worry will make sensitive people the world over have nightmares – has quickly become the symbol of our current anxiety. The body of a small three-year-old boy lying facedown on the shore. His tiny, fragile forehead dipped in the waves that washed his body back up on Turkish soil. The blue of his shorts and the red of his t-shirt seem to be calling out to the entire Bodrum Peninsula.

Later it became known that his name was Aylan. From Syria. Together with his five-year-old brother Galip and his mother Rehan he was drowned when the dinghy carrying them capsized. They were heading for the island of Kos in Greece, just four kilometers away, but did not make it. Only the father, Abdullah, was saved. There were 12 refugees in two crowded dinghies, eight of them children.

It is not easy for us to ask, let alone answer, what will happen to the tragic father. 'Everything I was dreaming of is gone', was all he could say after burying his sons and his wife. He is returning to Syria.

The fateful day was 2 September 2015, early autumn in Greece. Abdullah had once longed for a calm future and seasons in Canada:

he left his homeland destroyed by the bitter war between 'IS', *ad-Dawlah al-Islāmiyah* and government forces, the rebels and the Kurdish forces, and much else besides. But Canada, with cold-hearted bureaucracy, rejected Abdullah and his family's application.

So they tried to find another country, via a corner of Turkey, crossing the Aegean Sea and reaching the island in Greece where Hippocrates, the father of medicine, once lived. They were like thousands of other refugees now breaking through the margins of Europe – queues of hope that turn into long queues of mourning. Mourning the destruction of thousands of homes and devastation of their homelands. Mourning the exiled, the shattered Middle East, Africa struck by savagery, countries torn apart by ferocious opposition to authorities, countries ripped to shreds by religious fanaticism run rife, cursed by the greed for acquisition of land, oil and position, and ignited by long-suppressed vengeance.

We, even so far away, are part of those queues of mourning, like it or not. Not only for Aylan. We also mourn for Abdullah who said 'Everything I was dreaming of has gone'. Because what will become of people's dashed hopes – after the world heaved a sigh of relief 25 years ago because nuclear war did not break out and yet life turned out to be no further from despair?

That photo, the photo in the wet sand. Aylan.

'Every child comes with the message that God is not yet discouraged of man', the famous Bengali poet Rabindranath Tagore is supposed to have said. Tagore always had sophisticated, bright, sweet phrases – intoxicating, even. But perhaps this was because he had not seen little Aylan sprawled, face down. Aylan who had come with a message of good but was suddenly gone.

There on that continental shore, is God still not discouraged of man? On the other hand, is mankind still not discouraged of God, when children can so quickly and easily become victims of large, brutal forces – in a world they neither choose nor understand, just as they do not choose or understand the message of God – if indeed there is one?

Perhaps that message, if there is one, is indeed stark and depressing. But history always shows that at the same time, the stark and depressing can hold a commitment; what is born can be soon lost, the innocent and the sinful cannot endure, and yet what lives is worth holding on to.

Only those who have once been in the queue of hope and mourning can experience this contradiction with resolve and stillness: resolve that whispers like prayer.

I think this is what is in the lines of Auden's poem 'Lullaby', which he wrote in years threatened by war and death, the 1930s-1940s. He could not produce Tagore's optimism. But he was also far from bitter towards life, even in a flawed world.

Perhaps we can read 'Lullaby' and remember Aylan smiling in the photo with his brother Galip before his mother and father left on their refugee journey:

... and the grave
Proves the child ephemeral:
But in my arms till break of day
Let the living creature lie,
Mortal, guilty, but to me
The entirely beautiful.

March 2015

Pegida

History roars in the cold

    -- Sitor Situmorang (1923-2015*)*

I n the cold that night, there was not just one history roaring in the old square in Frankfurt. There were two, three, or maybe more.

Around 17,000 people crowded Römerberg, in the middle of the 10,000-square-meter complex. Protecting themselves from the drizzle and 2-degree cold, they were there to state that they, Germans and inhabitants of Frankfurt, opposed the anti-Islam movement, Pegida, which the same night planned to gather 500 of its supporters in another area of town.

There were speeches, applause, songs and music, and I saw a child holding a poster: *Gehört Islam zu Deutschland?* Is Islam part of Germany? And beneath, in large red letters, was written: Yes.

That night, the word 'Yes' felt startling. Here, an antithesis was going on. Pegida, the acronym for *Patriotische Europäer Gegen die Islamisierung des Abendlandes* (Patriotic Europeans Against Islamization of the West), which began in Dresden in October 2014, has revived its opponents. They are coming in a larger wave, seeing the growing support for 'patriots' who want to protect Europe from 'Islamization'.

Pegida does hold an attraction. Successful political movements always begin by filling a hole that appears because something has been wrenched from the dream of the masses. Pegida supporters are coming with the motto, 'Oppose religious fanaticism . . . together without violence'. Or 'Oppose religious warfare on German soil'.

Meaning that Pegida is attractive because of the fanaticism and violence shown by some Muslims – and that attraction is universal.

But what is 'universal' cannot long coexist with paranoia. Paranoia can very quickly fuse with hatred, and hatred can be strong because of conviction. And the end point of all this is the collapse of the 'universal'. History will then note two sad events: destruction and/or defeat.

On that cold night in January 2015, the people of Frankfurt gathered in Römerberg around the 'Fountain of Justice' because they are worried about what will happen with hatred. The *Gerechtigkeitsbrunnen,* which is the German name for the fountain decorated with the goddess of justice, was built 600 years ago. In the past, when the Kaiser was crowned, the fountain would flow with wine. The people celebrated. But it was not a story of celebration forever. The religious wars broke out in the 17th century, when for a period of 30 years Catholics and Protestants killed one another, spreading death and destruction in Frankfurt too. The statue on top of the *Gerechtigkeitsbrunnen* was one witness to this. In 1863, Friedrich Stoltze, a local poet, described it mockingly in bitter terms: 'This is the Lady of Justice! She looks like something terrible; the scales are gone, the goddess is wretched, and, devil take it, she's missing half an arm."

While not all the 17,000 people of Frankfurt might remember the Thirty Years War, they certainly do remember World War II: almost all the buildings around the square were almost completely razed to the ground by British and American bombs. The destruction began when Hitler wanted to strengthen Germany with cries of justice, but the scales of justice in his hand were destroyed because his Germany was a country with hatred.

If a large number of Germans today reject – with dread – the direction Pegida is taking, this is certainly because they remember hatred, Auschwitz, and the other concentration camps where Jews and 'non-Germans' were exterminated. And it is not easy for them to forget Dresden and Berlin that were smashed to smithereens with the fall of Hitler and the Nazi Party.

But memory is always accompanied by forgetting, and hatred can reappear in its cracks.

This is not because in history eternal hatred sticks fast. What appears to repeat is actually not repetition, but rebirth that is different from what went before. In the 17th century in Leibniz, a philosopher who felt he had to defend Protestantism saw Islam as a 'plague', *la peste de mahometisme*. He lived when there was a strong sense of a Turkish military threat in Europe. Today, the phobia towards Islam is raging because of the IS terror, Bako Haram barbarism and the fanaticism of the Taliban and their supporters.

So along with hatreds that are different, alliances of hatreds can also change. The supporters of Pegida are now allying with some Zionists who consider terror as an essential part of Islam. In former times, and still today, some Muslims condoned the Nazis because they viewed the Jews in essential terms as necessarily to be hated.

In the cold, in the warm, history indeed never roars alone.

September 2015

Mohamet

In April 1741, a play about 'Mohamet' was performed in a theatre in Lille, in the north of France. Its writer would go on to be remembered for centuries to come (even though this particular play was rarely discussed), because he was Voltaire, and because Voltaire always put forward intelligent ideas, at times profound, at times shallow, and he could be funny or rude, but generally disturbing. Especially about something that has continued right up to the 21st century: humanity and fanaticism and cruelty.

He began working on this play, *Le Fanatisme, ou Mahomet le Prophète* (Fanaticism, or Mahomet the Prophet') in 1739. The title alone shows that he was linking fanaticism to the Prophet who brought Islam to the world.

The play, in five acts, tells of Mahomet's plan to defeat Zopir, the governor of the city of Mecca. In Act 4, Zopir is murdered by a young man of whom he is fond named Seid, who is actually his own son but has become a follower of Mahomet and is now faithfully carrying out Mahomet's orders. Seid is then poisoned by Omar, a trusted follower of Mahomet. Seid dies slowly. He has to be got rid of in order to separate him from Palmira, the young woman with whom the Prophet is in love. At the end of the play, Palmira refuses Mahomet and kills herself.

I don't know whether *Mahomet* was one of Voltaire's best works: the play was never as well known as his others, *Candide* for instance, even though it was frequently performed. But the play did have one critic whose opinion is worth hearing even though he was not from literary circles, and was quoted almost a century later: Napoleon Bonaparte.

When Napoleon met Goethe in 1808 in the town of Erfurt, he declared that he did not like the play – even though it was Goethe who had translated it into German. It was a 'caricature', Napoleon said – and I can understand why. *Mahomet* is not profound, its bias is predictable, its protagonist almost completely one- dimensional. It is like a melodrama. Or propaganda.

Goethe did not disagree. He respected Voltaire, but also had strong sympathy for Islam: he was even nicknamed 'Meccarus' because of this. It is not surprising, then, that he tried to change the figure of Mahomet in the German version of the play. Goethe did not want to reproduce Voltaire's 'crudeness'. While in the original text Mahomet tells Zopir 'I will be more implacable, more cruel, even than thyself' (*Je serai plus que toi cruel, impitoyable*), in Goethe's translation we find, 'you invite me to cruelty' (*Du forderst selbst zur Grausamkeit mich auf*).

Unlike Voltaire, Goethe saw that in the history of Islamic violence occurred because of something from outside. But along with Voltaire, he rejected faiths that produce cruelty, and religions that depend on power that rejects interrogation.

In *Mahomet,* the main character declares his ambition: he, with his 'purer faith' (*culte épuré*) wants to establish a universal empire. Probably this is why Goethe interpreted *Mahomet* as a veiled criticism of the Catholic Church even though, strangely, Voltaire offered his work to Pope Benedict XIV. This might have been his way of avoiding the censors. The enmity between Voltaire and the Church was renowned, and although power in the name of religion might be considered stupid, it was still a real threat: the Paris Parliament ordered a public burning of one of Voltaire's poems on 23 January, 1759.

Voltaire to Goethe – a reasonably long time. But something

continued: the desire for spiritual life different to what religions instruct. Historians say that this desire was born with the Enlightenment which prioritized human reason. But I think it was not limited to that period. Whenever religions start to become mechanisms of revenge, then there is a longing for God in other ways.

Voltaire rejected religions, and at the same time he rejected atheism. He called himself a 'theist'. Around 1750 he stated what he meant by 'theism'.

'The theist is a man firmly persuaded of the existence of a Supreme Being . . . who punishes crimes without cruelty, and rewards virtuous acts with kindness. The theist does not know how God punishes, how he rewards, how he pardons, for he is not presumptuous enough to flatter himself that he understands how God acts; but he knows . . . that God is just'.

Voltaire: almost three centuries on. It feels like something is wrong these days when, from France, it seems necessary to repeat those words once more.

February 2015

The Shepherd

In a sandy desert, a shepherd withdrew from a prophet's anger. In Jalaluddin Rumi's—the 13th century's foremost Islamic poet— well-known story – from the *Masnavi* – Moses hears a shepherd uttering a strange prayer: 'Oh God, show me where thou art, that I may become Thy servant. I will clean Thy shoes and comb Thy hair, and sew Thy clothes, and fetch Thee milk'.

Moses saw this passionate prayer as the seed of heathenism. To compare God to a person who needs milk was irreverent.

So he shouted: 'Gag your mouth! If you do not block your throat vomiting such words, a fire will come and burn people up . . .'

Hearing this, the shepherd stopped his prayer: 'Ah, Moses, you have burned my soul with repentance . . .'

The shepherd tore his robe, and heaving a huge sigh he looked out at the desert and left at once.

At that moment, as Rumi tells the story, God rebuked Moses: 'O Moses, why hast thou sent my servant away? Thou hast come to draw men to union with me, not to drive them far away from me. So far as possible, engage not in dissevering; the thing most repugnant to me is divorce. To each person have I allotted peculiar forms . . . I am exempt from all purity and impurity, I need not the laziness or alacrity of my people . . .'

Upon hearing God's rebuke, Moses ran into the desert chasing the shepherd. When they met, Moses told him the good news: 'I was wrong. God has revealed to me that there are no rules for worship. Say whatever and however your loving tells you to'.

But – and this comes unexpectedly in Rumi's story – the

Shepherd replies, 'Moses, Moses, I've gone beyond even that: I am now drowning in my tears'.

The shepherd does not want to return to Moses's frame of reference, for Moses is still relying on 'permission', authorization and commands. In other words: rules. The shepherd prefers total intimacy with the God he loves. Rumi's *Masnavi* seems to be pointing out that Moses – who the Bible depicts as the recipient of the Ten Commandments – does not fully understand what God has said: 'They that know the conventions are of one sort, they whose soul and spirit burn are of another sort'.

The shepherd does not want to surrender to the path he sees as linear: the law. He chooses to remain in the desert. In the midst of sand hills and rocks, limits are unclear. And unimportant. Straight lines can be drawn without any west or east. Where is the orientation for facing God? 'Inside the Ka'bah', Rumi wrote, 'it doesn't matter in which direction you pray'.

I once read a discussion about this part of the *Masnavi*, which saw the desert as an important metaphor speaking about faith – which is often simplified and called 'religion'.

Centuries after Rumi, Derrida brought up this image again. In his discussion about human religious experience in *La Religion,* he mentions the 'desert within the desert': when humans experience total 'nothingness', when the 'I' in this mystic experience seems to disappear without trace, melting into the bosom of The Other.

That 'desert within the desert', as is usual with religions, holds 'messianistic' promise and hope: that later, far off on the horizon, under the rainbow, there will be The Other, which those of us who are steadfast and trusting will reach. But that promise cannot be depicted in advance. It symbolizes something infinite.

At the same time, the 'desert within the desert' is also the *khôra*: the 'place' that is no place, something entirely different from anything else. In other words, faith always holds within it things that cannot be condensed but which call us to continue searching. And with this, too, we recognize and value what is impossible but worthwhile – for instance, the promise of Justice to come.

Faith therefore holds courage – which usually fades once faith is condensed into a system and ordered with laws that safeguard straight paths. John D. Caputo, in his book *The Prayers and Tears of Jacques Derrida: Religion without Religion*, describes religion in Derrida's thinking as 'a universal messianicity despoiled of all messianism, as a faith without dogma advancing in the risk of absolute night . . .'

Night in the desert . . .

Far from desert sands, living as we do among islands and oceans, for us here in Indonesia probably a better metaphor to depict faith without dogma is the sea. Faith that is not limited by systems is an ocean that is a vast vessel of never-ending movement. Only the stars give direction. The waves appear always the same, even though they are actually forever different, changing. This is why the oceans, which collect water from all the different rivers, had no names until the conquerors and mapmakers came along.

Faith was indeed labeled later ('Islam', 'Christianity', 'Judaism', 'Hinduism' and so forth). It was mapped. But like the ocean, it still holds risk. 'Load the ship and set out. No one knows for certain whether the vessel will sink or reach the harbor'.

And it is in that very uncertainty that belief, or faith, declares itself. This means it is stronger than concepts and teachings. 'Enough of these phrases, conceit and metaphors, I want burning, burning, burning. — *Masnawi* 2: 1760.

January 2015

Shoes

There's an old pair of shoes that became famous, far beyond the thoughts of their unknown maker.

In 1886, the Dutch artist Van Gogh, who was then living in Paris, went to a flea market. He saw a pair of shoes and bought them. One rainy day he went out walking in them, and walked for a long time. He wanted to wear the shoes out – before painting them. It is claimed he said, 'Dirty shoes and roses can both be good in the same way'.

Some have theorized that he painted the shoes to depict his hardship in life. I am not convinced. Van Gogh frequently painted still life, and painted boots and farmers' shoes a number of times without signifying anything in particular: these things fascinated him, as though he were looking at them for the very first time. He felt that every single day there was something he could be thankful for. This was where his creativity sprang from: the ability to be moved by and to move something worthless. '. . . all that I seek in painting is a way to make life bearable' he wrote in a letter to his younger brother Theo in August, 1888.

The old shoes have no purpose: they are detached from the feet of their wearer, cut from the intention of their maker. Now they live alone in a painting that is stored and exhibited from one museum to the next. They are nobody's object. But also they do not become a subject directed at anyone. They do not direct nor are they directed.

In 1930, the philosopher Martin Heidegger looked at this painting in an exhibition in Amsterdam. The painting moved him, and drove him to write – and interpret, of course. He saw, from the visible worn inside of the shoes, a life story: these were the shoes of a peasant woman, he saw 'toilsome tread' and 'accumulated tenacity'. In the leather he saw 'the dampness and saturation of the soil.' Under the soles he imagined 'loneliness of the field-path as the evening declines.'

In the shoes', Heidegger wrote, 'vibrates the silent call of the earth.' The shoes 'belong to the earth and [are] protected in the world of the peasant woman.'

Of course the two-dimensional pair of shoes in the picture – which seemed to have spurred the musings of a philosopher and made him link them with a certain life – are from start to finish completely still. It is the philosopher alone who forms words; he built an image about the world of peasants in winter, about toilers loyal to the earth where they live – and the fascination of all that.

Heidegger was of course not wrong – but who can say that his interpretation was right? Some think that his perspective reflects the trend in Germany in the 1930s, when the Nazis were proclaiming loyalty to *Blut und Boden,* 'blood and soil', a metaphor for untainted origins. Heidegger himself enjoyed life commonly thought of as 'pure': he owned a hut in the Black Forest in Schwarzwald, near Freiburg, that blended with the hills and trees. This was where he wrote his reflections. And this is also where he was recorded as being a Nazi.

These days, people are probably beginning to forget Heidegger and tales of untainted origins. The shoes in Van Gogh's painting are today the shoes of an exhausted man or woman who has trekked from Syria or Sudan to the edge of the continent, leaving origins behind. Our era no longer offers the luxury and peace of a territory. And what is the meaning of loyalty to 'blood and soil' when what comes from it is merely hatred, suicide bombs and slaughter?

Migrants are walking, seeking new territories, seeking space that is not necessarily God-promised earth.

Of course, they are not new actors or sufferers in history. For centuries, demographies have been shaped by waves of migration, the movement of wanderers, the stamina of nomads, of all those who leave. Indeed, those who give sermons on the ideology of purity frequently shout, 'return to the primal letter, to pure origins, cling fast to your roots'. But humans are not trees with just one root.

Deleuze, who spoke so fluently and well about 'deterritorialization' was probably the thinker most in touch with today's voice of anxiety, when thousands of migrants are crossing borders that in fact also keep changing. "We should stop believing in trees, roots and radicles', he said.

Even though actually there is something odd in those words: for a tree is also a life story, a forest is also an event, always 'becoming'. Something grows after the pollen flies away, moves, carried by the wind, carried by birds. Without shoes.

Or more precisely, without Martin Heidegger's shoes.

May 2015

Silence

An old man, almost mute, his memory gone, and so too his son in a terrifying history: the senile man in Joshua Oppenheimer's film, *The Look of Silence*.

In Oppenheimer's film, which sets out to show the cruelty in Indonesia in the mid-1960s, this semi-paralyzed figure seems like an allegory of the horror and silence of the past.

I watched *The Look of Silence* at a cinema in Glasgow, Scotland, three weeks ago. The majority of the audience was not familiar with Indonesia. Oppenheimer's film seemed to be their first introduction to the distant, complex, exotic and troubled archipelago.

The opening scene: a video recording of two men in their seventies. We come to know that they live in Deliserdang, thirty kilometers from Medan. Proudly, they relate how they used to kill 'communists' on the banks of the Ular River.

Then we are shown the two old men going to the river. Their story takes on more detail: for instance, to kill a victim who was strong, they would cut his genitals from behind. The killers imitate the sound of the murdered men as they cried for help.

In another scene, one of the killers shows a thick book where he wrote down his experiences, complete with pictures of scenes of his savagery.

In another section, the other killer relates how he cut off a woman's breasts before he slaughtered her. Whenever he killed someone, he would drink the blood of his victim. So he would not go mad, he said. Another old man, sitting beside his son, related how he would always take a glass with him when he was going to kill. Where did they tap the blood? From a hole in the throat. Once he had even sent a head to a shop owned by a Chinaman; just to terrify him.

The Look of Silence: an outstanding cinematic work. The camera angles are wonderful, the pictures brilliant, the characters have great presence, and the editing builds amazing suspense. The construction of the film is so good that the world it records seems as though it could turn into a story,

It is impressive indeed that Oppenheimer managed to bring these figures of terrible history together with Adi. He is a 44-year old man whose uncle, Ramli, was killed. Adi has questions for these old men; he tries to get them to say they are sorry, and pushes them to talk about this brutal past.

The film's story is built from there.

After watching the film, as a guest in the Discover Indonesia festival I was asked to answer questions. I immediately realized there was a huge gulf of information between *The Look of Silence* and the stunned audience. The people of Glasgow did not know who those killers were: were they farmers, laborers, land owners, professional executioners? Why were they proud of their savagery? The killers declared that they were anticommunist. But it was not clear why merely being anticommunist would turn them into fanatical killers. Where did this intense hatred spring from?

On the way back home, a member of the audience asked about something else: who were the killers' victims, actually? Well, I said, they were considered to be members of the Communist Party. But my answer was not good enough, it seemed. Was the Communist Party illegal at the time; was it a secret enemy organization? No. The Communist Party was one of a few strong political parties in the 1960s, I answered. In the film, you see that the victims and their killers had long lived together as neighbors and so they must have already known their respective political party affiliations. How then, did this urge to eliminate them suddenly arise? And why did the Communist Party not fight back?

I wanted to explain – but I knew that then I would have to give a long lecture about the history of Indonesian politics (only half of which I recall). And I would have to explain social history: audiences not familiar with language, dialect and social differences in Indonesia – reading only the English subtitles – would not know that Adi's mother was speaking in Javanese and his father, the old man whose memory had gone, was probably a worker brought from Java who had lived for years in the Malay and Tapanuli territory; the only thing he could still remember was a Malay song. Why he was there, why the family was there, and whether bitter conflict could arise because of origins, were things about which I could merely guess.

What is clear is that I could not explain why Ramli, Adi's older brother, was hunted down and eventually killed. And I remained silent when an even more fundamental question arose: what is the point of bringing up the past if the result is not reconciliation, or even regret – but rather disturbance and even a reemergence of hatred?

That past is a 'wound', a man who escaped the genocide at Ular River says. An old wound, says one of those who motivated the slaughter. And the one who sliced the woman's breast was angry when Adi started to probe further about what happened. Adi's mother was afraid. There was anxiety that if the wound were reopened, it would fester all the more.

But to Adi and Joshua, opening the bandage of that wound would actually heal it. Forget the danger, for otherwise such cruelty could happen again.

But maybe this is because they stand outside the wound. They themselves did not experience the bitterness, the complexities, and the savagery; they were born after 1965. Joshua is from Texas and Adi was born after Ramli's death. They just want to know.

Knowledge is of course different to memory. To know is to control reality; to remember is not always to control the past.

'To remember all things is a form of madness', Hugh the old drunk schoolmaster says in Brian Friel's play *Translations*, whose story is based in the bloody conflict in Ireland.

In *The Look of Silence*, the semi-paralyzed old man, Adi's father, is not mad. All he can remember is a song.

September 2015

Essays and their Sources

Pg.	English Title	Original Title	Publication date in *Tempo* (or elsewhere)	Appearance in *Catatan Pinggir* (CP) series
ix	Books	Buku	2 May 2010	CP IX (601-4)
3	Native Land	Tanah Air	20 May 2000	CP V: (485-7)
6	Becoming	Kejadian	27 July 2014	*)
10	Coconut Juice	Air Kelapa	15 June 2014	*)
13	Crush!	Ganyang!	13 October 2013	*)
17	Arrows	Panah	9 October 2011	CP X (163-6)
21	Cradling	Memangku	20 March 2011	CP X (47-50)
25	Names, or why Juliet got it Wrong	Nama, atau mengapa Juliet salah	12 September 2010	CP IX (679-84)
31	Darkness	Gelap	23 May 2010	CP IX (613-6)
35	Indonesia	Indonesia	23 August 2009	CP IX (201-4)
38	That Name	Nama Itu	27 September 2009	CP IX (477-80)
41	Debris	Puing	17 February 2008	CP IX (129-32)
45	From Ambon and Scorched Ruins	Dari Ambon dan Gedung Hangus	21 August 2006 (not from column)	(Not from column)
51	Etc.	Dll.	27 August 2006	CP VIII (245-8)
55	Not	Bukan	25 June 2006	CP VIII (213-6)
59	Azahari	Azahari	27 November 2005	CP VIII (89-92)
63	1965	1965	10 October 2004	CP VII (273-6)
67	Papua	Papua	10 December 2000	CP V: (589-91)
70	Dur	Dur	8 July 2001	CP VI: (39-42)
73	Han Sui	Han Sui	15 February 1992	CP IV: (267-9)
76	La Patrie	La Patrie	(*Suara Independen*, 1 June 1995)	(Jakarta: *Kata Waktu*, 1120-2)
79	Imogiri	Sejarah	15 October 1988	CP III: (443-5)
82	The Death of Sukardal	The Death of Sukardal	19 July 1986	CP III: (99-101)
86	The Believer	PKI	5 October 1985	CP III: (37-9)
89	Ruins	Puing	9 February 1985	CP II: (637-9)
92	The Violent	Yang Keras	6 October 1984	CP II: (567-9)
95	Cities	Kota	23 June 1984	CP II: (511-3)
98	Twilight in Jakarta	Senja di Jakarta	10 April 1982	CP II: (119-20)

*) Not yet published in the *Catatan Pinggir* book series.

Pg.	English Title	Original Title	Publication date in *Tempo* (or elsewhere)	Appearance in *Catatan Pinggir* (CP) series
100	The Closing of the Newspapers 1978	Ketika Koran-koran ditutup, 1978	28 January 1978	CP I: (241-3)
102	Malay	Melayu	4 April 1987	CP III: (221-3)
106	Douch	Douch	16 February 2014	*)
110	Dirt	Kotor	29 June 2014	*)
113	Laws	Undang	11 May 2014	*)
117	History	Sejarah	27 October 2013	*)
120	Lies	Perang	24 March 2013	*)
123	Rushdie	Rushdie	16 December 2012	CP X (415-8)
126	Akhenaten	Ikhnaton	8 April 2012	CP X (271-4)
130	And then	Kemudian	5 February 2012	CP X (235-8)
134	Tintin	Tintin	4 December 2011	CP X (195-8)
137	Ten years on	11/9	18 September 2011	CP X (151-4)
140	Srebenica	Srebrenica	31 July 2011	CP X (123-6)
143	Taking Sides	Memihak	14 June 2009	CP IX (413-6)
147	Barbarians	Barbar	14 January 2007	CP VIII (327-30)
150	Jeremiah	Jeremiah	22 April 2007	CP VIII (383-6)
154	Shanghai	Shanghai	11 March 2007	CP VIII (359-62)
158	Cartoons	Karikatur	19 February 2006	CP VIII (141-4)
161	Amsterdam	Amsterdam	4 June 2006	CP VIII (201-4)
164	Sex	Seks	19 March 2006	CP VIII (157-60)
168	Bandung	Bandung	10 April 2005	CP VII (383-6)
172	Sharp Times	Begu Ganjang	20 February 2005	CP VII: 355-8
176	Abu Ghraib	Abu Ghraib	16 May 2004	CP VII (189-92)
180	Troy	Troya	28 June 2004	CP VII (209-12)
184	Zhivago	Zhivago	20 June 2004	CP VII (197-200)
188	America	Amerika	6 April 2003	CP VI: (397-400)
191	Baghdad	Bagdad	23 February 2003	CP VI: (371-4)
194	Bombs	Bom	8 December 2002	CP VI : (323-6)
197	Territorium	Territorium	13 January 2002	CP VI: (139-42)
201	Republics	Republik	31 March 2002	CP VI: (185-8)
204	Darwish	Darwish	5 May 2002	CP VI: (201-4)
208	Baku	Baku	3 February 2002	CP VI: (151-53)
212	Icarus, One Day	Pada Suatu Hari, Ikarus	5 January 2003	CP VI: (341-6)
217	Baucau	Baucau	9 September 2001	CP VI: (75-7)
220	Osama	Usamah	9 December 2001	CP VI: (119-22)
223	Menopause	Menopause	28 January 2001	CP V: (615-8)
226	Athena	Athena	27 February 2000	CP V: (437-9)

Pg.	English Title	Original Title	Publication date in *Tempo* (or elsewhere)	Appearance in *Catatan Pinggir* (CP) series
229	Mirror	Kaca	1 February 1992	CP IV: (259-61)
232	Khomeini	Khomeini	24 June 1989	CP III: (549-51)
234	The West	Barat	12 May 1984	CP II: (487-9)
238	Imagination not just Blood and Iron	Imajinasi, bukan hanya darah dan besi	20 August 1983	CP II: (341-3)
241	In Granada	Di Granada	13 November 1982	CP II: (195-7)
244	Graham Greene, White Man in Indochina	Orang putih Graham Greene di Indocina	20 January 1979	CP I: (445-7)
248	Mecca	Mekah	11 November 2012	CP X (395-8)
252	Leda	Leda	23 September 2012	CP X (367-70)
255	Sirius	Sirius	24 June 2012	CP X (315-8)
258	Myth	Mithos	13 January 2013	*)
261	Abraham	Ibrahim	28 November 2010	CP IX (727-9)
264	Casting Stones	Perajam	4 October 2009	CP IX (481-4)
268	Atheists	Atheis	5 August 2007	CP IX (13-6)
272	Dialogue 7	Percakapan 7	24 September 2006	CP VIII (261-4)
276	Laozi	Laozi	12 February 2006	CP VIII (137-40)
280	Prayer	Doa	4 September 2005	CP VIII (41-4)
284	Seven	Tujuh	6 November 2005	CP VIII (77-80)
288	Tso Wang	Tso Wang	21 December 2003	CP VII (99-102)
291	Horror	Horor	8 February 2004	CP VII (133-6)
295	Trees	Pohon-pohon	16 November 2003	CP VII (79-82)
298	Allah	Allah	30 November 2003	CP VII (87-90)
302	Soroush	Soroush	23 December 2001	CP VI: (127-30)
305	Jerusalem	Yerusalem	29 October 2000	CP V: (565-7)
308	The Body	Tubuh	6 February 2000	CP V: (425-7)
311	Visnu	Visnu	5 November 2000	CP V: (569-71)
314	God	Tuhan	19 December 1992	CP IV (371-3)
317	Saladin	Saladin	19 January 1991	CP IV (105-7)
320	Family	Keluarga	3 August 1991	CP IV (189-91)
323	Ego	Ego	15 April 1989	CP III: (517-9)
326	The Cube	Kubus	15 August 1987	CP III: (277-9)
329	Wounds	Luka	3 November 1984	CP II: (583-5)
332	Solar Eclipse over Borobudur	Gerhana Matahari di Borobudur	18 June 1983	CP II: (311-3)
335	Mosques	Masjid-masjid	24 November 1979	CP I: (619-21)
338	Sacred Poetry	Puisi Kitab Suci	(*Harian Kami*, 1968)	(Jakarta: Kata Waktu, 19-21)

Biographical Information

GOENAWAN MOHAMAD (b 1941) is an acclaimed Indonesian writer and man of letters. He has been at the forefront of Indonesian intellectual and cultural life since his early twenties, and a crusader for press freedom since his university days. He was founder of the Indonesian language weekly journal *Tempo* in 1971 and its chief editor from 1971-94, when the magazine was shut down by the Suharto regime. From 1994-98 he was involved with activist activities against the regime, and then stepped back as chief editor of *Tempo* for one year when the magazine resumed publication in 1998.

Since that time, Goenawan has been more involved with establishing alternative spaces for cultural and intellectual activity in Jakarta (Utan Kayu center and the Salihara complex) writing (essays, poetry, plays and librettos) and as theatre director and producer. He is frequently invited nationally and internationally as guest speaker and commentator, and has received numerous prestigious awards. He was Nieman Fellow at Harvard University (1989), Fellow at the Institute for the Humanities at the University of Michigan USA (2002) and in 2001 was honored as the Regent Professor of the University of California.

JENNIFER LINDSAY studied in New Zealand, the United States and Australia. She first went to Indonesia in 1971 and has lived there at various times since in various guises, including student, researcher, diplomat, and foundation program officer. She has translated many literary and academic works from Indonesian into English, and is a regular translator and columnist for Indonesia's weekly magazine, *Tempo*. Jennifer is a Research Affiliate in the School of Culture, History and Language at The Australian National University, and her academic writing focuses on Indonesian culture, language and history. From 2008-2010 she co-led an international research project into Indonesia's cultural history from 1950-1965, and was contributing editor to the volume produced from that project, *Heirs to World Culture: Being Indonesian 1950-1965* (KITLV 2012). She also directed (2010) a documentary about the Indonesian national cultural missions abroad of this time, (*Presenting Indonesia: Cultural Missions Abroad 1952-1965*). Jennifer now divides her time between Indonesia and Australia.

TERENCE WARD is a writer, documentary producer, and a cultural consultant. Born in Colorado, Terence grew up in Arabia and Iran. He graduated from the University of California, Berkeley, and also attended the American University of Cairo, specializing in political Islam. His book, *Searching for Hassan: A Journey to the Heart of Iran* is a literary chronicle of his odyssey back to Iran after 30 years. Currently, he is producing *Talk Radio Tehran,* a documentary film that follows the lives of three Iranian women. His latest book, *The Guardian of Mercy*, a true story centered on a painting of Caravaggio in Naples, will be published in 2015. Ward is an International Trustee of the World Conference of Religions for Peace.